D. H. LAWRENCE
AND THE
PARADOXES OF
PSYCHIC LIFE

SUNY series in Psychoanalysis and Culture
Henry Sussman, editor

D. H. LAWRENCE AND THE PARADOXES OF PSYCHIC LIFE

BARBARA ANN SCHAPIRO

State University
of New York
Press

Published by
State University of New York Press, Albany

© 1999 State University of New York

Production by Susan Geraghty
Marketing by Patrick Durocher
Cover photo courtesy of the Hotel La Fonda De Taos.

Printed in the United States of America

For information, address State University of New York
Press, State University Plaza, Albany, N.Y., 12246

Library of Congress Cataloging-in-Publication Data

Schapiro, Barbara A.
    D. H. Lawrence and the paradoxes of psychic life / Barbara Ann
Schapiro.
        p.   cm. — (SUNY series in psychoanalysis and culture)
    Includes bibliographical references and index.
    ISBN 0-7914-4297-7 (hc : alk. paper). — ISBN 0-7914-4298-5 (pb :
alk. paper)
    1. Lawrence, D. H. (David Herbert), 1885–1930—Knowledge-
-Psychology. 2. Psychoanalysis and literature—England-
-History—20th century. 3. Psychological fiction, English—History
and criticism. 4. Psychology in literature. I. Title. II. Title:
DH Lawrence and the paradoxes of psychic life. III. Series.
PR6023.A93Z8653 1999
823′.912—dc21   98-43560
                                                                      CIP

10 9 8 7 6 5 4 3 2 1

In memory of my grandfather,
Julius Cohen,
whose fascination with psychoanalysis
and whose love of a good story
I carry on.

CONTENTS

Acknowledgments   *ix*

Chapter 1   Introduction   1

   Lawrence and This (Female Psychoanalytic) Reader   1
   Lawrence and Psychoanalytic Relational Theories   3
   Intersubjectivity   5
   Intersubjectivity, Gender, and Domination:
     Jessica Benjamin's Theory   7
   Lawrence's Biography   11
   Previous Psychoanalytic Criticism of Lawrence   15
   An Intersubjective Approach to Lawrence:
     Polarities and Paradoxes   17

Chapter 2   *Sons and Lovers*   21

   Gertrude and Paul: The Depressed Mother and the
     Dependent Child   21
   Miriam and Paul: Self-Mistrust and the Failure of
     Otherness   37
   Clara and Paul: Depersonalization and the Psyche/Soma
     Split   44
   Walter, Baxter, and Paul: The Rejected Father and the
     Need for Recognition   48
   Paul: The Maternal Heritage   51

Chapter 3   The Short Stories   55

   "New Eve and Old Adam," "Odour of
     Chrysanthemums," "The Shadow in the Rose
     Garden," "Sun": Mutual Recognition and the
     Bodily Self   55
   "The Prussian Officer," "The Blind Man," "The
     Princess," "The Woman Who Rode Away":
     Intersubjective Collapse and the
     Domination-Submission Polarity   61
   "The Horse-Dealer's Daughter": Confronting Shame
     and the Struggle to Love   73

Chapter 4 *The Rainbow*   79

    Tom and Lydia: Sustaining the Maternal Identification
       and the Development of Faith   79
    Anna and Will: Deficiency, Shame, and the Will to
       Dominate   85
    Ursula and Others: Intersubjectivity and the Quest
       for Authenticity   89

Chapter Five *Women in Love*   103

    Gerald and Gudrun: The Sadomasochistic Scenario   103
    Birkin and Gerald: Seeking the Narcissistic Ideal   117
    Birkin and Ursula: Maintaining the Vital Tension   120

Epilogue   131

Notes   133

Works Cited   143

Index   151

ACKNOWLEDGMENTS

Portions of chapters 2 and 3, in slightly altered form, have appeared in *Scenes of Shame: Psychoanalysis, Shame, and Writing*, ed. Joseph Adamson and Hilary Clarke (SUNY Press). The section of chapter 3 on "The Woman Who Rode Away" was also published in *Psychoanalyses/Feminisms*, ed. Andrew Gordon and Peter Rudnytsky (SUNY Press). My thanks especially to Joseph Adamson and Peter Rudnytsky for their careful editing of those sections. I am grateful as well to Lynne Layton, who read and offered many valuable suggestions on the first chapter.

Additionally, I would like to express my appreciation to the Rhode Island College students in my graduate seminar on Lawrence in the spring of 1997. Their lively dialogue helped stimulate and refine my thinking. Special thanks to Liz Noren, a member of that seminar, for her research assistance. My gratitude also to Rich Weiner, dean of Arts and Sciences, and to the administration at Rhode Island College for supporting my sabbatical leave in the spring of 1995. That time allowed me to establish the groundwork for this project. I would also like to thank Henry Sussman and James Peltz at SUNY Press, along with Jeff Berman, for their encouragement and support. Finally, my husband, Scotty, and my children, Owen and Mira, were very understanding of the many hours I spent glued to the computer, and for that I am deeply grateful.

CHAPTER 1

Introduction

LAWRENCE AND THIS
(FEMALE PSYCHOANALYTIC) READER

I've always liked Lawrence. Yet as a woman, a Jew, and particularly, a psychoanalytic critic, I epitomize what Lawrence often venomously attacked. The following address to the reader in his novel *Mr. Noon*, I admit, makes me wince: "You sniffing mongrel bitch of a reader, you can't sniff out any specific why or any specific wherefore, with your carrion-smelling psychoanalysing nose, because there *is* no why and wherefore" (205). But Mr. Lawrence, I want to protest, you yourself are supremely interested in the whys and wherefores, in all the intricate play of conflicting passions and multiple, competing motivations beneath the conscious surface of our lives.

I also want to reassure him that psychoanalysis has changed considerably since the time he was alive. Freud's mechanistic model of the psyche as a system of hardwired sexual and aggressive drives has been radically revised. One of the premises of this study, in fact, is that psychoanalytic theory has only recently caught up with many of the insights about psychological life that Lawrence articulated over seventy years ago: that identity is profoundly relational, that the self cannot be realized outside the context of the other—"We have our very individuality in relationship" ("We Need One Another" 190); that affects are inextricably entwined with the body—"The body's life is the life of sensations and emotions. . . . All the emotions belong to the body" ("A Propos of *Lady Chatterley's Lover*" 492)—and that the spontaneous expression of affective, bodily life is essential for healthy living; and finally, that both psychological and moral life, at the deepest level, concern shifting dialectical tensions—"Life is so made that opposites sway about a trembling centre of balance" ("Morality and the Novel" 529).

As a reader/critic of Lawrence, my gender and my feminist values present, of course, another prickly issue. One wonders if there can possibly be anything more to say about Lawrence and women. Since his death the debate has swirled about two poles: on the one hand, Lawrence's strong feminine identification and empathy with women, and on the other, his undeniable misogyny. Anaïs Nin believed that

1

Lawrence achieved "complete realization of the feelings of women" (57) in his work, and even more recent critics, such as Carol Dix, have stressed the formative influence of his deep-rooted female identification. Other women readers have focused on Lawrence's insistence on female otherness, his terror of female power and dominance, and his celebration of the phallus. Of the criticism that indicts Lawrence for his misogyny, Kate Millett's *Sexual Politics* (1969), which casts him as a sadistic pornographer, is by far the most stinging; it has also proved exceptionally influential, determining the censorious direction of feminist criticism of Lawrence for the succeeding two decades.[1]

Now, in the nineties, some feminist critics are seeking to reappropriate Lawrence. Carol Siegel's *Lawrence among the Women*, for instance, looks at Lawrence's fiction in the context of female literary tradition, emphasizing how "real female voices successfully compete with Lawrence's dictatorial male pronouncements" (9) and how "his female characters deconstruct from within the fictions that (attempt to) contain them" (16). While she admits that his work "contains a full measure of misogyny," she contends that it is "too fluid, changeable, and even self-contradictory" (183) to fit the developmental pattern of progressive hostility toward independent women that other feminist critics have argued. Cynthia Lewiecki-Wilson also stresses how the narration in Lawrence's texts "combines both omniscient point of view and subjectivity, resulting in a textual voice that authorizes each character's experiences as equally legitimate, presenting competing centers of 'authenticity'" (70). Linda Williams makes a similar point in her intriguing application of psychoanalytic feminist film theory to the study of the female gaze in Lawrence's fiction. She discusses the "multiple positions" of the female subject in his texts, and like Siegel, asserts that Lawrence "writes against himself": "Despite his protestations for an essential difference between the sexes, the shifting focus of desire in Lawrence's fantasy texts betrays the fact that identity is not so fixed or divisible" (138).

The views of these feminist critics fit the postmodern perspective of Lawrence that Peter Widdowson has labelled "radical indeterminacy." They also complement a current direction in Lawrence criticism that uses Bakhtin's dialogic theory to illuminate the diverse and competing discourses in Lawrence's texts.[2] It is into this recent conversation on Lawrence that I wish to enter with the following study. I bring to the table current psychoanalytic theories that highlight the importance of dialectical play in unconscious life. Such dialectical play, I believe, can help us more fully appreciate those opposing voices and identifications so crucial to Lawrence's art. These theories also describe the rigid polarities that result when dialectical tensions break down: my thesis is that Lawrence's work reveals the effects of breakdown as well as the continual effort to maintain tension. His fiction involves us in what psychoanalyst Michael Eigen calls "the interlocking of rigidity and fluidity" that constitutes the very nature of psychic life (*Psychotic Core* 346).

My critical position thus itself depends on maintaining the tension of oppositions and paradoxes. It argues for a view of Lawrence in which gender identity is at once fluid and rigid. Gender identity is also not the only story in the psychology of Lawrence's fiction. Those inner experiences of which Lawrence speaks to me most intensely and intimately are not gendered: they have to do with feeling fully and authentically alive, with understanding emotional aliveness in relation to the body, and with tolerating the conflictual, contradictory nature of passionate life. Contemporary psychoanalytic theory has helped me better understand those particular dimensions of Lawrence's art and my experience of them.

LAWRENCE AND PSYCHOANALYTIC RELATIONAL THEORIES

A paradigm shift, as I have discussed in *Literature and the Relational Self*, has occurred in psychoanalytic thinking. For the majority of contemporary psychoanalytic theorists, the psyche is now understood more as a matter of internalized relational configurations than of inherent drives, and process and context are emphasized over universal psychic structures. The term "relational," as Emmanuel Ghent explains, stresses

> relation not only between and among external people and things, but also between and among internal personifications and representations. It stresses process—as against reified entities—and the relations among processes all the way along the continuum from the physical and physiological, through the neurobiological, ultimately the psychological, and, for some, even the spiritual. Everything is context dependent; nothing has meaning without relation to other processes. ("Forward" Skolnick and Warshaw xx)

This perspective resonates with Lawrence's repeated emphasis in his writing on relationship and flow, on the "intertwining flux" of all things and the context-dependency of all meaning. "Nothing is true, or good, or right, except in its own living relatedness to its own circumambient universe" ("Art and Morality" 525).

It is precisely the retreat from connection, from our natural bonds, and from the flow of passionate life in general, that Lawrence identified at the source of a modern malaise, a cultural pathology. Although he does not use the clinical term, Lawrence diagnosed modern Western society as schizoid: our culture's overvaluation of abstract rationality and autonomous individuality, he believed, betrayed an emptiness, a hollowness at the core, and a tragic incapacity for real relationship. The cultural and the personal are always intertwined. Lawrence understood this condition so well because he too suffered from it.[3] His fiction represents a creative response; it depicts a brilliant, if arduous, struggle to recover authenticity of being through relationship.

The hollow self condition that Lawrence critiques, and that also imbues so much modernist literature and art, has become for the contemporary psychoanalyst the very definition of psychopathology. As Stephen Mitchell notes, "Psychopathology, in the contemporary psychoanalytic literature, is often defined not in terms of pieces of conflictual, unwanted fragments intruding into experience; psychopathology is defined by a missing center or lack of richness throughout experience" (*Hope and Dread* 24). Mitchell is also helpful in addressing the postmodern contention that there is no center, "core" or "true" self at all. He suggests that we think about the self in temporal rather than spatial terms, as a matter of experience in time rather than of reified structures:

> Thinking about the self in terms of time rather than space provides a more useful way of approaching the important issue that the search for the core of the self was meant to solve—the need to distinguish among degrees of authenticity in experience. . . . Speaking of authenticity versus inauthenticity or true versus false experience frees us from the spatial metaphor in a way that speaking of a true or false self or a "core" or "real" self does not. (*Hope* 130–31)

My psychological discussion of the nature of selfhood in Lawrence's fiction assumes this perspective: it focuses on felt *experience*. To the person who experiences some vital lack or deficiency, who feels empty and unreal, the theoretical debate about whether a real or core self actually exists matters little—it is irrelevant to the person's subjective experience of emptiness and unreality. From the temporal point of view, in fact, Mitchell shares the postmodernist position on the multiple and discontinuous dimension of selfhood:

> The view of self as multiple and discontinuous is grounded in a temporal rather than a spatial metaphor: Selves are what people do and experience over time rather than something that exists someplace. Self refers to the subjective organization of meanings one creates as one moves through time, doing things, such as having ideas and feelings, including some self-reflective ideas and feelings about oneself. . . .
> . . . Each relational configuration yields two ways of being in the world; each actual relationship may contain multiple self-organizations; and there may be many such relationships. The result is a plural or manifold organization of self, patterned around different self and object images or representations, derived from different relational contexts. (*Hope* 101, 104)

In contradistinction to the postmodernist view, however, Mitchell believes that such multiplicity exists along with the continuity of a self-reflective and organizing "I," an "I" that creates meaning and organizes the diverse experiences and manifold self-other configurations: "there is a sense that the 'I' that is creating meaning today, processing and organizing experience, is a continuation of the 'I' that created subjective experience yesterday and the day before. By recognizing the 'I' that organizes my experience, I recognize myself as myself" (109).

To posit such an organizing "I" is not to assume an essential unified subject, the sort of mythical harmonious identity to which postmodernists so object. As Jane Flax has pointed out, the postmodernist perspective tends to confuse the concept of a "unitary" self with that of a "core" self—a basic continuity of being. The lack of such a "core" experience of being, Flax argues, leads to "a terrifying slide into psychosis" (218–19). Both Lawrence's fiction and psychoanalytic relational theories explore how affects and the body are deeply implicated in the self's experience of its own core being or reality. Our earliest self experiences are overwhelmingly physical. The bodily experiences of infancy set the stage, or the metaphors, for the imaginative development of our particular subjectivity. As Mitchell explains, "Our early life is dominated by powerful and absorbing physical events—eating, urinating, defecating, arousal, quiescence—and these events and processes become the basic categories, the underlying metaphors through which all subsequent experience is patterned" (*Hope* 125). Similarly, Eigen asserts, "The infant lives from and through the body before the body is represented as a physical body with specific limits and functions. However, once self-other awareness emerges, body feelings become a part of momentous dramas beyond them" (*Psychotic* 153–54).

If we think of the core self in terms of core experience, then that experience is bodily. Donald Winnicott, one of the most important influences for contemporary relational theorists, best articulates this position: he describes the psyche as "the imaginative elaboration of somatic parts, feelings, and functions, that is of physical aliveness. . . . [T]he live body, with its limits, and with an inside and outside, is felt by the individual to form the core for the imaginative self" (*Through Paediatrics* 244). Most importantly, Winnicott and relational theorists argue that the earliest experiences of these bodily functions and processes are suffused with affect. And affects, rather than biological drives, are what most profoundly determine psychic growth.

INTERSUBJECTIVITY

Many relational theorists, such as Robert Stolorow and George Atwood, highlight "the shift from drive to affect as the central motivational construct" (26) for contemporary psychoanalysis. Affects, moreover, are embedded in the interpersonal context. Stolorow and Atwood explain: "Affectivity, we now know, is not a product of isolated intrapsychic mechanisms; it is a property of the child-caregiver system of mutual regulation. . . . The 'affective core of the self' derives from the person's history of intersubjective transactions, and thus the shift from drive to affect resituates the psychoanalytic theory of motivation squarely within the realm of the intersubjective" (26). Stolorow and Atwood define "intersubjectivity theory" as a systems or field theory that understands psychic phenomena "as forming at the interface of reciprocally interacting subjectivities" (1).

For the intersubjective theorist, psychic reality is both interpersonal and intrapsychic: it focuses on "*both* the individual's world of inner experience *and* its embeddedness with other such worlds in a continual flow of reciprocal mutual influence" (18). One of the most crucial factors in the development of a sense of subjective reality, of subjective meaning or authenticity, is what intersubjective theorist Daniel Stern calls "affect attunement"—a sharing or communing between infant and caregiver of internal affect states. Such matching of feeling states is our first and most important form of sharing subjective experiences, and it serves to authorize our experience of ourselves, to validate our very being.

Stolorow and Atwood emphasize that "the caregiver's affect attunement is communicated primarily through holding and other sensorimotor contacts with the infant's body. Early deficits in such attunement show themselves in various deformations of the child's body-self and/or in an incomplete attainment of the sense of indwelling" (46). "Indwelling" is a term coined by Winnicott to refer to the integration of the psyche and the soma—"the in-dwelling or the inhabitation of the body and the body functioning," the opposite of which would be "depersonalisation" and "loss of contact with the body and body functioning" (*Psychoanalytic Explorations* 261–62). It is precisely this state of indwelling that Lawrence's fiction persistently seeks to restore. His railing against loss of contact with the body is indeed a kind of battle cry against depersonalization on the personal as well as the cultural level.

Intersubjective theory, furthermore, focuses on the mutual influence and interrelations of *subjects*. This perspective differs significantly from the traditional psychoanalytic view of a subject relating to its objects. One of the most radical aspects of Stern's theory (which is based on laboratory studies of mother-infant interactions) is its rejection of the longheld assumption of the infant's initially merged or symbiotic state with its first object, the mother. Ego psychologists such as Margaret

Mahler posit a linear continuum of psychological development that begins with a primary undifferentiated phase and moves gradually toward separation and the establishment of an autonomous ego. In contrast, contemporary infant research, as Eigen explains, "suggests that at least an area of differentiation exists from the beginning. During the time period Mahler calls autistic, the infant perceives and tracks objects, shows object preferences, and interacts with its milieu in finely tuned ways. The infant seems both separate and permeable from the outset" (*Psychotic* 151).

Thus the key psychological issue, as intersubjective theorist Jessica Benjamin asserts, is not only how we separate "or become free of the other, but how we actively engage and make ourselves known in relationship to the other" (*Bonds of Love* 18). Psychic maturation is less a matter of a linear movement from oneness to separateness than a matter of negotiating back-and-forth tensions. These tensions are a natural product of the infant coming to realize its own subjectivity in a world of other subjectivities; its own feelings and desires inevitably bump up against the independent, divergent feelings and desires of those on whom it depends. As Charles Spezzano states, "There is always a part of the affective orientation of others that leads them to look beyond us" (174).

Relational and intersubjective theories accentuate the dialectical tensions at the heart of psychic and emotional life. Spezzano believes that the best way to conceive of human psychology is as "shifting dialectical arrangements of affective states" (214). For many theorists, Spezzano notes, those opposing states have to do with "self-creation" on the one hand and "affiliation" on the other. Similarly, Jay Greenberg defines the essential dialectical feeling states as "safety"—which concerns security in our relations with others—and "effectance"—which aims toward self-sufficiency and autonomy. Mitchell's terms are slightly different, but they basically express the same tension: "The self operates in the intricate and subtle dialectic between spontaneous vitality and self-expression on the one hand and the requirement, crucial for survival, to preserve secure and familiar connections with others on the other" (*Hope* 133).

INTERSUBJECTIVITY, GENDER, AND DOMINATION: JESSICA BENJAMIN'S THEORY

Jessica Benjamin has introduced her own variation of this basic dialectic in which the opposing positions are even more fluid and interdependent. For her, the central conflictual tension involves "self-assertion" and "mutual recognition." What she calls "mutual recognition" is a version of Stern's affect attunement: "mutual recognition includes," she says, "a number of experiences commonly described in the research on mother-infant interaction: emotional attunement, mutual influence, affective mutuality, sharing states of mind" (*Bonds* 16). She stresses, however, that assertion and recognition are not only oppositional but mutually dependent. The assertion of our selves, the expression and realization of our subjective agency, is paradoxically contingent on the recognition by and of an independent other. "Recognition is that response from the other which makes meaningful the feelings, intentions, and actions of the self. . . . But such recognition can only come from an other whom we, in turn, recognize as a person in his or her own right" (*Bonds* 12).

Benjamin studies how this fundamental intersubjective dialectic has become at once gendered and disrupted in our culture. The cultural denial of self-assertion and agency to women breaks the tension and upsets the balance. If women are the primary caretakers but only men are granted subjectivity, then everyone suffers from this subject/object split. Benjamin compares the problem to Hegel's formulation of the master-slave dynamic, with women in the position of the slave. The master's domination and objectification of the slave deprive the master himself of what he most needs: recognition from an other who is strong and independent enough to give it. A mother's recognition of her child is not simply a matter of her acting as a mirror: her "recognition will be meaningful only to the extent that it reflects her own equally separate subjectivity" (*Bonds* 24).[4]

The lack or impairment of maternal subjectivity has far-reaching psychological effects. The recognition process breaks down: for the infant, there is no intact other to withstand, recognize, and therefore validate the assertion of the infant's bodily and passionate being. Benjamin draws on Winnicott's concept of "object use" in her discussion of this issue. Winnicott's terminology is somewhat misleading since he actually means the opposite of what we might normally associate with the phrase "object use." He does not mean manipulating or exploiting the other as an object. On the contrary, the concept refers to the infant's ability to experience the other as an independent, separate being in his or her own right; "use" suggests the ability *to benefit from* relationship with a real, external other.[5] In order to reach that stage, however, the infant must first psychically "destroy" the other and the other must survive. Benjamin explains:

> Winnicott is saying that the object must be destroyed inside in order that we know it to have survived outside; thus we can recognize it as not subject to our mental control. . . . [I]f I completely negate the other, he does not exist; and if he does not survive, he is not there to recognize me. But to find this out, I must try to exert this control, try to negate his independence. (*Bonds* 38)

The infant's psychic destruction of the other, in other words, is a form of ruthless self-assertion. In order for the baby to "use" or discover the real other, the other must survive this ferocious assertion of self. Failure to survive, in Winnicott's view, does not only refer to traumatic death or absence, but more generally, to the mother's emotional rejection or withdrawal in the face of the baby's fierce assertion. The mother's ability to survive depends on her own healthy self-assertion, on her comfort with her own physicality and emotional expression, including the expression of anger and aggression. The cultural discomfort with female assertiveness and with the mother as an embodied subject of desire are at the crux of Benjamin's argument. "The negation of the mother's independent subjectivity in social and cultural life," she claims, "makes it harder for her to survive her child's psychic destruction and become real to him" (*Bonds* 214).

The discovery of real otherness is profoundly liberating; this is indeed one of Lawrence's most insistent themes.[6] His work equally dramatizes, however, the failure of discovery and its brutal consequences. His stories and novels often demonstrate what happens when the discovery process is thwarted, and what happens is the seesaw dynamic of domination and submission, the trap of sadomasochism. Benjamin's work offers an illuminating new framework for exploring the problem of domination and the sadomasochistic strains in Lawrence's writing. Beneath the sadomasochistic dynamic that frequently complicates his fiction, as the following study will show, is a desperate desire to discover the other and to be discovered or recognized by the other. His work vividly illustrates Benjamin's contention that "The underlying theme of sadism is the attempt to break through to the other. The desire to be discovered underlies its counterpart, namely, masochism" (*Bonds* 71–72).

The breakdown of the assertion-recognition dialectic and the collapse of intersubjectivity result not only in the domination-submission polarity but in a rigidified gender polarity as well. Benjamin maintains Irene Fast's differentiation model of gender identity, which posits an early feminine identification in boys: "Rather than male and masculine in earliest gender orientation, children are hypothesized to be overinclusive in their experience, not attuned to sex difference or aware of the limitations inherent in belonging to a particular sex" (Fast 22). The process of gender differentiation, Fast argues, is thus primarily "a recognition of limits, that some sex and gender characteristics, uncritically assumed for themselves, belong exclusively to persons of the other sex, and is associated in both girls and boys with feelings of loss, denial, envy, and so forth" (4). The optimal development of gender differentiation does not involve repudiating the other sex but giving up or renouncing the narcissistic overinclusiveness and achieving what Fast calls "sec-

ondary identification": "The trait or capacity learned in primitive identification with the parent [such as, for boys, a procreative or nurturing
potential in relation to the mother] is integrated into one's own individual and separate self" (103).

Such secondary identification—a holding of simultaneous likeness
and difference—is the hallmark of intersubjectivity. Contrarily, intersubjective failure is marked by repudiation and by omnipotent narcissistic fantasies. For Benjamin, the fantasy of the omnipotent mother is
not, as much psychoanalytic and feminist theory has assumed, psychic
bedrock. The "fantasy of omnipotence is not an originary state but is a
reaction to confronting the other . . . a defensive reaction to disappointment" ("The Omnipotent Mother" 134). The fantasy is a response to
narcissistic injury. Benjamin believes maternal repudiation occurs pre-
dominantly during the oedipal phase.

> The boy displaces the mother's envied power onto the father and then
> identifies with it rather than finding a way out of that power strug-
> gle. . . . [T]he Oedipus complex does not dissolve narcissism; it dis-
> places it. The seldom recognized effect of the oedipal phase is to shift
> the form of omnipotence. Whereas the child in the preoedipal phase is
> overinclusive and wishes to be "everything" . . . the oedipal child repu-
> diates all that is other and insists that what he (or she) has is "the only
> thing." . . . Traditional oedipal theorizing states that the boy realizes
> he cannot have mother, accepts the limit that father sets, and so gives
> up omnipotent control over the primary object. But at another level,
> omnipotence is restored through the repudiation of the mother,
> whereby that which he gives up is turned into nothing, and indeed,
> father now has "everything," the phallus. ("Omnipotent" 139–40)

Benjamin's analysis of this type of oedipal dynamic in which narcissism is displaced or transferred can shed light on those idealized, dominating male figures who tread so heavily through Lawrence's fiction. Like
the omnipotent mother of narcissistic fantasy, these imposing father-fig-
ures embody a profound ambivalence, often inspiring as much dread as
desire. The threat is not just castration but (again as in relation to the
omnipotent mother) utter annihilation, a total loss of self in the other. The
rich complexity of Lawrence's fiction, however, is such that it also *resists*
the omnipotent fantasies; the striving for intersubjectivity competes with
the omnipotent tendencies. The repudiation of mother/woman in his fiction does not succeed in completely negating the positive, nurturing, and
empathic aspects of that primal identification; there is indeed frequent evidence of Fast's notion of secondary identification. In his most interesting
work, the narcissistic domination fantasies are tempered by the equally
Lawrencian passion for mutuality and balance, for the otherness that limits narcissism and makes real relationships possible.

LAWRENCE'S BIOGRAPHY

The purpose of this study is to use an intersubjective lens to explore the psychological dynamics, both interpersonal and intrapsychic, of Lawrence's fiction. My focus is not biographical; my aim is not to psychoanalyze Lawrence the man. Nevertheless, the author's life is implicit in my analysis, and if one were to examine the biography, one would expect to find confirming patterns. I will thus look briefly at the formative relationships in Lawrence's life, relying primarily on John Worthen's consummate volume on Lawrence's early years.

Worthen's portrait of Lawrence's mother Lydia is most pertinent to my argument. While the majority of Lawrence criticism highlights the controlling, domineering aspect of Lydia and her fictional counterpart, Gertrude Morel in *Sons and Lovers*, what is most striking in Worthen's portrayal is Lydia's extreme reticence, her shyness and emotional reserve. She was indeed nicknamed "The Mouse" as a child. Worthen quotes Lawrence's younger sister Ada describing Lydia "as having 'a rather quiet, reserved and ladylike nature. . . . She was never effusive or demonstrative in any way'" (15). Above all, the sense of Lydia that emerges in Worthen's account is that of a thwarted life, a life constricted on several levels and disappointed at all stages.

Lydia's emotional constriction was likely due, at least in part, to her strict, puritanical upbringing. She was also constrained by her family's diminished economic and social position; her father's family had been relatively well-off, but due to a collapse in the lace industry, they had lost almost everything. Lydia's parents were acutely sensitive to their loss of social position and esteem, and they habitually lived beyond their means. In Worthen's view, Lydia's father George suffered from "restlessness" and a "hurt pride" (13) that undoubtedly affected the children. When Lydia was nineteen, George was permanently lamed in an accident at work. The family was now forced to depend on the support of relatives—a further blow to the family's already injured pride. Lydia would have liked to have been a teacher (she had taught briefly when she was younger); nevertheless, she went to work with her sisters in a lace factory.

Four years later Lydia met Arthur Lawrence, and it appears that he may have represented her best opportunity for escape. Though he was only a collier, a miner's wages in those days were relatively high. There is further evidence to suggest that Arthur misrepresented his position to Lydia as something more than merely that of a collier. He led her to believe that he owned his house and furniture as well, when in actuality they belonged to his mother. "While it is impossible to be certain about what Arthur Lawrence told Lydia," Worthen concludes, "or what she may have wanted to hear, it is important that she came to believe that she had been deceived" (15). Her dashed expectations compounded a pattern in her family history of loss and humiliating disappointment.

In addition, when Lydia married Arthur, she was forced to leave her family's community and move to Eastwood. Worthen emphasizes her almost complete isolation. She "had relatively few friends in Eastwood, where she lived for twenty-six years. . . . To be more exact, she never accepted that Eastwood was her community" (23). Lawrence—or "Bert" as he was known to the family—was the fourth child born to this isolated and apparently bitter and depressed mother. In my analysis of *Sons and Lovers* I intend to show how the mother's wounded narcissism and depression are key factors in her son Paul's identity and relational problems. It is precisely the reality of the mother's thwarted life, her fractured subjectivity, that gives rise to the fantasy of her devouring omnipotence.

For Lydia, Arthur most likely represented an escape not only from poverty, but quite possibly from her cramped emotional life as well. From all accounts Arthur was an exuberant, highly sensual man, who drank and danced with abandon. Lydia's initial attraction to these qualities, however, soon gave way to her bitterness at being deceived and a growing antagonism toward both Arthur and the whole mining community. The marriage thus proved to have the opposite emotional effect; far from liberating her, it served only to rigidify her defenses, to increase her inwardness, isolation, and need for control. "She became sterner as she got older," Worthen notes, "and forgot her original reaction to her husband's charm and good humour" (18). Her children, as *Sons and Lovers* makes clear, became her allies and her refuge. The mother's overinvestment in her children and the shackling quality of her love are a direct product of the paucity of her life. The imperiousness and pride for which she was known may have been her best defense against a much deeper sense of injury and shame; and it is the mother's shame, not really her power, that is the legacy her son wrestled with most profoundly in his fiction.

Quoting from Lawrence's letters, Worthen maintains that we can see in the young Lawrence "a child's version of his mother's feelings; he grew up with a 'distaste for being caressed (except on occasions)' (i. 51), with a strong sense of untouchableness which was his 'sort of pride' (i. 165)" (59). The writer who came to champion touch and bodily, sexual expression was struggling against his own heavy sense of shame and deeply ingrained inhibitions. "Loving Lydia Lawrence meant not only remaining a responsible son and becoming a salary earner," Worthen suggests, "it meant inhibiting his own carelessness, impulsiveness, anger and (in particular) sensuality" (156). In Lawrence's life, and later in his imaginative work, his father came to represent everything that was denied and repressed: instinctive physicality, sensuality, and spontaneous emotional expression. Worthen thus sees the homoerotic strains in Lawrence's work as arising out of his particular parental conflict.

> We should see him, therefore, not as a "repressed homosexual," nor as a "latent homosexual," or indeed as a homosexual at all, but as a man caught between his habitual, torturing detachment, and his passionate longing for attachment: between the self who, like his mother, looked on and coolly understood and appreciated things—and the self much closer in sympathy to the more immediate, warmer and less articulate Arthur Lawrence. . . . He seems to have been particularly haunted by an acute nostalgia for being a man simple, sensual and whole: one who loved, and who was loved, physically and undemandingly in a way which he found, in his adolescence, more characteristic of his father than of his mother, and of men than of women. (158)

While I basically agree with this perspective, it does not account for the intense ambivalence toward homosexual love that also shows up in much of Lawrence's writing, in his letters and his fiction. Such ambivalence, furthermore, cannot be attributed simply to fear of social convention (Lawrence was hardly one to let societal pressures affect his choices). Rather, I think we need to look to the dynamics of infantile narcissism—particularly shame and splitting—in order to understand Lawrence's repulsion as well as attraction to the homoerotic bond.

As I will show in my analysis of his texts, Lawrence's idealized male characters are essentially idealized self-projections. Such idealization is a defense; it is a reaction to loss and deficiency, and thus it is invariably threatened by the shame and envy that initiated it. The empty, deficient self dreads being overwhelmed by the very power and vitality it has projected outward, onto the idealized other. For Lawrence, homosexual love was as ambivalently bound up with narcissistic projections as heterosexual love. While loving another man was connected in his mind with an infusing male potency, it was also tangled up with profound narcissistic shame, with self-contempt, and with a terror of dissolution and absorption: hence, as his letters reveal, his dreams of beetles and his associations of swamps and "marsh gas" with homosexual love.[7]

What the self lacks internally it craves in the external world, and thus it risks being overpowered or enslaved precisely by what it so urgently seeks. Worthen describes Lawrence's extreme reaction to watching Sarah Bernhardt perform onstage. In a letter (I 59) Lawrence refers to Bernhardt as "the incarnation of wild emotion," and discusses his extraordinary fascination with her performance: "I could love such a woman myself, love her to madness; all for the pure, wild passion of it. Intellect is shed as flowers shed their petals." He also describes rushing from the theater in fright lest he become "enslaved" to such a woman. As Worthen notes, "He was fascinated by the idea of being enslaved, and of having his own intellectual detachment stripped from him. And he did not know if he wanted it, or if he wanted to run away from it. That was the excitement of Bernhardt" (147). That is also the excitement that inspires much of the tension and dynamics of his fiction; it fuels conflict, moreover, in regard to both his male and female characters.

Worthen sees Lawrence's detachment from his own feelings as the most traumatic aspect of his young life. Underlying such detachment is a smoldering sense of shame connected with emotional and bodily expression. Lawrence was excruciatingly sensitive throughout his early years to feeling exposed and humiliated. His weak lungs and the many illnesses that plagued him from the time he was two weeks old contributed significantly to the problem, exacerbating his sense of deficiency and bodily shame. The rage that inevitably accompanies such shame became increasingly apparent when Lawrence entered his early twenties. The emotional constraint and the seeming gentleness and asexuality of his manner were periodically giving way to violent outbursts and angry, irrational fits. These were frequently directed at Jessie Chambers, the model for Miriam in *Sons and Lovers* and with whom Lawrence had an intensely ambivalent attachment. It wasn't until he met Frieda Von Richthofen Weekley, who was as impulsive and as sensually and emotionally uninhibited as his father, that Lawrence found a relationship that, though still perpetually conflicted, was genuinely liberating. Worthen believes that *Mr. Noon*, a thinly veiled fictional account of Lawrence's first trip abroad with Frieda, "suggests how Lawrence's life with Frieda was also important in making him show (not control) his feelings, and in making him come to terms with bottled up rages by being violently angry" (414).

Lawrence and Frieda's relationship was notorious for its violent rows. Yet they remained devoted, if not always (primarily in Frieda's case) sexually faithful to one another. The ability to tolerate tension is central to my thesis about Lawrence's literary genius; Frieda's ability to tolerate such extreme tension in their actual relationship is perhaps testament to her personal genius as well. Some of the paradoxes in Lawrence's fiction are equally apparent in his married life. While he could strike Frieda and furiously demand her submission, he simultaneously thrived on her ability to fight back and *not* cave in to his demands. He needed her fierce self-assertion to counter his own and thus save him from himself and a destructive solipsism. He could rant ludicrously about male mastery, yet he actually valued her feistiness and depended on her toughness and tenacity. He remarked to a friend that had he married Jessie Chambers rather than Frieda, "'I should have had too easy a life, nearly everything my own way, and my genius would have been destroyed'" (Maddox 399). Mark Kinkead-Weekes, in his biography of Lawrence's middle years, concurs with this view. "Frieda's greatest gift to him," he says, "was to refuse to let him dominate, and to fight him into self-exposure and self-knowledge" (*D. H. Lawrence* 23).

Lawrence, moreover, did not treat his wife as a slave or domestic servant; on the contrary, he defied conventional male working-class roles by doing his own cooking, sewing, and cleaning throughout his adult life. He enjoyed these domestic, traditionally female activities, just as he enjoyed the company of his many female friends. In his life as in his fiction, Lawrence's identification and empathy with women existed alongside his fear and anger toward them—one disposition did not extinguish the other. With both people and animals he could be tender and nurturing as well as savage and cruel, and these contradictions are creatively reenacted in his art. The man who struggled with emotional detachment and fear of exposure wrote novels especially notable for their passion and frankness, for their bold, uncensored expression of feeling. His fiction, as a result, offers an exceptionally candid view of the often contradictory needs and desires that drive human affective life.

PREVIOUS PSYCHOANALYTIC CRITICISM OF LAWRENCE

Lawrence's antagonism toward psychoanalysis has not prevented critics from applying various psychoanalytic theories to his work. Daniel Weiss's *Oedipus in Nottingham* (1962) was the first extensive Freudian study, while Marguerite Beede Howe's *The Art of the Self in D. H. Lawrence* (1977) uses Erikson, Jung, and Laing to examine Lawrence's existential anxieties about identity and relationship. Like virtually all of the psychoanalytic critics of Lawrence—both Freudian and post-Freudian—Howe highlights the fantasies of regressive merging and the fear of maternal engulfment that run throughout his work. Murray Schwartz defines the psychological "meta-theme" of Lawrence's fiction as that of oscillation between two poles: "the desire for oceanic merger and the desire for dominant autonomy, between boundarilessness and isolation, between oneness with an (idealized) other and separation created by (my/his/her) rage. At either extreme of these polarized states of being, Lawrence seems to lose his sense of personal existence. Yet he moves continually between the poles, and it is this movement that gives his style its distinctive rhythm" (219). Schwartz also notes the important affininities between Lawrence and Winnicott: both locate the heart of creative living in relationship, in the dynamic interaction between self and other.

Accordingly, several psychoanalytic studies in the recent past have focused on the preoedipal dynamics in Lawrence's work, and they make profitable use of Winnicott and other object relations theorists. Daniel Dervin (*A Strange Sapience* 1984) applies Winnicott's ideas to an exploration of Lawrence's creative process, illuminating the relationship between destructiveness and creativity. Dervin also understands Lawrence's trademark phoenix imagery as symbolic of the emergence of a nuclear, assertive self. Judith Ruderman's influential *D. H. Lawrence and the Devouring Mother* (1984) applies preoedipal theory, particularly Mahler's ego psychology, to the works of Lawrence's "leadership period." She sees the search for a strong, patriarchal leader and the worship of the phallus that distinguish these middle-period works as essentially defensive; the idealized male fantasies protect against the more fundamental, underlying fantasy of the powerful, primitive mother and the annihilation of regressive merging that she represents.

Margaret Storch (*Sons and Adversaries* 1990) shares Ruderman's view, though she relies primarily on Melanie Klein's theories to illuminate the idealization and splitting apparent in Lawrence's characterizations and imagery. She finds ample evidence in Lawrence's texts of Klein's paranoid-schizoid position in which breast/mother is split into good and bad, and like Ruderman, she sees the paranoiac projection of the omnipotent, "bad," devouring mother as giving rise to the defense of idealized masculinity. The sense of emptiness, the feeling of inauthenticity and lack of sensuous contact that Lawrence suffered from and railed against, Storch believes, is "grounded upon threatened masculinity, castration fear, and the mother who overpowers the father" (14).

Storch concludes by arguing that *Lady Chatterly's Lover*, unlike the strident masculine fantasies of the leadership novels, achieves a "sustained fantasy of masculine strength" (188) that finally allows for some integration of the loving, good mother. John Clayton makes a similar claim about Lawrence in his object relations study of the modern novel (*Gestures of Healing* 1991). He argues that Lawrence "is the only modernist who can take blessing from his father. It is what permitted him to identify with the center rather than long for the center, to assert knowledge rather than uncertainty" (195). Lawrence, he maintains, was able to keep the modernist anxiety of emptiness and engulfment "at bay by identifying with a mythologized father" (195).

My psychoanalysis of Lawrence's texts comes to a different conclusion. Identification with an idealized father is not what resolves splitting or protects against emotional void. Like Benjamin, I do not see the traditional oedipal solution as the only way out of the primitive narcissistic fantasies of the early mother-child dyad. As Winnicott has shown, limits and reality can be discovered *in* the dyad, through the interactions of symbolic play. Lawrence's very ability to symbolize his narcissistic conflicts, to represent and transform them so creatively in his art, attests to at least some degree of internalization of the good mother from the beginning, to a holding and sustaining maternal presence that is not wholly dependent on the later paternal identification. The psychological achievement of his fiction does not lie in his identification with a mythologized father but in his ability, in his best work, to identify with his female characters as subjects of desire and to maintain the values of tenderness and nurture in his male and paternal characterizations.

This is not to deny the maternal repudiation, the defensive male idealizations, and the ubiquity of the bad, devouring mother fantasies that Ruderman and Storch so persuasively detail. Rather, my point is that the paranoid-schizoid fantasies exist in tension with more highly developed intersubjective strivings. The narcissistic domination fantasies compete with an empathic identification in which maternal/female subjectivity is recognized and valued. Benjamin in fact sees the tension between the intersubjective, relational world and the omnipotent fantasy world "as roughly equivalent to that between the depressive and schizoid positions in Kleinian theory, which are no longer understood as successive but as dialectically alternating or complementary" ("Omnipotent" 132), a view that is increasingly holding sway in contemporary psychoanalytic thought.[8]

Psychoanalytic criticism of Lawrence has focused almost exclusively on the omnipotent fantasies. Those fantasies represent only one side, however, of a psychological dialectic that is crucial to appreciating Lawrence's fiction. In his greatest work, the subjective reality of the characters—that is, the realization of their complex inner lives, of their fully human suffering—competes with and ultimately withstands the polarized narcissistic fantasies that are also projected onto them. While the leadership novels reflect a breakdown in tension and are admittedly weighted on the side of schizoid or narcissistic fantasy, his best works hold and play with oppositional pressures; they maintain, in Lawrence's own words, "the trembling instability of the balance" ("Morality and the Novel" 528).[9]

AN INTERSUBJECTIVE APPROACH TO LAWRENCE: POLARITIES AND PARADOXES

Intersubjective theory thus broadens the focus and uncovers new territory for psychoanalytic investigation of Lawrence's work. If the omnipotent mother fantasy does not represent bedrock, and if symbiosis with the mother does not represent an original, universal condition, then the

Lawrencian fantasies of maternal omnipotence and of merging become available for still further analysis. These fantasies do not necessarily reflect an originary psychological position but may in fact be retroactive, signifying a breakdown of particular relational dynamics and interactions. We thus need to attend more closely to the specific modes of mother-child and self-other interaction in Lawrence's fiction, looking especially at difficulties in attunement and recognition.

An intersubjective approach will also expose some surprising psychological ironies. Beneath the fantasy of the dominating, devouring mother is the experience of a wounded, fragile mother whose impaired subjectivity is vital to understanding Lawrence's imaginative world. The overriding anxiety is that the fragile m/other cannot survive the destructiveness of a ruthless self-assertion. The full, unchecked release of bodily impulses and desires, the self unconsciously fears, will overwhelm and devastate the other on whom it depends. My textual analyses hope to prove how this anxiety plays an important role in the formation of Lawrence's sadomasochistic fantasies.

Identification with the mother's shame and suffering is deeply implicated in, though not eradicated by, the male domination fantasies. Such identification can help to illuminate the irony that Lawrence biographers have noted: the writer best known for his celebration of sexuality and uninhibited bodily expression in his art was in many respects quite puritanical and fastidious in his life. As Worthen mentions, Lawrence disliked being touched or caressed, and he hated being kissed on the mouth. Jeffrey Meyers points out how Lawrence made Frieda wear austere, starched underwear and once chided a female houseguest for entering the sitting-room in her ankle-length petticoat—"He disapproved," he told her, "of people appearing in their underclothes" (125). As Meyers wryly observes, "He could be a prude as well as a priest of love" (125).

The irony is apparent in the fiction as well. Beneath the urgent promotion of spontaneous sensual expression in the texts is a profound sense of shame over bodily, passionate life and a concomitant narcissistic rage. Sexuality is bound up with such shame and rage for Lawrence, and thus it can prove to be a source of terror, of dread and repulsiveness, while simultaneously representing the locus for narcissistic repair, for idealization and salvation of the self.

Finally, by examining the role of the mother in Lawrence's fiction not only as a psychic object but as a subject, and in particular, as a wounded or fractured subject, I hope to cast fresh light on the contradictions in Lawrence's relations with women. His work reveals how a breakdown of balanced subject-subject relations, or intersubjectivity, can give rise to defensive, destructive polarities—specifically, rigid polarities of gender and of domination and submission. At the same time, however, the subjective universe of his fiction reflects an unusually fluid gender identity and a psychic flexibility that can accommodate, indeed play, with dialectical tension, with deep ambivalence, and with paradox. In Lawrence's finest works, the paradoxes take precedence over the polarities.

The following study will thus focus on what I (and the majority of critics) consider Lawrence's most accomplished fiction: *Sons and Lovers, The Rainbow, Women in Love,* and a number of short stories. In line with my theoretical perspective, the analyses of these works will be structured in terms of relationships—interpersonal relations between characters as well as intrapsychic relational dynamics apparent in the specific language and imagery of the texts as a whole. While the characters fall into certain recurring relational patterns and are often trapped in polarized narcissistic fantasies, the narrative perspective frequently resists and counters those fantasies by encompassing them within a larger intersubjective awareness. By exhibiting dynamic tension on a number of levels, Lawrence's best works dramatically reenact the competing forces of psychic and relational life: the opposing identifications, positions, and desires operating within any single psyche, as well as the tension between internal and external—between projection of the inner world and awareness of the outer—and between assertion of the self and recognition of the other. His work alerts us to the need for that difficult but vital tension between self and other when both are recognized equally as subjects of desire.

CHAPTER 2

Sons and Lovers

GERTRUDE AND PAUL:
THE DEPRESSED MOTHER AND THE DEPENDENT CHILD

Critics have generally recognized *Sons and Lovers*, Lawrence's third novel, as one of the author's most finely observed and moving works. It has nevertheless provoked controversy over the question of aesthetic control: Does the novel lose command of tone and point of view? Many readers have noticed the contradictions between the dramatic presentation of the characters and the interpretive commentary on them. As H. M. Daleski observes, "The weight of hostile comment which Lawrence directs against Morel is balanced by the unconscious sympathy with which he is presented dramatically, while the overt celebration of Mrs. Morel is challenged by the harshness of the character in action" (43). Mark Schorer indeed proclaims the novel a technical failure because of such contradictions; the "psychological tension," he believes, "disrupts the form" of the novel (167).

Conversely, more recent critics commmend the novel expressly for its manipulation of narrative point of view. Helen and Carl Baron, in their introduction to the Cambridge University Press edition of the novel, stress the deliberate "ambiguity" in the narrative perspective, a "blending of the way people perceive each other," such that the reader is invited to "notice how feelings are silently passed between people so that they are unconsciously affected by each other's emotions" (xxx–xxxi). Other critics emphasize that Paul's perspective should not be confused with that of the author or the omniscient narrator. Geoffrey Harvey, for instance, argues that "Paul's point of view is by no means the only one. . . . His version of the truth of his story is centrally important and a crucial means of gaining sympathy for him, but it is endlessly qualified by other competing perspectives, and in control of these viewpoints is the implied author, who is concerned throughout to testify to the complexity of the truth" (69). Harvey's position is similar to Cynthia Lewiecki-Wilson's claim, quoted in my introduction, that the "narration combines both omniscient point of view and subjectivity, resulting in a textual voice that authorizes each character's experiences as equally legitimate, presenting competing centers of 'authenticity'" (70).

The authorization of each character's subjective authenticity—the affirmation of the character's compelling inner life, of his or her needs and desires even as they conflict with the needs and desires of the character most ostensibly identified with the author—reflects, in the language of my critical framework, an intersubjective consciousness. Such intersubjective consciousness functions simultaneously with the projection of unconscious narcissistic fantasies—fantasies most associated with the authorial alter ego character—onto all of the characters. The result is a conflictual, sometimes contradictory character portrayal that is nevertheless true to the complex dialectic of projection and awareness—projection of one's own inner world and empathic awareness of the inner world of the other—that distinguishes real human relationships. The tension between intersubjective consciousness and narcissistic projection is especially apparent in the characterization of Mrs. Morel.

Judith Arcana has traced what she sees as a tradition of "wholesale mother-blaming" in *Sons and Lovers* criticism. She ties this phenomenon to an "oedipalized mother-blaming" in our culture-at-large (139). The view of Gertrude Morel as the destroyer of her husband and the devourer of her sons, she argues, "ignores one basic conflict the novel presents: the intensity and power of Gertrude Morel thwarted by the utter impotence of her situation" (143). She quotes Lydia Blanchard's description of Gertrude ("Love and Power" 435) as "'a woman trapped in a marriage she does not want, hemmed in by a world that allows her no positive outlets for her talents and energies, who must live a vicarious existence through her sons'" (146).[1]

This is indeed the perspective that the novel's first three chapters in particular present. The mother is depicted not merely as an object of anger or desire for her husband and children but as a suffering subject in her own right. The compassionate rendering of Mrs. Morel's inner pain is a predominant feature of the early chapters. Granted this focus is not sustained throughout the novel—Paul's subjectivity becomes the reigning perspective of part 2—but to ignore the sensitive portrayal of the mother's distress in part 1, as Arcana asserts, is to neglect a vital aspect of the novel.

While I disagree with Arcana that the fantasy of the mother as destroyer and devourer is only projected onto the novel by critics brainwashed by oedipal theory (the fantasy is there in the text, too), I do believe that *Sons and Lovers* demonstrates how that fantasy is grounded in the mother's thwarted subjectivity. The first chapter emphatically establishes the mother's lack of "I-ness," her sense that she has no self, no individual agency or authentic being in her own right:

And looking ahead, the prospect of her life made her feel as if she were
buried alive.

. . . She seemed so far away from her girlhood, she wondered if it
were the same person walking heavily up the back garden at the Bottoms,
as had run so lightly on the breakwater at Sheerness, ten years before.

"What have I to do with it!" she said to herself. "What have I to
do with all this? Even the child I am going to have! It doesn't seem as
if I were taken into account."

Sometimes life takes hold of one, carries the body along, accomplishes one's history, and yet is not real, but leaves one's self as it were
slurred over. (14)

Because the mother does not feel herself "real," the discovery of reality
for the child she carries will prove to be exceedingly difficult. Lack of
faith in the mother's independent reality and the comcomitant sense of
one's own insubstantiality or hollowness constitute the core problem for
Paul; it is indeed the fundamental problem that Lawrence's fiction
repeatedly, and so creatively, addresses.

Lawrence is astutely aware of the social and economic circumstances contributing to the mother's narcissistically impaired state.
Gertrude's economic dependency in a loveless marriage keeps her powerless, angry, and resentful. As a woman, her options for self-realization
and expression are limited to her role as mother and, as Blanchard notes,
to a vicarious experience of achievement through the lives of her sons:

The world seemed a dreary place, where nothing else would happen for
her—at least until William grew up. But for herself, nothing but this
dreary endurance—till the children grew up. And the children! She
could not afford to have this third. She did not want it. The father serv-
ing beer in a public house, swilling himself drunk. She despised him,
and was tied to him. The coming child was too much for her. If it were
not for William and Annie, she was sick of it, the struggle with poverty
and ugliness and meanness. (13)

By presenting Mrs. Morel's perspective, the narrative displays an
empathic understanding of the mother's resentment of her fetus, Paul.
This is rather remarkable given the autobiographical nature of the novel
and the authorial identification with Paul. The fact that Mrs. Morel "did
not want," indeed "dreaded this baby" (50) is repeated several times in
the opening chapters. We are also told of her great shame and guilt over
feeling such antipathy toward her baby, and we will certainly see Paul
suffer the consequences. As Jeffrey Berman points out, Gertrude is an
"alternately overloving and underloving" mother (205). The narrative
identification with the mother's anguish in this first part of the book,
however, resists a simplistic interpretation of the novel that "blames"
Gertrude Morel for her failures as a mother.

Sons and Lovers dramatizes Mrs. Morel's rigidity and lack of sensuality, but it also allows the reader to see the mother herself as the
beleaguered child of a cold, harsh parent—her overbearing father,
George Coppard: he is described as "proud in his bearing, handsome,
and rather bitter; who preferred theology in reading, and who drew near
in sympathy only to one man, the Apostle Paul; who was harsh in gov-
ernment, and in familiarity ironic; who ignored all sensuous pleasure"
(18). Though we are told Gertrude preferred her mother and "hated her
father's overbearing manner towards her gentle, humorous, kindly-
souled mother" (15–16), it is her father's emotional legacy that she
bears: "She was a puritan, like her father, high-minded, and really
stern" (18). If one is assigning blame, in other words, one must look to
Lawrence's explicit representation of the repressive, patriarchal culture
of which Gertrude is a product.

The narrator also informs us that before meeting Walter Morel,
Gertrude had loved a young man, John Field, whom she was prevented
from marrying by economic constraints and by Field's own rigid, auto-
cratic father. When Field tells her he would like to go into the ministry,
Gertrude responds, "Then why *don't* you—why don't you. . . . If *I* were
a man, nothing would stop me" (16). Field replies, "But my father's so
stiff necked. He means to put me into the business, and I know he'll do
it" (16). Field's father loses the business, but Field pursues neither the
ministry nor Gertrude: he becomes a teacher and marries an elderly
woman with property. "And still," the narrator asserts, "Mrs. Morel
preserved John Field's bible. . . . [She] kept his memory intact in her
heart, for her own sake. To her dying day, for thirty-five years, she did
not speak of him" (17).

The portrait of Gertrude that emerges in this first chapter allows the
reader to understand her brittleness. The hard, affectless surface or shell
protects against deep disappointment and personal diminishment,
against the emotional rejection she suffered as a daughter and a woman
in a father's world. After marrying Walter, she again experiences humiliation and betrayal when she learns that the house she believed was her
husband's does not actually belong to him: "Gertrude sat white and
silent. She was her father now. . . . She said very little to her husband,
but her manner had changed towards him. Something in her proud,
honorable soul had crystallised out hard as rock" (21).

Lawrence's fiction regularly portrays characters whose souls have
hardened and "crystallised" as a result of severe narcissistic injury. A
shameful feeling of rejection—rejection of her feeling, desiring self—
underlies Mrs. Morel's proud, impenetrable surface. The condition
infuses much of Lawrence's fiction. It fits Harry Guntrip's description of
schizoid phenomena in which the self, by warding off its intolerable,

painful feelings, becomes insulated from all emotion, indeed from the affective core of its being. The predominant subjective experience for the schizoid individual, and for so many Lawrence characters, is consequently one of emptiness or inner void.

Gertrude was originally attracted to Walter because he promised to fill the void by representing precisely what she (and her father) lacked— spontaneous, emotional and physical expressiveness: "the dusky, golden softness of this man's sensuous flame of life, that flowed from off his flesh like the flame from a candle, not baffled and gripped into incandescence by thought and spirit as her life was, seemed to her something wonderful, beyond her" (18). As Lawrence came to recognize so clearly, however, another person can never complete or fill the void in the self. Selves can only balance and complement one another. The empty or fractured self may typically seek to absorb or devour the other in an attempt to compensate for the deficiency, but Lawrence shows again and again how that sort of relationship is doomed.

Because Gertrude "had no life of her own," the narrator explains, "she had to put her own living aside, put it in the bank, as it were, of her children. She thought and waited for them, dreamed what they would do, with herself behind them as motor force, when they grew up. Already William was a lover to her" (44). *Sons and Lovers* is indeed the quintessential oedipal novel; it demonstrates exactly how the oedipal fantasy becomes bloated and inflamed by the mother's wounded narcissism or impaired subjectivity. The early scenes in the novel consistently spotlight Mrs. Morel's subjective experiences of loss, exclusion, and betrayal. In the scene in which Morel chops off William's baby curls, for instance, the narrator focuses on Mrs. Morel's emotional devastation:

> It was her first baby. She went very white, and was unable to speak. . . .
> "Oh—my boy!—" she faltered. Her lip trembled, her face broke, and,
> snatching up the child, she buried her face in his shoulder and cried
> painfully. She was one of those women who cannot cry: it hurts as it
> hurts a man. It was like ripping something out of her, her sobbing. . . .
> [S]he knew, and Morel knew, that act had caused something momen-
> tous to take place in her soul. She remembered the scene all her life, as
> one in which she had suffered the most intensely. (24)

Her reaction may in fact be irrational and excessive, but her pain, as the narrative enforces, is nonetheless real. Prior to the incident we are told of Gertrude's loneliness and isolation "miles away from her own people"; her passionate bond and identification with her male child provide the only sense of meaningful connection and value in her life: "He came just when her own bitterness of disillusion was hardest to bear; when her faith in life was shaken, and her soul felt dreary and lonely.

She made much of the child, and the father was jealous" (22). The narrator, however, does not blame Morel—cutting the child's hair was not a malicious act. The reader may even feel, like the critic Harvey, that Morel "has as much right as she has to decide when the baby's hair will be cut; that his desire to observe social convention is not unreasonable; and that his wife's overreaction is made to seem tragically absurd by his stunned silence" (70). Nevertheless, the narrative choice to describe the event primarily from Mrs. Morel's point of view is significant and reflects empathy with the mother's profound sense of loss, however irrational that feeling may be.[2]

The other scene that vividly depicts the mother's desolation, one of the most famous in all of Lawrence's fiction, is that of Mrs. Morel and the white lilies. Once again the emotional context for the scene is rejection and betrayal: Mrs. Morel has been locked out of the house by her drunken husband. Outside, she is struck by the brutal light of the moon just as she had been struck by her husband's brutal treatment: "Mrs. Morel, seared with passion, shivered to find herself out there in a great, white light, that fell cold on her, and gave a shock to her inflamed soul" (33). She wanders around in a "delirious condition," mentally reenacting the painful scene until, as usual, she has successfully numbed the pain through defensive, "mechanical" mental effort: "mechanically she went over the last scene, then over it again, certain phrases, certain moments coming each time like a brand red hot, down on her soul: and each time . . . the brand came down at the same points, till the mark was burnt in, and the pain burnt out" (33–34). Finally,

> She hurried out of the side garden to the front, where she could stand as if in an immense gulf of white light, the moon streaming high in face of her, the moonlight standing up from the hills in front, and filling the valley where the Bottoms crouched, almost blindingly. . . .
>
> She became aware of something about her. With an effort, she roused herself, to see what it was that penetrated her consciousness. The tall white lilies were reeling in the moonlight, and the air was charged with their perfume, as with a presence. Mrs. Morel gasped slightly in fear. She touched the big, pallid flowers on their petals, then shivered. They seemed to be stretching in the moonlight. She put her hand into one white bin: the gold scarcely showed on her fingers by moonlight. She bent down, to look at the bin-ful of yellow pollen: but it only appeared dusky. Then she drank a deep draught of the scent. It almost made her dizzy.
>
> She looked round her. The privet hedge had a faint glitter among its blackness. Various white flowers were out. In front, the hill rose into indistinctness, barred by high black hedges, and nervous with cattle moving in the dim moonlight. Here and there the moonlight seemed to stir and ripple.

Mrs. Morel leaned on the garden gate, looking out, and she lost herself awhile. She did not know what she thought. Except for a slight feeling of sickness, and her consciousness in the child, her self melted out like scent into the shiny, pale air. After a time, the child too melted with her in the mixing-pot of moonlight, and she rested with the hills and lilies and houses, all swum together in a kind of swoon. (34)

Critics all agree that the imagistic rendering of Mrs. Morel's interior state here is extraordinary; they disagree, however, over the exact meaning or interpretation of the images.[3] I would like to emphasize two major points. First, the mother's initial subjective state—her forlorn, outcast position and her sense of violation and helpless fury—echoes that of a narcissistically injured child. Throughout Lawrence's work, the mother is repeatedly cast as the object of the child's narcissistic rage; in this scene the mother is *both* the suffering subject and the hated object—represented by the archetypally maternal moon, here figured as a cold, aggressive, and blinding force.[4] The mother's internal suffering is foregrounded even as the scene symbolically projects the external image of a remorseless and overpowering mother. Second, the merging fantasy with which the scene culminates is directly related to the condition of narcissistic injury with which the scene begins.

As discussed in the introduction, the prevailing psychoanalytic view of merging fantasies today is that they represent less a regression to an actual prior symbiotic state than a reaction to early failures of attunement and recognition. If the infant's assertion of its spontaneous, physical and emotional being is not recognized by the attuned response of the other, the baby experiences narcissistic rejection, a denial of its affective vitality or being. The child, moreover, may feel that its experience of bodily feelings and desires is shameful and must be kept hidden and rigidly in check. The result is a loss of the sense of subjective reality or authenticity. Such a state can trigger the opposite fantasy: the fantasy of letting go and abolishing all barriers and boundaries as one seeks the bodily, affective affirmation of self that was experienced as denied or withheld.

The lily scene paradoxically casts the mother herself in the role of the maternally rebuffed and bereft child. The imagery of the first part of the scene also enacts a basic assertion-recognition dynamic. The tall white lilies reeling and stretching in the moonlight suggest a passionate (indeed phallic) self-assertion that both mirrors and balances the powerful assertiveness of the white moon. Beneath the exterior whiteness of the lilies, associated like the moon with coldness and chastity, is an interior of yellow pollen and perfumed scent, connoting a "dusky" sensuality (and echoing the sensuous "dusky, golden softness" of Mr. Morel, quoted earlier). Mrs. Morel's reaching in to touch and then deeply inhaling the scent represent an attempt to access a hidden, repressed sensuality or bodily vitality. The explicitly oral metaphor—"she drank a deep draught of the scent"—also ties the scene psychologically to the primary mother-child relationship and its initial oral mode of connection.

The act of imbibing the pollen leaves Mrs. Morel in a dizzy, disoriented state, and the two paragraphs that follow describe a blurring of boundaries and a mystical, melting fluidity. The fantasy emphasizes a profound relaxing of restraints and a surrendering of mental defenses— "she lost herself awhile. She did not know what she thought"—(recall Mrs. Morel's exhausting mental efforts earlier to defend against emotional pain). The moonlight at the end is no longer aggressive but holding and containing—a "mixing-pot of moonlight" in which "she rested with the hills and lilies and houses." The regressive fantasy of merging or melting, again, does not reflect a desire to return to an actual former state of bliss or oneness with the mother; as this scene makes clear, it is a reaction, an imaginative effort to reverse an actual former state of emotional, bodily frigidity and nonattunement, and to dissolve the rigid mental barriers defending against pain and rejection.

The fantasy of idealized attunement and perfect harmony, however, cannot be sustained. When Mrs. Morel finally leaves the garden she is once more feeling fatigued and desolate: "she was tired and wanted to sleep. In the mysterious out-of-doors she felt forlorn" (35). Mrs. Morel's depression is key to understanding the psychological problems of her sons and the symbolic imagery of the above scene. Gertrude's lost contact with her own authentic emotional and bodily life will make it difficult for her to recognize the passional life of her sons. Paul will himself continually reenact the dynamics of the lily scene as he struggles to assert himself and be recognized by mother/moon/woman. He too will seek to recover a lost authenticity and hidden sensuality with a desire so intense it threatens boundaries and loss of self. His experience of his mother as withdrawn and withholding both excites acute narcissistic rage (most often projected in the image of a hostile, rejecting mother) and exacerbates the oedipal desire to penetrate, merge with, and possess her.

The narrative shows Paul even as an infant as heir to his mother's stunted life, to her sadness and shame. Mrs. Morel notes "the peculiar heaviness of its [the baby's] eyes, as if it were trying to understand something that was pain. . . . It had blue eyes like her own, but its look was heavy, steady, as if it had realised something that had stunned some point of its soul" (50). She decides to call him Paul, "she knew not why" (51). The name, however, echoes her father's affinity with the cold, harsh Apostle Paul "who ignored all sensuous pleasure." The mother cannot help but bequeath to her son her own puritanical, affectively impoverished heritage.

Mrs. Morel's depression is mirrored in her child who, the narrator tells us, trotted after her "like her shadow" and "would have fits of depression" that were particularly unsettling for his mother: "It made her feel beside herself. . . . She would plump him in a little chair in the yard, exclaiming, 'Now cry there, Misery!'" (64). Because Mrs. Morel has defensively warded off her own deep sadness and shame, she is unable to tolerate or empathize with her son's negative affects—his feelings of grief and anger—as well. Throughout his life Paul is unable to tell his mother about any of his failures or disgraces: "he never told her anything disagreeable that was said to him, only the nice things, trying always to make her believe he was happy and well-liked, and that the world went well with him. . . . He brought her everything, except his small shames and ignominies" (135).

Unable to express himself fully in relation to his mother, Paul never feels fully recognized or realized by her. Only his mother holds the power to confer reality and authenticate his experience of himself. "The children," the narrator relates, "alone with their mother, told her all about the day's happenings, everything. Nothing had really taken place in them, until it was told to their mother" (87). For Paul, "There was one place in the world that stood solid and did not melt into unreality: the place where his mother was. Everybody else could grow shadowy, almost non-existent to him, but she could not. It was as if the pivot and pole of his life, from which he could not escape, was his mother" (261). The mother's dependence on her children—particularly her sons—to provide her own missing self-esteem makes it difficult for her children to discover their own independent selves, and thus they remain resentfully dependent, unable to "escape" her orbit.

The mother will assume gigantic, fearsome proportions in fantasy precisely because of the belittlement and self-suppression she suffered in reality. Paul's crippling dependence on her is thus paradoxically due to his sense that she is vitally dependent on *him*—that he is responsible for filling her emptiness, providing her missing self-esteem, and relieving her suffering. "It hurt the boy keenly, this feeling about her, that she had never had her life's fulfilment: and his own incapability to make up to her hurt him with a sense of impotence, yet made him patiently dogged inside. It was his childish aim" (91). This is also the obsessive aim of the boy Paul in the story "The Rocking-Horse Winner." The scene in part 2 of *Sons and Lovers* where Paul and his mother view the Lincoln cathedral symbolically captures the psychological dilemma of a child's dependence on a depressed mother.

The scene imagistically parallels the mother and the cathedral:

He looked at his mother. Her blue eyes were watching the cathedral quietly. She seemed again to be beyond him. Something in the eternal repose of the uplifted cathedral, blue and noble against the sky, was reflected in her, something of the fatality. What was, was!—with all his young will he could not alter it. He saw her face, . . . her mouth always closed with disillusion; and there was on her the same eternal look, as if she knew fate at last. He beat against it with all the strength of his soul.

"Look mother how big she is above the town! Think, there are streets and streets below her: she looks bigger than the city altogether."

"So she does!" exclaimed his mother, breaking bright into life again. But he had seen her sitting, looking steady out of the window at the cathedral, her face and eyes fixed, reflecting the relentlessness of life. And the crow's-feet near her eyes, and her mouth shut so hard, made him feel he would go mad. (280–81)

The passage emphasizes, above all, the mother's remoteness in relation to her son. Like the cathedral, she seemed "to be beyond him," excluding him, shutting him out with her hard, "fixed" stoicism. Due to maternal depression, the child experiences the mother as affectively closed-off and hopelessly inaccessible. The experience arouses intense narcissistic fury and ignites the oedipal desire to penetrate her barriers. The boy tries to reach the mother by praising the cathedral's grandeur and power, declaring how much "bigger than the city" it looks. He is, in essence, trying to enhance the mother's self-esteem, to make her feel important and powerful. Although she brightens briefly, Paul realizes that her other look of tight constraint and disillusion represents the hard reality he is powerless to change.

"The Rocking-Horse Winner," as mentioned, is also about a child's furious and futile attempt to access a depressed mother. The story, unlike *Sons and Lovers*, does not give much attention to the sources of the mother's calcified inner state. Only the opening paragraph offers a succinct assessment of her condition:

There was a woman who was beautiful, who started with all the advantages, yet she had no luck. She married for love, and the love turned to dust. She had bonny children, yet she felt they had been thrust upon her, and she could not love them. They looked at her coldly, as if they were finding fault with her. And hurriedly she felt she must cover up some fault in herself. Yet what it was that she must cover up she never knew. Nevertheless, when her children were present, she always felt the centre of her heart go hard. This troubled her, and in her manner she was all the more gentle and anxious for her children, as if she loved them very much. Only she herself knew that at the centre of her heart was a hard little place that could not feel love, no, not for anybody. (790)

Berman is correct, I believe, in pointing out the similarity between the mother in this story and Mrs. Morel (209). Arcana, on the other hand, makes a distinction between the story and the novel, claiming that the story is indeed "mother-blaming": the text of the story "never redeems her, and the mother's utter inability to respond to him [her son] turns us away from empathy with her character" (146–47). Though the focus of the story is on the boy's inner world, not the mother's, the narrative tone is not accusatory. In the above paragraph, the mother's condition is simply observed and reported. The narrative makes it clear, furthermore, that the mother's emptiness and inability to feel represent a loss for her as well as her children. The issue of blame seems to me more a matter of the reader's projection than an actual concern of the narrator or implied author.

Like Gertrude Morel, the mother in this story is trapped in a loveless marriage and by a maternal role she feels has "been thrust upon her." Without any sense of her own effective agency, life seems to her a matter of "luck," that is, of forces beyond her control. She feels subject to a fate that is either benevolent or withholding, with no power to affect or influence that fate herself. From a psychoanalytic perspective, such a state suggests a child's dependence on a nonattuned other, an other whom the child experiences as nonresponsive and beyond her control. The other's lack of response to the child's agentic expression ultimately has a nullifying, numbing effect. Time and again in Lawrence's fiction we see a woman forced into a childlike position of dependency in marriage and in a culture that refuses to recognize her as a subject in her own right—a situation that repeats and telescopes a narcissistically wounded infantile state. Although the story, unlike the novel, does not pursue the roots of the mother's emptiness in empathetic detail, the opening paragraph does place her condition in context. Lawrence seems aware, as usual, that the inability to feel is always a response and a defense.

"The Rocking-Horse Winner" is about the child's battle to break through the mother's defensive numbness and receive the affective recognition he craves. Paul's childlike association of "luck" with "lucre," along with his mother's anxiety about money, make him believe that he could fill his mother's affective hollowness by winning at the horse races and thus providing her with "luck." The desire to compensate the mother's emotional shortage and "fill" her himself is inevitably sexualized, evident in the orgasmic imagery of the child's feverish, back-and-forth riding on his wooden horse. The masturbatory, mechanistic, mentally controlling nature of the child's riding represents a state of being that Lawrence revolted against repeatedly in his writing. Paul's state also implies the sort of fusion Lawrence dreaded: the boundaries between the internal and the external have collapsed. The self's inner wishes magically affect the outside, material world. The story thus allows us to glimpse the emotional and relational origins of that state of solipsistic isolation and omnipotent control toward which Lawrence was powerfully drawn as well as repulsed.

The sexual implications of Paul's rocking-horse riding, furthermore, cannot be wholly explained by the oedipal drive. Sexuality, as Stephen Mitchell has discussed, is a prime arena for the playing out of basic self-other boundary issues. "Sex," he explains, "is a powerful organizer of experience. Bodily sensations and sensual pleasures define one's skin, one's outline, one's boundaries" (*Relational Concepts* 103). The pleasurable release of tension, according to Mitchell, is not the fundamental aim of sexuality; rather, it is "the establishment and maintenance of relatedness," of emotional responsiveness and connection (*Relational* 107). Thus the interpretation of Lawrence's story need not begin and end with the sexual symbolism and the oedipal fantasy. The sexual and the oedipal are informed by still deeper emotional and relational dynamics. The frenzied fantasy of sexualized union with the mother reflects a more profound need to fill the mother's emptiness and heal her wound, to unfreeze her affective core and secure her emotional response, her recognition.

The scene near the story's end, when the mother finally discovers her son wildly "plunging to and fro" on his horse, symbolically enacts the longed-for recognition originally impeded by the mother's emotional frigidity: "Then suddenly she switched on the light, and saw her son, in his green pyjamas, madly surging on the rocking-horse. The blaze of light suddenly lit him up, as he urged the wooden horse, and lit her up, as she stood, blonde, in her dress of pale green and crystal, in the doorway" (803). The son has finally obtained the mother's recognition. The light and color imagery conveys the basic psychological dynamic. Mother and son are at last united and in harmony, connected by the blazing light that illuminates them each together and by their matching green attire. Unlike the light, however, the green is not a "blazing," vital hue but "pale green and crystal," evoking the affectively frozen conditon that provoked the son's frenzied activity in the first place. Soon after this scene the boy dies. The child cannot fill the void in the mother's self, though he was willing to sacrifice his own self in the effort.

The enraged hostility and aggression toward the mother apparent throughout Lawrence's writing emerge, therefore, less in response to the mother's real power or strength than as a reaction to her impaired state, to her emotional calcification and psychic fragility. In *Sons and Lovers* such maternally directed violence is expressed symbolically in two scenes—the broken doll and bread-burning episodes. In the first incident, after Paul accidentally breaks Annie's doll, he conducts a strangely sadistic doll-sacrifice ceremony:

He made an altar of bricks, pulled some the shavings out of Arabella's body, put the waxen fragments into the hollow face, poured on a little paraffin, and set the whole thing alight. He watched with wicked satisfaction the drops of wax melt off the broken forehead of Arabella, and drop like sweat into the flame. So long as the stupid big doll burned he rejoiced in silence. At the end he poked among the embers with a stick, fished out the arms and legs, all blackened, and smashed them under stones.

"That's the sacrifice of Missis Arabella," he said. "An' I'm glad there's nothing left of her."

Which disturbed Annie inwardly, although she could say nothing. He seemed to hate the doll so intensely, because he had broken it. (82–83)

Psychoanalytic critics have generally interpreted the doll in this scene as representative of the mother and the ritual sacrifice as a reflection of Paul's enraged and destructive feelings toward her.[5] I have also discussed the episode briefly in *Literature and the Relational Self* (67–68). There I stress the importance of Annie's assertion that Paul "seemed to hate the doll so intensely, because he had broken it," and I argue that Paul's sadism reflects his fear and hatred "of his own destructive rage and the fragile vulnerability of mother/self" (68). I would like to extend that interpretation here by considering the scene in relation to Winnicott's concept of object use. As discussed in the introduction, Winnicott argues that the infant needs to "destroy" the object psychically and the object must survive in order for the infant to "use" or discover the real object—an object whose existence is independent of and outside the infant's mental control.

Michael Eigen offers a wonderfully evocative description of this process:

A kind of psychic explosion takes place in which one lets go as fully as possible. In the other's survival, otherness is born (or reborn) and the self quickens. In such an instance fury or rage is deeper than hate. . . . The baby's wrath plays a role in exploding fantasy and reaching the realness of himself and others. An explosion clears the air. The discovery that the other continues to be alive in spite of one's fantasy of destruction creates or ratifies a joyous shock of difference. One is liberated by the other's survival and aliveness. (*Psychotic* 179–80)

The doll episode, I believe, displays the emotional and psychic consequences of the mother's *failure* to survive. Annie's observation that Paul hates the doll so intensely *because* he had broken it is key. Storch and Dervin conflate the original breaking of the doll with the sadistic ritual, seeing both as reflective of the son's murderous fury toward the mother. A distinction, however, needs to be made. Paul does not originally break the doll out of hate; rather, the doll gets broken in the wake of a Winnicottian destructiveness—a furious, assertive physicality, an unrestrained "letting go." The doll, hidden under a cover, indeed breaks when Paul is jumping excitedly on the sofa. The child is then horrified and enraged at the doll's failure to survive. In Winnicott's terms, the doll/mother has failed to survive the child's ruthless self-assertion. Without the mother's intact externality or otherness, there are then no limits or bounds to the child's own terrifying destructiveness. At this point, in Eigen's words, "fury turns to hate" and "the child becomes addicted to omnipotent fantasy control" (181), of which the sadistic doll-burning ritual is a powerfully vivid example.

This interpretation can help illuminate, I believe, the sadistic strains that run throughout Lawrence's fiction. Ghent has also written about sadism as a breakdown product of failed object use. "If the subjective object never becomes real . . . and externality is not discovered," Ghent explains, then the subject is "made to feel that he or she is destructive; and finally, fear and hatred of the other develops, and with them, characterological destructiveness comes into being. In short, we have the development of sadism . . . the need to aggressively control the other as a perversion of object usage" ("Masochism" 124). Because the construction of the mother's own psychic world is so brittle, she cannot withstand the child's psychic destruction. Thus beneath the fantasy of maternal omnipotence in Lawrence's fiction is ironically just the opposite experience: an experience of the mother's acute vulnerability, of her inability to tolerate the child's furious assertion of his bodily, passionate self.

The same unconscious experience of the mother is apparent in the bread-burning episode. Paul is assigned the task of tending to his mother's loaves of bread baking in the oven. He is joined at home first by Miriam and then by the coquettish young woman Beatrice. Paul flirts with the seductive Beatrice, and Miriam angrily notices "his full, almost sensual mouth quivering. He was not himself" (244). Miriam then reminds him of the bread, which Paul discovers to his horror has charred and burned. He wraps up the most severely burnt loaf in a damp towel and hides it in the pantry. A bit later, alone with Miriam, Paul feels anxiously conflicted over his desire to kiss her: "Her dark eyes were naked with their love, afraid, and yearning. . . . She lost all her self control, was exposed in fear. And he knew, before he could kiss her, he must drive something out of himself. And a touch of hate for her crept back again into his heart" (247). At this point he suddenly remembers the bread, and Miriam observes "something cruel in the swift way he pitched the bread out of the tins" (247). When his mother returns home, Paul notices that she is looking especially frail and ill, "bluish round the mouth" (249), and he fears that she may have a serious heart problem.

Storch interprets the bread-burning episode as another vengeful fantasy against the powerful mother. The loaves, she says, symbolize "maternal power," and "[t]he burning of the loaves and the burial of the shrouded or swathed loaf is a reflection of the unthinkable and the unapproachable: the wish for the death of the repressive mother who curtails desire" (103). As with the doll episode, however, I believe a distinction needs to be made between the initial destructive act, the burning, and the consequent symbolic act of swathing the loaf and burying it in the pantry.

I agree that the "desiccated loaf . . . swathed up in the scullery" (248) likely reflects a sadistic death wish, but that wish follows a symbolic expression of maternal vulnerability, not maternal power. As a result of Paul losing himself, as Miriam bitterly notes, of relaxing his mental defenses—his conscious, vigilant self—and indulging his sensuality, the bread is ruined. The loaves are indeed associated with the mother, and once again, in Winnicott's terms, she has failed to survive. The burned loaves reflect an unconscious fear, not a wish: the fear that one's spontaneous passion is lethal, that the release of any erotic or aggressive impulse will destroy the other. A sadistic fantasy follows, just as the "hate" Paul feels toward Miriam and the cruelty she observes in his handling of the second batch of loaves follow his experience of Miriam as exposed, undefended, and perilously vulnerable. Finally, the mother's return is marked by her debilitated state and impaired heart, a confirmation of her terrible fragility.

This psychological dynamic can also help make sense of a curious scene in "The Fox." When Henry sees March for the first time in a dress, rather than the "hard-cloth breeches . . . strong as armour" that she was accustomed to wear, he suddenly loses his desire for her and is stricken with a "grave weight of responsibility. . . . She was soft and accessible in her dress. The thought went home in him like an everlasting responsibility" (49). This sentiment is repeated throughout the next several pages: "Since he had realised that she was a woman, and vulnerable, accessible, a certain heaviness had possessed his soul. . . . She was the woman, and he was responsible for the strange vulnerability he had suddenly realised in her" (53). This burdensome sense of the woman's vulnerability is exactly what inflames Henry's need to dominate and control. Without faith in the woman's otherness or ability to survive, he cannot let go himself nor can he let the woman go. In Benjamin's terms, the assertion-recognition dialectic breaks down and is reconfigured in the polarized dynamic of domination and submission.

In *Sons and Lovers* Paul experiences both his mother and Miriam as repressive because he fears they cannot withstand the uninhibited expression of his passionate, bodily being, the abandonment of mental restraints or "letting go" that sexuality entails. His occasionally vicious treatment of Miriam, which I will examine in the next section, is a result of what he experiences as her infuriating frailty and is related to the sadistic symbolic fantasies discussed above. Nevertheless, the narrative also displays an empathic identification with the mother and with Miriam which functions simultaneously with the unconscious anger, resentment, and sadistic fantasies of omnipotent control. The narrative presentation of Mrs. Morel is astute and emotionally honest even while we see the distortions created by Paul's unconscious fears and desires.

At times Paul's defensive misrepresentations of his mother strikingly contradict the dramatic presentation of her. At one point he characterizes her as a basically "jolly" woman (216), and another time he tells Miriam, "See, my mother looks as if she'd *had* everything that was necessary for her living and developing. There's not a tiny bit of a feeling of sterility about her" (362). The reader, at least this reader, balks at that representation. Paul needs to believe that his mother is jolly and fulfilled because the burden of the opposite reality is so intolerable to him: the mother's depression, her emptiness and emotional sterility, are precisely what the text so effectively portrays.

Paul's internal world mirrors his mother's. Gertrude Morel's narcissistically wounded condition, the lack of recognition and the consequent shame and rage she suffers are reproduced in her son. The subjective experience of emptiness and the detachment from affective, bodily life are passed down relationally from mother to child. Paul battles against his identification with his depressed mother as he seeks to assert himself and realize his own authentic life. The battle is one that Lawrence continually waged himself thoughout his life and his art. In his best work, the identification with the mother's shame and depression is relinquished without a wholesale repudiation of his maternal ties.

The conflictual relationship between Paul and Mrs. Morel reflects, finally, the crucial tensions of psychic life: the "intricate and subtle dialectic," in Mitchell's words, between "spontaneous vitality and self-expression" and the need to "preserve secure and familiar connections with others" (*Hope* 133). Or, in Benjamin's and Winnicott's terms, the dialectical needs of recognizing and being recognized by the m/other while also asserting the self and indeed psychically "destroying" her. Paul's faith in his mother's "survival," despite her actual death, is hard-won, but the end of the novel, as well as Lawrence's very ability to write so creatively and productively, suggest that such faith ultimately prevailed.

MIRIAM AND PAUL:
SELF-MISTRUST AND THE FAILURE OF OTHERNESS

The most common critical view of Miriam is that she represents simply one more version of the stifling and possessive mother.[6] Seeking to rescue Miriam from the prevailing negative perspective, Louis Martz argues that her character is far more complex than either Paul or most critics allow. Martz points, for instance, to the scene in which she overcomes her fear of letting the hen peck corn from her hand. The scene demonstrates, he says, Miriam's "extreme sensitivity, along with her shy desire for new experience," and that "for all her shyness and shrinking she is nevertheless capable of a strong response" (51). Martz believes that the complex view of Miriam recedes as the narrator becomes less objective and more identified with Paul in part 2 of the novel.

Tension exists throughout the novel, I believe, between an empathic rendering of Miriam's complex inner life, her dynamic subjectivity, and her status as the object of Paul's narcissistic projections. As much as Miriam is another version of the devouring mother, she is equally another version of Paul himself. In many respects her conflicted subjectivity mirrors his. Ross Murfin has observed that "the very words [Lawrence] uses to criticize Miriam are nearly identical to those Lawrence has used to characterize Paul" (65). Murfin notes such words as "tight," "intense," "hyper-sensitive," and "suffering." The fact that Miriam's interior life is so identified with Paul's is precisely what dooms their relationship: neither feels fully real or alive, and neither fully trusts in the other's independent reality.

Paul's contempt for Miriam's intensity and suffering reflects, above all, his own self-contempt. "Paul hated her," the narrator asserts, "because, somehow, she spoilt his ease and naturalness. And he writhed himself with a feeling of humiliation" (217). Miriam indeed holds up a mirror to his own (and his mother's) constrained emotional life and bodily shame, to his very lack of ease and naturalness. Paul complains about Miriam's heated, "overcharged" intensity—"There was no looseness or abandon about her" (184)—but he shares that hot intensity far more than he likes to admit. At one point, when reflecting on his response to the "cool" Clara, he does in fact acknowledge it: "He marvelled at her [Clara's] coldness. He had to do everything hotly. She must be something special" (307).

Miriam's anxieties are typical of those that torment so many Lawrence characters. The scene in which Paul pushes her on the swing, for instance, symbolically plays out the intense fear of sexual release—of physically and emotionally "letting go" and surrendering to the other—that runs throughout Lawrence's fiction. Miriam is terrified of abandoning herself: "Down to her bowels went the hot wave of fear. She was in his hands. Again, firm and inevitable came the thrust at the right moment. She gripped the rope, almost swooning" (182). In this scene Paul is granted the looseness and abandon that are typically craved, but the narrative is concentrated on Miriam's point of view, on her interior state, not Paul's. The flood of fear and yearning that rises within her is the most characteristically Lawrencian aspect of the scene.

> There was something fascinating to her in him. For the moment he was nothing but a piece of swinging stuff, not a particle of him that did not swing. She could never lose herself so. . . . It roused a warmth in her. It were almost as if he were a flame that had lit a warmth in her, whilst he swung in the middle air. (182)

This is one of the most familiar relational scenarios in Lawrence's fiction: the other possesses an unselfconscious spontaneity, warmth, and animal vitality that the self lacks. The cold, deficient self is deeply attracted, compelled by the other's radiating warmth, but also dreads being overwhelmed by the other's very potency and vitality. This dynamic, as I will discuss in a later chapter, propels such short stories as "The Prussian Officer," "The Blind Man," and "The Princess." The deficient self in these stories, as elsewhere in Lawrence's fiction, is sometimes male and sometimes female. In the confrontational scenes between the deficient self and the idealized other, however, the locus of authorial identification and narrative perspective is primarily with the fearful, conflicted self. In the swing scene it is Miriam, not Paul, who represents that essential subjective position.

The narrative in *Sons and Lovers* displays an empathic understanding of the roots of Miriam's inner deficiency (as it does with Mrs. Morel) in her thwarted life as a female in a house ruled by males. We see her ridiculed and emotionally abused by her rough and insensitive brothers, much like Mabel in the story "The Horse-Dealer's Daughter." Miriam is also keenly aware of her inferior status in the larger world. Deprived of opportunity for self-expression and achievement, she is angry and bitter. She protests to Paul that she has been denied the chance "'of learning—of doing anything. It's not fair, because I'm a woman'" (185). The mental, imaginative realm becomes her only recourse, her only means of compensating for the self-denigration and persistent narcissistic wounding she has suffered:

> She hated her position as swine-girl. She wanted to be considered. She wanted to learn, thinking that if she could read . . . the world would have a different face for her, and a deepened respect. She could not be princess by wealth or standing. So, she was mad to have learning whereon to pride herself. (174)

Lawrence thus shows Miriam's injured narcissism as having both familial and cultural roots. Because others did not recognize or believe in her, she "did not believe in herself, primarily" (255). Paul accuses her of not wanting to love, but of having an "abnormal craving" to be loved: "You absorb absorb, as if you must fill yourself up with love, because you've got a shortage somewhere" (258). And Miriam herself suspects the truth of this accusation:

> Perhaps he could not love her. Perhaps she had not in herself that which he wanted. It was the deepest motive of her soul, this self-mistrust. It was so deep she dared neither realise nor acknowledge it. Perhaps she was deficient. Like an infinitely subtle shame, it kept her always back. (260)

Yet Miriam also wonders if the same might not be true of Paul. "Was *he* deficient in something? Perhaps he was" (261). Paul indeed confesses to his mother, "I think there must be something the matter with me, that I *can't* love" (395). Just as Paul accuses Miriam of abstracting him and of failing "to realise *him*" in their lovemaking (227), so Clara accuses Paul of the very same things: "'About *me* you know nothing,' she said bitterly—'about *me*!' . . . 'you've never come near to me. You can't come out of yourself, you can't'" (406–7).

If Miriam in her innermost being feels defective and ineffectual, she also discovers a similar emotional reality at the heart of Paul. In a quietly moving scene in the novel, Miriam silently watches as Paul stands in the middle of the road, doggedly working on a broken umbrella. The umbrella had significantly once belonged to William:

> Turning a corner in the lane, she came upon Paul who stood bent over something, his mind fixed on it, working away steadily, patiently, a little hopelessly. She hesitated in her approach to watch. He remained concentrated in the middle of the road. Beyond, one rift of rich gold in that colourless grey evening seemed to make him stand out in dark relief. She saw him slender and firm, as if the setting sun had given him to her. A deep pain took hold of her, and she knew she must love him. And she had discovered him, discovered in him a rare potentiality, discovered his loneliness. Quivering as at some "Annunciation," she went slowly forward. (201)

In this scene Miriam indeed "discovers" Paul in all his vulnerability and loneliness—his hopelessness yet persistence at repairing what he cannot fix, at restoring what is irreparably damaged or lost. His mother's love was originally focused on William, not him, and he cannot bring William back nor secure his mother's unconditional love in the same way, no matter how assiduously he tries. The broken umbrella, like the impaired bond with his beloved mother, is stubbornly resistant to his most determined efforts. Miriam intuitively recognizes this even before she learns that the umbrella was originally William's. She has discovered him, exposed and vulnerable, which the image of him standing out in solitary relief against the evening sky enforces. Such deep, intimate knowledge of the other can indeed be described as love. The reference to the Annunciation, however, poses a question: Is it Miriam's love for Paul that is self-sacrificial and Christ-like or Paul's for his mother? Both possibilites are equally plausible, a point that further emphasizes the deep alliance and indentification of these two characters.

It is little wonder that Jessie Chambers failed to recognize herself in the portrait of Miriam: though the character is based on the external facts of her life, Miriam's conflicted inner life most powerfully resembles Lawrence's own. The author indeed grants Miriam subject status by endowing her with his own inner complexity and allowing her to suffer *like* his protagonist self. Paul, however, is never able to relate to Miriam as *other* than self, as other than the object of his narcissistic projections. For the reader, though, Clara's character once again serves as a corrective, highlighting the limitations in Paul's perception of Miriam. When Paul complains about Miriam's wanting "a sort of soul union," Clara responds:

> "But how do you know what she wants?"
> "I've been with her for seven years."
> "And you haven't found out the very first thing about her."
> "What's that?"
> "That she doesn't want any of your soul communion. That's your own imagination. She wants you."
> He pondered over this. Perhaps he was wrong.
> "But she seems—" he began.
> "You've never tried," she answered. (321)

Clara's comments reflect an awareness that Paul's problems with Miriam are more likely due to his own fantasies and projections than to Miriam's actual character. Paul is oblivious, Clara suggests, of Miriam's real desires, of her separate reality apart from *his* fears and desires. Paul momentarily considers this possibility, just as the narrative has made the reader aware of it as well. An intersubjective awareness, in other words, has temporarily interrupted Paul's more habitual narcissistic projections in relation to Miriam. Paul is not identical with the narrator, however, and the narrator, unlike Paul, continually plays with the tension between these two modes.

Paul's failure to comprehend Miriam's separate reality or otherness in fact fuels his sadistic bullying of her. He sees in her only a mirror of his own vulnerability, shame and fear, which arouses intense narcissistic rage. What he perceives as her terrible fragility again reflects his experience of his mother as too fragile to withstand the uninhibited expression of his passionate, bodily self. These narcissistic dynamics are especially apparent in the algebra lesson scenes, which Millett describes as "some of the most remarkable instances of sexual sadism disguised as masculine pedogogy which literature affords" (355).

Paul's sadistic fury is aroused precisely by Miriam's submissiveness and humility in the face of these lessons:

> It made his blood rouse to see her there, as it were at his mercy, her mouth open, her eyes dilated with laughter that was afraid, apologetic, ashamed . . . [T]hings came slowly to her. And when she held herself in a grip, seemed so utterly humble before the lesson, it made his blood rouse. He stormed at her, got ashamed, continued the lesson, and grew furious again, abusing her. . . . Once he threw the pencil in her face. (187–88)

Paul's expressions of rage and contempt when confronting Miriam's humiliating self-abasement are a defensive response to his own underlying shame. According to Andrew Morrison, rage and contempt are the affects most frequently associated with shame; they may, in fact, represent attempts to rid the self of shame: "underlying many expressions of rage is a feeling of shame—a feeling that reflects a sense of failure or inadequacy so intolerable that it leads to a flailing out, an attempt to rid the self of the despised subjective experience. . . . Contempt represents . . . an attempt to 'relocate' the shame experience from within the self into another person, and thus, like rage, it may be an attempt to rid the self of shame" (13–14).

Interestingly, at the beginning of the novel, William exhibits similar bullying behavior toward his nightschool students. He would issue "snorts of impatience and disgust," and call names: "'You great booby, you block-head, you thundering idiot and fool'" (71). Léon Wurmser also discusses contempt as one of the most prominent "masks" of shame: it "lies in shaming others, in turning contempt from the self toward others. It is defense by reversal" (24). Mrs. Morel's sons are caught up in the vicious cycle of shame, both their own and their mother's. The mother's deep feelings of narcissistic inadequacy, of emotional and bodily shame, are passed down relationally to the children who depend on and identify with her.

Miriam, too, suffers from a similar debilitating shame. Her fear of sexuality is essentially a fear of her own narcissistic inadequacy. When she considers having sex with Paul, she admits that she "was not afraid of people, what they might say. But she dreaded the issue with him. . . . He would be disappointed, he would find no satisfaction, and then he would go away" (328). Her sense of profound self-deficiency, her fear, as quoted earlier, that "she had not in herself that which he wanted," proves once more to be the real source of her sexual inhibitions.

Miriam's perilous fragility again serves to infuriate Paul. In the scene leading up to their lovemaking, Paul's perception of Miriam's defense-lessness is associated with images of death and destruction, and it char-acteristically provokes aggressive behavior. After climbing a cherry tree,

> He looked down. There was a faint gold glimmer on her face, that looked very soft, turned up to him.
> "How high you are!" she said.
> Beside her, on the rhubarb leaves, were four dead birds, thieves that had been shot. Paul saw some cherry-stones hanging quite bleached, like skeletons, picked clear of flesh. He looked down again to Miriam.
> . . .
> She seemed so small, so soft, so tender down there. He threw a handful of cherries at her. She was startled and frightened. He laughed with a low, chuckling sound, and pelted her. (329)

Aggressive feelings and destructive fantasies emerge, once again, not from the experience of female/maternal power but from the experience of acute female vulnerability. Miriam is in the lowly, submissive position, seeming "so small, so soft, so tender down there." Paul is in the position of power, and it is the unconscious fear of overpowering and destroying the other through one's own greedy, thieving love (like the birds, and as in the doll and bread-burning episodes) that gives rise to the deathly asso-ciations and, in this case, to the playfully aggressive behavior.

When the narrator allows us inside Miriam's consciousness, how-ever, we discover that she is neither as defenseless nor as vulnerable as Paul assumes. Her psychological defenses, in fact, are quite similar to his. Just as Clara accuses Paul of never coming out of himself or coming near to her, so too Miriam holds herself back and never truly achieves intimacy with Paul. Her inner reserve protects against the fear of being dominated by him (just as Paul holds back out of fear of being domi-nated by women in general):

> She knew she felt in a sort of bondage to him, which she hated because she could not control it. She had hated her love for him from the moment it grew too strong for her. And, deep down, she had hated him because she loved him and he dominated her. She had resisted his dom-ination. She had fought to keep herself free of him, in the last issue. And she *was* free of him, even more than he of her. (340)

Miriam finally confesses openly that their relationship "has been one long battle," that "he had always fought away from her," and that there had never been any real intimacy or "perfect times" between them, as Paul would like to believe. This revelation, so unsurprising to the reader, is utterly shattering to Paul. He is "aghast," stunned: "She whose love he had believed in when he had despised himself, denied that their love had ever been love. . . . Then it had been monstrous. There had never been anything really between them—all the time he had been imagining something where there was nothing" (341). Once again Paul is confronted with his own false projections. He does not blame himself, however, but Miriam. He feels deceived and betrayed. "*You* never believed in me," he charges. "She had despised him when he thought she worshipped him" (342).

The accusation that Miriam "never believed in" him calls to mind a scene from a later novel, *Kangaroo*. Here the Lawrence alter ego character, Richard Somers, has a disturbing dream in which a woman resembling both his wife, Harriet, and his mother appears "sullen and obstinate against him, repudiating him. . . . [H]er face was swollen and puffy and almost mad or imbecile, because she had loved him so much, and now she must see him betray her love." He cries to her, "'Don't you believe in me? Don't you *believe* in me?'" But the woman turns away "to the sullen and dreary, everlasting hell of repudiation." He wakes and immediately thinks of Harriet and his mother: "the two women in his life he had loved down to the quick of life and death," and yet he feels, "They neither of them believed in me" (96–97).

The mistrust of women so distinctive of Lawrence's work rises out of this deep-rooted conviction that his mother did not "believe in" him, that for all her narcissistic investment in him, she never trusted in his individual integrity or believed in him as a separate being in his own right. Nor does he have faith in her integrity as a separate, independent subject: the fantasy of Somer's dream is that the woman's mental disintegration results from his bad or untrustworthy love. The dream exposes, as does so much of Lawrence's fiction, the psychic consequences of failed intersubjectivity: the collapse into the oppressive, narcissistic polarity of idealization and repudiation—the all-good and all-bad splitting of the paranoid-schizoid state.

Miriam's worshipping love, like the dream woman's, proves to be false and empty. She had never really "believed in" him. Yet we have also seen how Paul has failed to believe in or fully comprehend Miriam's separate subjectivity, her independent reality or otherness. Paul and Miriam, finally, have never really believed in themselves or the other. In the last, pathetic scene between them toward the novel's end, each longs for the other's self-assertion to compensate for their own inability to claim themselves as subjects of desire. "He would leave himself to her," Paul thinks. "She was better and bigger than he. He would depend on her" (457). Each wants to be claimed, wholly and unequivocally, by the other—a dynamic that prefigures the theme of masochistic submission in much of Lawrence's later work.

Miriam sorely wants to put her arms around Paul's body, to "take it up, and say 'It is mine, this body. Leave it me!' . . . But she crouched and dared not. She was afraid he would not let her. She was afraid it was too much" (462). The fear, once again, is that asserting one's real bodily passions and desires will be "too much": it will overwhelm, "destroy," or be rejected by the other. Rather, Miriam wants him to claim her: "Oh, why did not he take her! Her very soul belonged to him. Why would not he take what was his!" (462). Paul, however, "could not bear it, that breast which was warm and which cradled him without taking the burden of him. . . . She could not take him and relieve him of the responsibility of himself" (462).

Both Miriam and Paul suffer from such severe narcissistic loss and inner deficiency that neither can provide what the other needs. Both want the other to assume the "burden" of their tormented selves. Both are terrified of claiming themselves—of fully asserting their bodily, passionate being—and thus they look to the other to assert what they feel incapable of asserting. Miriam is as much a twin to Paul—a mirror of his tormented subjectivity—as she is the object of his rage and defensive projections. Jessie Chambers may not have felt rewarded by Lawrence's portrait of Miriam, but by granting Miriam an inner life so like his protagonist's, Lawrence is acknowledging an extreme closeness, indeed identification, with her character. Miriam's deep sense of shame, her self-mistrust, and her crippling inhibitions are the very problems with which Paul so exhaustingly struggles. His ultimate repudiation of her reflects a repudiation of his own projected weaknesses.

Yet Miriam's character is more than merely a bundle of Paul's projections. As with Mrs. Morel's character, the narrative presents her particular history, her psychological and emotional conditioning, with compassionate insight. It also allows us to see Paul's misperceptions and misjudgments of her. In the end, Paul's repudiation of Miriam is balanced by the narrator's empathic recognition of the complexity and depths of her pain. By recognizing her suffering, her inner world, the narrator is recognizing Miriam's subjectivity as both like and separate from Paul's. The intersubjective consciousness of the narrative thus stands in tension with Paul's narcissistic projections, recreating for the reader a dynamic tension fundamental to human relational life.

CLARA AND PAUL:
DEPERSONALIZATION AND THE PSYCHE/SOMA SPLIT

If Miriam's hot intensity uncomfortably mirrors Paul's inner shame and anxiety, making her a reflection or projection of his own undesirable self, then Clara, in her cool confidence and independence, represents for Paul a desirable otherness.[7] Clara's very remoteness and inaccessibility are indeed what make her so desirable to him. These qualities, first of all, duplicate those of his emotionally withdrawn mother. In the scene in which Paul and Clara attend the theatre, Paul's experience of Clara watching the play echoes, in several important respects, his experience of his mother viewing the Lincoln cathedral:

> And he loved her as she balanced her head and stared straight in front of her, pouting, wistful, immobile, as if she yielded herself to her fate because it was too strong for her. She could not help herself—she was in the grip of something bigger than herself. A kind of eternal look about her, as if she were a wistful sphinx, made him mad to kiss her. (375)

As in the cathedral scene, the woman's "immobile" stoicism, her fatalism, as well as her "eternal" and mysterious quality of inaccessibility are stressed. In this case, a merging fantasy immediately follows:

> He was Clara's white, heavy arms, her throat, her moving bosom. That seemed to be himself. . . . There was no himself. The grey and black eyes of Clara, her bosom coming down on him, her arm that he held gripped between his hands were all that existed. Then he felt himself small and helpless, her towering in her force above him. (375–76)

The merging fantasy is provoked, once more, by the experience of the other's affective remoteness and impenetrability. We see here, as so often in Lawrence's fiction, the fantasy of the woman's "towering" force over the "small and helpless" self. Yet that fantasy significantly occurs in the context of Paul's perception of the woman's own helplessness, of Clara's yielding "to her fate because it was too strong for her." Again, the text makes us aware of an ironic reality: the boy/man's fantasy of the woman's dangerous omnipotence is precipitated by the reality of the woman's powerlessness and her stoic suffering in the face of it.

Clara's cool remoteness, however, also serves to make sex less threatening because Paul can more easily keep her depersonalized and invulnerable. Whereas Paul can never forget Miriam's neediness and personal frailty, Clara's detachment and seeming self-sufficiency allow him to unleash his sexuality without fear of destroying her. We are told that for Clara, "The naked hunger and inevitability of his loving her, something strong and blind and ruthless in its primitiveness, made the hour almost terrible to her" (397). Yet unlike Miriam, Clara can more easily contain and absorb this terrible, primitive force.

The peewits "screaming in the field" during Paul and Clara's love-making symbolically project the terror that is always bound up with sexuality for Lawrence. If a ruthless sexuality is to be unloosed, however, then that terror must be allowed expression as well, and the effect of such full-blown self-expression is liberating. A primitive, blind, and ruthless force has been released, and neither self nor other has been destroyed. As the following beautifully lyrical line suggests, a thrusting, assertive sexuality is safely contained—embraced within a balanced, wheeling universe: "They had met, and included in their meeting the thrust of the manifold grass stems, the cry of the peewit, the wheel of the stars" (398). The narrator indeed remarks a few lines later, "The night contained them" (398).

The "baptism of fire in passion" that Paul experiences with Clara, however, is utterly without intimacy: "But it was not Clara. It was something that happened because of her, but it was not her. They were scarcely any nearer each other" (399). For Paul, as for many Lawrence characters, an uninhibited self-assertion is possible only in the context of a depersonalized relationship in which neither self nor other is personally vulnerable. Depersonalization is also a characteristic defensive response to early narcissistic injury. If the infant's bodily being has not been recognized or affirmed, the child experiences his/her body and bodily functions as objectionable, shameful, and "bad." The continuity of the psyche/soma, in Winnicott's terms, is disrupted; the soma is split off from the psyche—one's body is not felt to be an integral part of one's personal subjectivity or experience of self.

Throughout Lawrence's fiction sexuality represents a *healing* of this split through *recognition* of the bodily self. Such a fantasy is evident in the scene in which Paul caresses Clara's naked body:

> She stood letting him adore her and tremble with joy of her. It healed her hurt pride. It healed her, it made her glad. It made her feel erect and proud again in her nakedness. Her pride had been wounded inside her, she had been cheapened. Now she radiated with joy and pride again. It was her restoration, and her recognition. (383)

The relationship between Paul and Clara, however, is far more complex than this fantasy about the restorative power of sex suggests. The intersubjective perspective of the narrative again endows the woman with her own afflicted inner consciousness that counters many of Paul's projections and fantasies about her. Clara, in fact, battles Paul's depersonalization of her, and in the next chapter she charges that he has never truly recognized her at all. As quoted earlier, she cries, "'About *me* you know nothing . . . about *me*! . . . You can't come out of yourself, you can't. . . . I feel . . . as if it weren't *me* you were taking'" (406–7).

This failure of recognition—the feeling that the other has failed to see or acknowledge the separate, real *me*—indeed distinguishes all of the characters' relationships in this novel. Paul, in the end, makes the very same complaint about Clara:

> She wanted him, but not to understand him. He felt she wanted the
> man on top, not the real him that was in trouble. That would be too
> much trouble to her, he dared not give it her. She could not cope with
> him. It made him ashamed. (451)

The fear, as usual, is that the other can "not cope" with the "real" me—
the me that is troubled, anxious, and vulnerable, the me that is desperate for love. We see here the buried shame that rules the lives of so many
of Lawrence's characters and is a key factor in their fundamental feelings of unreality and powerlessness. In the above passage, Paul continues: "So, secretly ashamed because he was in such a mess, because his
own hold on life was so unsure, because nobody held him, feeling
unsubstantial, shadowy, as if he did not count for much in this concrete
world, he drew himself together smaller and smaller" (451).

Paul's experience of Clara, like his relationship with all the female
characters in this novel, is thus profoundly contradictory. While she represents, in her ripe sexuality, a towering, fearsome force, she is equally
felt to be too frail and shaky to withstand the force of his own terrible
needs and desires—"Clara could not stand for him to hold on to" (451).
The real issue, once more, is not the woman's power but the fear of her
not being strong enough and the shame over the self's unmet, unman-
ageable needs.

Finally, one other incident in Paul's relationship with Clara deserves
mentioning—the scene, recently restored in the unexpurgated Cambridge edition, in which Paul stealthily puts on Clara's stockings and is
sexually aroused (381). Angela Carter sees Lawrence's fixation on
women's clothes, particularly stockings, throughout his fiction as evidence of pure transvestism—"Lorenzo the Closet-Queen" (161–68). For
Carter, Lawrence's art of "female impersonation" only reflects a deeper
misogyny. Linda Williams interprets the stockings as a classic Freudian
fetish—a symbolic phallus that defends against the horror of the cas-
trated woman—while also emphasizing the multiple possibilities suggested by Paul's act: "the act manages to suggest narcissism, masturbation *and* straightforward heterosexual intercourse (Paul inserts himself
into the stockings, which stand in for the absent Clara). . . . Paul is both
his own masturbatory self as well as 'being' the sexiest part of Clara"
(133).

Paul is certainly deriving pleasure from his female identification
here, and perhaps it is pleasurable because he is alone and controlling it.
Two other instances in the text also suggest Paul's identification as a girl
in relation to both Clara and Baxter. At one point, the narrator states
that Clara "saw his neck in the flannel sleeping jacket as white and
round as a girl's" (384). Another time, when Paul runs into Baxter on

the stairs—"he almost collided with the burly metal-worker"—Paul is whistling a tune entitled "'Put me among the Girls'" (391). The wish to be a girl is part of the larger fantasy of being ravished by a powerful, animalistic male. To be penetrated by the other is a way of absorbing his power and bodily vitality, and thus of reclaiming it as one's own. The intense ambivalence that such a fantasy inevitably entails, however—the terror of being overwhelmed and annihilated by the very animalistic masculinity one seeks—is also apparent throughout Lawrence's fiction and will be discussed more fully later.

Though the text reveals Paul's fantasies of appropriating and controlling Clara's sexuality, those fantasies, as usual, do not contain the whole story. Clara is not merely a sex object, as Millett maintains, "whom Paul nonchalantly disposes of when he has exhausted her sexual utility" (358). As discussed, Clara frequently points up Paul's misperceptions and shortcomings. Her character stubbornly resists his attempts to depersonalize her. She is indeed the object of Paul's narcissistic fantasies, yet she also maintains her integrity as a separate subject who withstands his attempts to objectify and assimilate her to the particular drama of his inner world. In such resistance—in the woman's maintaining her externality and otherness—lies the potential for real relationship and the hope implicit in Lawrence's best fiction.

WALTER, BAXTER, AND PAUL: THE REJECTED FATHER AND THE NEED FOR RECOGNITION

The tension between repudiation and an empathic narrative identification also figures into the characterization of Walter Morel. Many readers, like Daleski, feel that the dramatic presentation of Morel's character is far more sympathetic than the view of him we get through Paul's (and his mother's) eyes. Even after Walter's most brutal act in the novel, throwing the drawer at Gertrude, the narrator draws us into Morel's pained consciousness and informs us that Morel himself was far more damaged by the deed than was his wife:

> He lay and suffered like a sulking dog. He had hurt himself most. And he was the more damaged, because he would never say a word to her, or express his sorrow. . . . Nothing, however, could prevent his inner consciousness inflicting on him the punishment which ate into his spirit like rust, and which he could only alleviate by drinking. (55)

The incident also evokes a familiar relational dynamic. The man comes to resent and dread the woman precisely because he has the power to harm or break her. The narrator comments: "He dreaded his wife. Having hurt her, he hated her" (57). As in the doll episode, hate for the female other emerges out of the experience of her destructibility, her vulnerability to one's own destructive impulses. In unconscious fantasy the woman is thus paradoxically at once powerful and powerless: the boy/man feels utterly dependent on her (she is all-powerful) but he has no faith in her dependability (she is powerless to withstand his self-assertive destructiveness). As Benjamin has argued, the mother's actual powerlessness and lack of agency in social and cultural life help create this trap by making it all the more difficult for her to survive her child's psychic destruction and become real to him.

Walter is caught in the polarizing stalemate that results from such intersubjective breakdown. Like his wife, he too "felt a sort of emptiness, almost like a vacuum in his soul" (63) which he attempts to dull through drink. His life with his mates at the pub becomes a refuge from the antagonism and emptiness of his home. The narrative nevertheless makes us aware of Morel's distinctly domestic, tender, and nurturing qualities—qualites that his children, particularly Paul, refuse to accept. When Paul is sick as a baby, we are told that "Morel wanted to hold the child, to soothe him. It would have done the man good to be able to nurse his sick baby. But the child would not be nursed by him. It would stiffen in his arms, and . . . would scream, draw back from the father's hands" (63). Later, when Paul is older and ill again, Morel stands hesitantly outside his door: "He felt his son did not want him" (91). Paul callously rejects all of his father's clumsy but touching attempts to comfort and reassure him.

The characterization of Morel is multidimensional, as is the psychology involved in Paul's rejection of him. Obviously Paul's emmeshment with his mother and her contempt for the father together play a vital role, as do oedipal rivalry and Paul's inflamed need to possess his mother totally. In my view, however, what most prevents Paul from accepting and identifying with his father is Morel's explosive temper, his wild and unrestrained outbursts of anger toward the mother. These attacks are terrifying for the boy; he now must protect his mother not only from his own destructive impulses but from his father's as well. Morel's fiery temper thus exacerbates Paul's anxiety over his mother's psychic fragility. For the boy who fears his own rage and destructiveness, his father's fury becomes another inhibiting factor, another obstacle to the identification with masculine sexuality and the spontaneous expression of passion.

This dynamic is most apparent in the scene in which Paul, awakened from sleep, listens in terror to the "shrieking" of the ash tree outside the house as his parents quarrel violently in the room below. The tree is associated with Morel: he likes its shrieking noise—"'It's music,' he said. 'It sends me to sleep'" (84). To Paul, however, the tree's noise is "demoniacal" and mixed up with his father's drunken, violent behavior:

> Then he heard the booming shouts of his father, come home nearly drunk, then the sharp replies of his mother, then the bang, bang of his father's fist on the table, and the nasty snarling shout as the man's voice got higher. And then the whole was drowned in a piercing medley of shrieks and cries from the great, wind-swept ash-tree. The children lay silent in suspense, waiting for a lull in the wind to hear what their father was doing. He might hit their mother again. There was a feeling of horror, a kind of bristling in the darkness, and a sense of blood. (84–85)

The narrator tells us that not until Paul and the other children heard the soothing sound of the tap water drumming into the ketttle "which their mother was filling for morning . . . could [they] go to sleep in peace" (85). Not until they were assured of their mother's safety, in other words, could they relax their defenses and allow themselves the self-abandonment of sleep.

Storch has also discussed the ash-tree's identification with the father. She associates it with a positive, specifically creative and liberating masculine force: Paul "must deny himself identification with this creative force and also with his father as a strong male. . . . Paul cannot identify with this liberating masculinity" (100). Paul is blocked from such identification, however, not simply by his mother's powerful hold over him and his father, as Storch maintains, but by the very nature of that masculinity itself, by its seemingly uncontrolled aggressiveness and frightening destructive potential.

Paul's dilemma is similar to that of a patient Winnicott discusses who was "in this position that he always protects the mother because he must preserve her in order to be able to have any rest or relaxation at all. He therefore has no knowledge that his mother might survive his impulsive act. A strong father enables the child to take the risk because the father stands in the way or is there to mend matters or to prevent by his fierceness" (Psychoanalytic Explorations 237). Paul has no faith in his father's ability to mend, prevent, or stand in the way of his (Paul's) own destructive impulses; on the contrary, the father's temper only intensifies Paul's anxiety over his mother's safety. Winnicott describes his patient as adopting "self-control of impulse at a very early stage" and as being severely inhibited: "The inhibition had to be of all spontaneity and impulse in case some particle of the impulse might be destructive" (237). The struggle against such inhibition is the very struggle that Sons and Lovers, indeed all of Lawrence's creative work, imaginatively enacts.

The son's rejection of his father, of course, only intensifies his need for paternal identificatory love. That need is made all the more desperate by the original failure of recognition in the mother-child relationship. Lawrence looks to an idealized father-figure not only to defend against the omnipotent mother of unconscious fantasy, as Storch and Ruderman insist, but also to bestow recognition of the bodily, passionate self that, having been unrealized, has become idealized.

Despite the overtly oedipal constellation of Paul's relationship with Baxter Dawes, the imagery and language of their fight scene (which prefigures the famous wrestling scene of Birkin and Gerald in *Women in Love*), suggest an even more primary, elemental desire at work. The fight is described in erotic, orgiastic terms that emphasize, above all, a perfect physical attunement and reciprocity between the two men:

> He [Paul] lay, pressed hard against his adversary, his body adjusting itself to its one pure purpose of choking the other man, resisting exactly at the right moment, with exactly the right amount of strength, the struggles of the other, silent, intent, unchanging, gradually pressing its knuckles deeper, feeling the struggles of the other body become wilder and more frenzied. Tighter and tighter grew his body, like a screw that is gradually increasing in pressure, till something breaks. (410)

To claim that this scene merely expresses Lawrence's latent homosexuality is analytically unsatisfactory—it doesn't explain enough. As James Cowan has discussed in relation to Birkin, the motives beneath the homosexual strivings are concerned not primarily with sexual gratification but with attempts to assuage early disturbances and divisions in the self—specifically, the split between the spiritual and the sensual, or the psyche and the soma ("Blutbrüderschaft" 200–201). The most blatant homoerotic scenes in Lawrence's novels—the bathing scene in *The White Peacock*, the wrestling scene in *Women in Love*, the sick-room scenes in *Aaron's Rod*, and the initiation rituals in *The Plumed Serpent*—all highlight the same fantasy: that of complete bodily attunement and mutual responsiveness between the self and an other like the self—an idealized masculine self. The homosexual fantasies, as Cowan argues, reflect, at the most fundamental level, attempts at magical, narcissistic repair. Because homosexuality is so tied up with narcissistic fantasies in Lawrence's fiction, it is prey to the same splitting and polarities—idealization and repudiation, domination and submission—that confound heterosexual relationships in his work. Paul's conflicted and erotically tinged relationship with Baxter raises issues that will be explored more fully in discussions of "The Prussian Officer" and *Women in Love*.

PAUL: THE MATERNAL HERITAGE

Both Mrs. Morel's death and the novel's final scene display the paradoxical tensions so definitive of Lawrence's art. Paul directly hastens his mother's death by feeding her the morphine-laced milk. The act, as Storch suggests, reverses and vengefully attacks the original oral relationship between mother and child: by "denying life to his mother at the fundamental level," Paul is "making a statement of violence against the mother-child bond itself" (107). As so often in Lawrence's fiction, however, the unconscious fantasy does not contain the whole story. The act is also done in an attempt to relieve the mother of her real, excruciating suffering; it is equally an act of almost unbearable empathy. While watching his mother die, "It was almost as if he were agreeing to die also" (436). By killing her he believes he will be killing a vital part of himself as well. Thus for Paul, his mother's death on the one hand liberates or releases him and on the other relegates him to a deathlike state of horrifying nothingness and unreality. "The real agony was that he had nowhere to go, nothing to do, nothing to say, and *was* nothing" (456).

Many critics read the last scene in which Paul, fists clenched, walks "towards the faintly humming, glowing town, quickly" as a final repudiation of the mother, an embrace of the father's world, and a determined movement toward life. Others emphasize the "drift towards death" and read the ending more ambiguously.[8] In this final scene contradictory forces are again at play. At the same time as we see the workings of a profound despair, we see the seed of faith. Not only is the despair rooted in the maternal relationship but so too is the faith. At the end, Paul renounces a limitless narcissistic identification with his mother and in so doing discovers a limited self. This is, I believe, the psychological significance of one of the novel's most moving passages:

> On every side the immense dark silence seemed pressing him, so tiny a speck, into extinction, and yet, almost nothing, he could not be extinct. Night, in which everything was lost, went reaching out, beyond stars and sun. Stars and sun, a few bright grains, went spinning round for terror and holding each other in embrace, there in a darkness that outpassed them all and left them tiny and daunted. So much, and himself, infinitesimal, at the core a nothingness, and yet not nothing. (464)

The paradox of "at the core a nothingness, and yet not nothing" captures an emotional reality that acknowledges loss without annihilation, aloneness without disintegration. Paul turns his back at the end on a merged or narcissistic identification with the mother and on the despair and darkness to which such an identification inevitably leads: "He would not take that direction, to the darkness, to follow her."

This type of renunciation is not the same thing as repudiation of the mother. Paul discovers that he can go on "being" in his mother's absence, and that discovery paradoxically implies her presence. Without some internalization of the loving, good mother, Paul would indeed have succumbed to the darkness.[9] Lawrence's faith in "being," his sense of belonging to a profoundly interconnected, living universe—in short, his religious sensibility—stems not from identification with an idealized father, as some have argued, but from hard-won faith in the primary maternal relationship.

In an object relational study of religious faith, John McDargh asserts, "Faith is integrally related to the development of the capacity to be alone" (81), which includes the "capacity to tolerate dependency" (83) and "the capacity to tolerate ambivalence" (92). Lawrence's fiction dramatizes the exquisite struggle involved in developing the capacity to tolerate dependency, ambivalence, and aloneness. That *Sons and Lovers* gives such full play to the opposing, ambivalent forces in this struggle is testament to the capacity itself.

CHAPTER 3

The Short Stories

"NEW EVE AND OLD ADAM," "ODOUR OF
CHRYSANTHEMUMS," "THE SHADOW
IN THE ROSE GARDEN," "SUN":
MUTUAL RECOGNITION AND THE BODILY SELF

Nowhere in Lawrence's fiction do intersubjective dynamics come into sharper relief than in the short stories. Due to the demands of the form, little is extraneous to the pivotal tension between the characters. The rhythm of breakdown and attempted repair of intersubjectivity frequently defines that tension. Time and again the stories portray characters urgently seeking self-realization, but that self-realization is possible only *in relation* to a fully recognized other, a separate, independent other capable of granting recognition to the self. The conflict or dilemma in the stories often assumes one of two forms: either the other lacks full subjectivity and collapses under the weight of the self's clamorous needs, or the other's independent subjectivity threatens to suffocate, constrain, or negate the self. The problems are interrelated since the fantasy of the other's overwhelming or destructive power stems from the failure of mutual recognition and the collapse of intersubjectivity in the first place. The dilemma in the stories unfolds, furthermore, in relation to male and female characters equally.

The conflict between the husband and wife in "New Eve and Old Adam" exposes the failed intersubjectivity that complicates love and power throughout Lawrence's work. Each character desperately wants to be recognized or realized by the other, but the other remains "unreal"—without a core self or separate subjectivity—and thus is incapable of such recognition. "You—you don't love. I pour myself out to you," the wife, Paula, complains, "and then—there's nothing there—you simply aren't there" (167). She insists, furthermore, that

> She had loved him, too. She had loved him dearly. And—he had not seemed to realise her. So that now she *did* want to be free of him for a while. Yet the love, the passion she had had for him clung about her. But she did want, first and primarily, to be free of him again. (169)

The conflict between intimacy and freedom, so definitive of Lawrence's work, emerges here as irreconcilable due to a frustration of mutual recognition. The husband, Peter, claims for his part that "There was no core to the woman" (177) and that she deceives herself about her ability to love: "She's got a big heart for everybody, but it must be like a common room: she's got no private, sacred heart, except for herself, where there's no room for a man in it" (176). He accuses her at the end of never having loved him: "You lie to yourself. You *wouldn't* love *me*, and you won't be able to love anybody else—except generally" (183).

The story highlights how essential the other's recognition is to the self's experience of its own bodily reality. When Peter, at his wife's insistence, leaves the house for the night, he goes to a hotel and attempts to revive a sense of physical vitality by taking a bath:

> He was trying, with the voluptuous warm water, and the exciting thrill of the shower-bath, to bring back the life into his dazed body. Since she had begun to hate him, he had gradually lost that physical pride and pleasure in his own physique which the first months of married life had given him. His body had gone meaningless to him again, almost as if it were not there. (171)

Without the other's recognition, the body goes "meaningless." For Lawrence this condition serves as creative tinder; it fuels the consuming struggle of his fiction to restore meaning to the body.

The omniscient narrator of "New Eve and Old Adam" allows both characters in this adversarial love relationship equal voice; neither seems solely to blame and both seem trapped in their own narcissism. The story presents a deeply ambivalent relationship from conflicting perspectives and without resolving the tensions. As so often in Lawrence's work, the narrative perspective reflects an intersubjective consciousness even as the characters themselves are blindly narcissistic. The story attests, furthermore, to the fact that the female characters are not the only ones who threaten to devour and absorb in Lawrence's universe. Like Skrebensky in *The Rainbow* or Gerald in *Women in Love*, Peter Moest in this story seeks to incorporate and possess the woman out of his own deficiency, his own lack of boundaries and separate subjectivity:

> He seemed to follow her so, to draw her life into his. It made her feel she would go mad. For he seemed to do it just blindly, without having any notion of her herself. It was as if she were sucked out of herself by some non-human force. . . . Perhaps he did not think of her, as a separate person from himself, sufficiently. But then he did not see, he could not see that she had any real personal life, separate from himself. (170)

The woman is a "New Eve" in her free and independent spirit, but the man is an "Old Adam" in his idea of the woman, as Paula charges, only as "an expansion, no, a *rib* of [him]self, without any existence of her own" (182). This is not a conception Lawrence advocates, despite his apparent fear of and anger at willful, independent women. In this story, neither the man nor the woman is "there" for the other—thus the impasse, the utter frustration experienced by both characters.

If the other is not realized in his or her external otherness and separate subjectivity, then the self too remains unrealized, blocked from experiencing its own authenticity or sense of aliveness. This is precisely the insight at which Elizabeth Bates agonizingly arrives at the end of "Odour of Chrysanthemums." As she views the naked, dead body of her husband, she realizes, with sudden, paralyzing fear and shame, that

> she had never seen him, he had never seen her, they had met in the dark and had fought in the dark, not knowing whom they met nor whom they fought. . . . She had denied him what he was—she saw it now. She had refused him as himself. . . . They had denied each other in life. Now he had withdrawn. An anguish came over her. (198–99)

As early manuscript versions reveal, Lawrence labored long over the ending of this story, revising and rewriting it numerous times. "The climactic scene," Keith Cushman contends, "constitutes a Lawrentian archetype that remained central to his imagination all his life" (48). That scene—the woman wincing "with fear and shame" at the revelation her husband's naked, dead body has forced upon her—is indeed fundamental to Lawrence's psyche. It expresses, once again, a devastating failure of mutual recognition—a failure to acknowledge and to be acknowledged by the real, separate other with whom one is erotically attached—and it lies at the heart of Lawrence's creative vision.

The haunting story "The Shadow in the Rose Garden" also ends with a woman in a state of paralysis and shock, though in this case the emphasis is not on the woman's failure to recognize, but on the failure of the beloved other to recognize her. The woman and her husband are vacationing in a seaside village where she had previously resided before her marriage. The breach in their relationship is immediately established: the husband is pacing about the garden in a state of angry "self-suppression" while the wife "looked apart from him and his world, gazing away to the sea" (121). The husband's rage and self-suppression, we understand, are directly related to his wife's refusal to acknowledge or direct her gaze on him. The wife, however, is in a similar state of tense self-suppression. She wanders off to the rose garden of the village rectory where, in her white muslim dress, she is compared to a white rose:

> a white rose that was greenish, like ice, in the centre . . . she went to a
> little seat among the white roses, and sat down. . . . She sat quite still,
> feeling her own existence lapse. She was no more than a rose, a rose
> that could not quite come into blossom, but remained tense. . . . She
> was not herself. (125–26)

The woman's state is a familiar one in Lawrence's work: the frozen
center, the lack of authentic self-experience, the feeling of one's existence lapsing into a white nothingness recall, for instance, Mrs. Morel's
thwarted emotional life and her swooning into the white lilies, as well
as the frigid lives and snowy deaths of Gerald in *Women in Love* and
Cathcart in "The Man Who Loved Islands." This story connects that
condition to a crushing failure of recognition. A shadowy figure appears
in the rose garden, and we soon learn that it is the woman's former
fiancé, a soldier, who according to rumor had died of sunstroke in
Africa. He is alive, but he is mad, deranged, a lunatic.

Lawrence spends several pages detailing the shattering impact this
discovery has on the woman. Her realization that this person—once the
object of her deepest passsion—cannot recognize her has the effect of
nullifying her entire existence:

> She looked up, blanched to the lips, and saw his eyes. They were black,
> and stared without seeing. . . . The whole world was deranged. . . . She
> wondered, craving, if he recognised her—if he could recognise her. . . .
> Could he recognise her, or was it all gone? . . . She sat motionless with
> horror and silence. . . . Her eyes searched him, and searched him, to
> see if he would recognise her, if she could discover him. "You don't
> know me?" she asked, from the terror of her soul, standing alone.
> (126–27)

She leaves in a "blind" haste, feeling totally depleted and drained,
"without any being" (128). The repeated emphasis on eyes—on seeing
and being seen by the beloved other—runs throughout Lawrence's fiction and draws its emotional and psychological force from the eye contact, the subtle but profound attunement play of early mother-child
interaction. Such attunement, as Stern and others have argued, sets the
very foundation for the development of a sense of a subjective self, the
base for how one experiences self in relation to other and external
world.

Christopher Brown has discussed the preponderance of eye imagery
in "The Fox," and he equates vision in that work with domination—"to
see is to dominate, to be seen is to be dominated" (61).[1] That equation,
however, is the result of a prior process gone awry, of a traumatic break,
as in "The Shadow in the Rose Garden," of attunement, of recognition
by and of the primary other. Thus the woman in the rose garden, unrec-

ognized by the other to whom she is erotically bound, is terrified and overwhelmed by his alien power: "She had to bear his eyes. They gleamed on her, but with no intelligence. He was drawing nearer to her. . . . Her horror was too great. The powerful lunatic was coming too near to her" (127).

Without attuned recognition, in other words, the erotic or desired other is experienced as a dominating, overpowering presence. The woman's failure to "discover" the other and to be "recognised" by him also leaves her with an unbounded hostility and destructive rage— "now she hated everything and felt destructive" (130). She turns this hostility on her husband and behaves coldly and cruelly toward him, just as he, out of an equivalent wound (her lack of recognition of him), seeks to hurt and control her. The erotic relationship thus dissolves into destructive power play, one of the most familiar scenarios in Lawrence's fiction.

Sadomasochistic fantasies play a critical role in many of Lawrence's short stories, and those fantasies emerge out of the breakdown of mutual recognition and the failure to "discover" the other or the self. Emmanuel Ghent argues that masochism is best understood as a distorted bid for recognition. Erotic submission, he believes, is the "defensive mutant" of the healthy and positive desire for "surrender"—for letting down the defensive barriers that inhibit authentic self-experience. Ghent could be describing any number of Lawrence's characters when he states, "There is, however deeply buried or frozen, a longing for something in the environment to make possible the surrender, in the sense of yielding, of false self" ("Masochism" 109). This longing is part of "an even more general longing to be known, recognized" and is "joined by a corresponding wish to know and recognize the other" (110). Thus masochism—enslaving oneself to a powerful master—is a "pseudo-surrender" and conceals "the longing for, the wish to be found, recognized, penetrated to the core, so as to become real, or as Winnicott put it in another context, 'to come into being'" (116).

Ghent's language here in fact echoes Lawrence's in his story "Sun"—a story precisely about the desire for and achievement of such self-surrender. The story begins with the character Juliet in a state of empty depression. She is debilitated by internal "anger and frustration" and by "an incapacity to feel anything real" (529). She also feels an oppressive, overwhelming responsibility for her child—"She felt so horribly, ghastly responsible for him: as if she must be responsible for every breath he drew" (529). On doctor's orders, she embarks with the boy to rest in the Mediterranean sun. The vibrant sexual imagery with which Lawrence depicts Juliet's nude sunbathing betrays the relational dynamic—the deep desire for surrender and recognition—at its source.

Lawrence emphasizes the sun's face and "look"; its phallic, penetrating ability is specifically associated with its ability to "focus on," see or "know" her to the depths of her being:

> Pulsing with marvellous blue, and alive, and streaming white fire from his edges, the sun! He faced down to her with his look of blue fire, and enveloped her breasts and her face, her throat, her tired belly, her knees, her thighs and her feet. . . . She could feel the sun penetrating even into her bones; nay, farther, even into her emotions and her thoughts. . . . And though he shone on all the world, when she lay unclothed he focussed on her. It was one of the wonders of the sun, he could shine on a million people and still be the radiant, splendid, unique sun, focussed on her alone. . . . [T]he sun knew her in the cosmic carnal sense of the word . . . (530–35)

By surrendering herself to the sun, Juliet is indeed "found, recognized, penetrated to the core" by the powerful, external other. Thus she "comes into being" and becomes "real." This story, and the symbolic function of the sun throughout Lawrence's work, also cast an interesting light on a detail in "The Shadow in the Rose Garden." The woman's fiancé, we recall, had gone mad from sunstroke. Perhaps the underlying fantasy is that he could not withstand the full force of erotic expression, neither the other's nor his own. This would further explain the woman's devastating sense of depletion and negation: the expression of her bodily, passionate being (as is feared so often in Lawrence's fiction) has proved to be "too much"; thus she feels denied and rejected at her vital, physical core.

In "Sun," once Juliet discovers her embodied, passionate self, she is also able to relinquish her overly possessive sense of responsibility for and control over her son. For all of his ambivalence toward mothers, Lawrence demonstrates in this story an implicit understanding of the importance of full maternal subjectivity. Juliet is able to allow her son the freedom to find and express his own being only after she has been allowed to discover her own. The end of the story reflects Lawrence's acknowledgment of the cultural constraints on such erotic wholeness and freedom for women. Juliet does not act on her desire to make love to a neighboring peasant whose blue eyes "flame" like the sun, but returns instead to her grey, "unsunned" husband Maurice: "her next child would be Maurice's. The fatal chain of continuity would cause it" (545).

Though "Sun" does reflect a masochistic fantasy—Juliet finds herself only by worshipful surrender to the more powerful male force—it also reveals the deeper affirmative longing behind this characteristic Lawrencian fantasy. It is the same fierce longing expressed in the story "Glad Ghosts." Here a man makes contact with the ghost of a woman who had died unfulfilled—a woman who had never been recognized or "worshipped" in her body so that even while alive, she had been a living ghost. For Lawrence, as for the character in this story,

> man in the body is formed through countless ages, and at the centre is the speck, or spark, upon which all his formation has taken place. It is even not himself, deep beyond his many depths. Deep from him calls to deep. . . . It is calling and answering, new-awakened God calling within the deep of man, and new God calling answer from the other deep. And sometimes the other deep is a woman, as it was with me, when my ghost came. (698)

The passage expresses a quintessential Lawrencian yearning: the yearning for mutual recognition, a calling and an answering, between self and other on a level that is felt to be at the deepest ground of existence—the level of the body.

"THE PRUSSIAN OFFICER," "THE BLIND MAN," "THE PRINCESS," "THE WOMAN WHO RODE AWAY": INTERSUBJECTIVE COLLAPSE AND THE DOMINATION-SUBMISSION POLARITY

The failure of mutual recognition and the collapse of intersubjectivity into erotic domination and submission distinguish a number of Lawrence's stories. The powerful, hypnotic "The Prussian Officer" is one of his most overt and intensely sadomasochistic works. The story concerns a Prussian captain who viciously torments his peasant orderly until the orderly finally revolts and strangles him to death. At the end, the two are laid "side by side" in the mortuary. As many critics have discussed, the homoerotic element is obvious. The orderly's person "was like a warm flame upon the older man's tense, rigid body" (3), and the orderly himself, despite his attempt to remain unengaged, feels a passionate hate grow "responsive to the officer's passion" (5). The young man indeed "felt he was connected with that figure moving so suddenly on horseback: he followed it like a shadow, mute and inevitable and damned by it" (2). The omniscient narrator, as usual, takes us into the minds of both characters, allowing us to understand the attraction-repulsion each feels toward the other as springing from the same torturously fevered soul.

The story dramatizes one of the most typical relational dynamics in Lawrence's short fiction: one character, the Captain, is an empty shell, "tense, rigid" and "suppressed" (4); the other, the young soldier, "seemed to live out his warm, full nature, to give it off in his very movements, which had a certain zest, such as wild animals have in free movement. And this irritated the officer more and more" (4). As usual, the empty character craves in the other what he himself lacks, but in this case, the envy and rage underlying such psychic hunger explode to the surface.

The Captain suffers from the paradigmatic Lawrencian condition: a suppression of passionate, bodily life and an incapacity to feel real. As a result, "reality"—the source of vitality and power—is projected as tantalizingly outside the self; it is experienced, like the remote, radiant mountains that frame the story, as external, ideal, and seductively inaccessible. The sadistic Captain is less a castrating oedipal father than an enraged, preoedipal child who has failed to discover the reality of self or other. The heavy oral imagery of the story also betrays its preoedipal roots.

The Captain's rage is most provoked at seeing the young man eat and drink: "To see the soldier's young, brown, shapely peasant's hand grasp the loaf or the wine-bottle sent a flash of hate or of anger through the elder man's blood. It was not that the youth was clumsy: it was rather the blind, instinctive sureness of movement of an unhampered young animal that irritated the officer to such a degree" (3). Orality is tied to a "blind, instinctive" sensuality and to a feeling of infuriating deprivation. Melanie Klein's descriptions of the splitting and sadistic projections that stem from oral rage and envy are certainly applicable to this story.[2]

The Captain, furthermore, is not the only one enraged by the oral satiation of the other. The orderly, in fact, is driven to his breaking point at the sight and sound of the Captain's eating and drinking: "he saw the thin, strong throat of the elder man moving up and down as he drank, the strong jaw working. And the instinct which had been jerking at the young man's wrists suddenly jerked free" (14). He significantly strangles the Captain to death, his hands gripping the older man's throat and jaw. The final section of the story repeatedly stresses the orderly's intense, raging thirst—"his brain flamed with the sole horror of thirstiness!" (20)—as he wanders deliriously through the forest. When he is finally found, collapsed on the ground, by the other soldiers, they "dropped him in horror" at the sight of his "open, black mouth" (20).

Although the orderly is originally endowed with a sensual reality and fullness the Captain lacks, the dominant fantasy is that the orderly is robbed by the more powerful man: "It was as if he was disembowelled, made empty, like an empty shell. He felt himself as nothing, a shadow creeping under the sunshine. And, thirsty as he was, he could scarcely drink, feeling the Captain near him" (11). The fantasy of being robbed by the more powerful masculine other, and the anal metaphor of disembowelment through which it is expressed, show up repeatedly in Lawrence's fiction. In *Kangaroo*, for instance, Somers has the following dream:

He was standing in the living-room at Coo-ee, bending forward doing some little thing by the couch, perhaps folding the newspaper, making the room tidy at the last moment before going to bed, when suddenly a violent darkness came over him, he felt his arms pinned, and he heard a man's voice speaking mockingly behind him, with a laugh. It was as if he saw the man's face too—a stranger, a rough, strong sort of Australian. And he realized with horror: "Now they have put a sack over my head, and fastened my arms, and I am in the dark, and they are going to steal my little brown handbag from the bedroom, which contains all the money we have." (144)

The anal and sexual symbolism here is almost laughably Freudian. The dream exposes, however, the deep dread that inevitably accompanies homosexual desire for Lawrence. The desire to have one's intellect stripped (as the sack over the head suggests), to be entered, indeed ravished, by the dominant, rough man is also felt to be a horrifying humiliation and violation—he is being "robbed" of all he has.

In "The Prussian Officer," both the orderly and the Captain are essentially operating out of the same schizoid, hungry, "empty shell" condition. The orderly's mesmeric attraction to the officer—"a handsome figure in pale-blue uniform"—as well as to the shimmering "pale blue" mountains suggest that he is as ambivalently drawn to the Captain as the external source of his own missing potency as the Captain is drawn to him.[3] Both are impelled by a profound sense of loss, a loss rooted in the first relationship between self and m/other and the initial oral mode of connection.

To the orderly, the radiant mountains at the end "seemed to have it, that which was lost in him" (20), just as from the Captain's perspective, the orderly holds the vital authenticity that is lost and inaccessible to him. The mountains, "blue and cool and tender," hold and withhold potency and love. The soldier "wanted them—he wanted them alone—he wanted to leave himself and be identified with them" (20). Underneath the Captain's abuse of the orderly lies the same erotic yearning for merged identification, a desire to surrender and lose the self in the other in order to find the self. The sadistic, dominating control of the other can also be understood as the flip side, the defense against, the masochistic desire/fear of loss of self in the other.

The merging fantasy springs, again, not from an original, blissful fusion with the m/other but from the frustrated desire for attunement, for recognition of one's full bodily, passionate being by a fully other, separate being like the self. In "The Prussian Officer" erotic desire is distorted by loss, envy, and rage—the residue of failed recognition and intersubjective breakdown. Desire thus results only in domination and destruction of the other, and in the corresponding annihilation of the self.

Similar dynamics figure in "The Blind Man," though here the climax is characterized by paralyzing fear and dread rather than the envious, destructive rage played out in the earlier story. Maurice Pervin, the blind man, lives in a dark, sensual "blood-contact with the substantial world" (54). The narrator tells us that "the rich suffusion of this state generally kept him happy, reaching its culmination in the consuming passion for his wife. But at times the flow would seem to be checked and thrown back. Then it would beat inside him like a tangled sea, and he was tortured in the shattered chaos of his own blood" (54). The suggestion here is that Maurice's depressions stem from the failure of the other to meet fully or recognize his authentic being, namely his physical, sensual, and erotic being.[4]

Lawrence's preoccupation with "blood-contact" and sensuality in all of his writing is not simply, as Storch has argued, a defensive response to castration anxiety and threatened masculinity. Although such anxiety plays a role, the origins of the fixation are deeper and precede the development of gender identity. The obsession is rooted in the clamorous demand for recognition of one's being, and for the infant, "being," as discussed in the introduction, is an intensely physical, embodied phenomenon. Recognition of the instinctive, bodily self, however, is only possible if the recognizing other feels authentic and comfortable in her or his own body and sexuality. Thus the cultural discomfort with female sexuality—particularly the madonna-whore split—has crippling psychological repercussions for everyone. If mothers are stripped of sexuality, of their full bodily, sensual life, then their children, male and female, will suffer from that impairment. A disembodied mother cannot recognize the bodily life of her child.

In "The Blind Man," Maurice's pregnant wife, Isabel, is afraid of the "hot animal life," the darkness and sensuality of the barn where Maurice spends most of his time. The story climaxes in the barn with a meeting between Maurice and Bertie Reid, a friend and distant cousin of Isabel's. Bertie is even more terrified than Isabel of the dark animality the barn represents. A cerebral lawyer, Bertie is described as harboring "an incurable weakness, which made him unable ever to enter into close contact of any sort" (58). His inner life is ruled by shame and fear: he "could not approach women physically. . . . At the centre of him he was afraid, helplessly and even brutally afraid. . . . At the centre he felt himself neuter, nothing" (58). Alone in the barn with Maurice, stripped of his intellectual and social defenses (Maurice accidently knocks off his hat), Bertie all but disintegrates.

In a rush of tenderness and desire for contact with the young man, Maurice asks Bertie to touch his eyes and his scar. Bertie is revolted but does so because "he was under the power of the blind man, as if hypnotised" (62). Maurice is excited by the intimacy, by the potential for mutual recognition that, for him, such intimacy represents: "'Oh, my God, we shall know each other now, shan't we? We shall know each other now,'" he exclaims. Bertie, however, remains "as if in a swoon, unconscious, imprisoned. . . . He gazed mute and terror-struck, overcome by his own weakness. . . . He had an unreasonable fear, lest the other man should suddenly destroy him" (62).

The scene depicts, once again, a collapsed intersubjectivity and the resulting dynamic of domination and submission. Though Maurice is only seeking recognition, he is experienced by Bertie as dominating because he (Bertie) lacks the "core"—the embodied, agentic selfhood—that would have made mutual recognition possible. The erotic element is also apparent. Bertie's "swooning" in contact with Maurice's powerful male animality, as well as his extreme revulsion and dread, all suggest an unconscious but terrified desire. As in "The Prussian Officer," the empty character desires in the other precisely what he himself lacks. His own deficiency and shame, however, pollute that desire and provoke the fantasy of annihilation.

Though the character of Bertie may have been modeled on Bertrand Russell, it is perhaps not coincidental that throughout Lawrence's boyhood he was known to his family and close friends as "Bert" or sometimes "Bertie." The loss of spontaneous, bodily and emotional self-experience—what Winnicott describes as "the true self"—typifies the modern schizoid condition. This is the condition Bertie represents and that Lawrence understood all too well. Dollie Urquhart in "The Princess" is another version of Bertie. In this New Mexico-set story, Lawrence provides more backround for understanding the relational origins of the "empty-shell" condition.

Dollie is the prized child of a man whom the narrator calls "just a bit mad." The most striking features of Colin Urquhart are his "vague blue eyes," eyes that seemed "to be looking at nothing" and his lack of physicality or somatic reality: he is described as a "spectre," an "echo . . . a living echo! His very flesh, when you touched it, did not seem quite the flesh of a real man" (159–60). After three years of marriage to this man, his wife, the narrator suggests, withers and dies from his very lack of substance. The child becomes his special doll—"My princess," he calls her.

The situation contains characteristic Lawrencian features. The child is passionately attached to and dependent on an other who is not "all there," who is disembodied and incapable of "seeing" or recognizing the child in her separate, real, and embodied self. She grows up with an "inward coldness" and an incapacity, like Bertie, for intimacy. As her father's narcissistic object, she suffers from both his grandiosity and his isolation. He tells her that they are the last of a "royal race," that they harbor royal "demons" within that sets them apart from ordinary, vulgar people. Despite her coldness and arrogance, however, there is that in Dollie which yearns for recognition and contact, for erotic expression and relationship that would bring her into being and make her "real."[5]

After her father dies, she visits a ranch in New Mexico and meets the Indian guide, Domingo Romero. She catches a "spark in his eye" and immediately recognizes his "fine demon." The narrator describes "an inter-recognition between them, silent and delicate" (170). Like Dollie, Romero is narcissistically wounded, arrogant, and isolated. His family had once been the owners of the ranch and the surrounding land, but they had now lost all to the white man. Romero's eyes are described as black, "half alive," "fatal," and hopeless, but at their center "a spark of pride. . . . Just a spark in the midst of the blackness of static despair" (168). Though both Dollie and Romero are only "half alive," existing in a state of frozen despair, that "spark" of potential life remains. Their attuned recognition provides the last chance for igniting desire and emerging into life for them both.

Dollie convinces Romero to take her into the mountains—"She wanted to look over the mountains into their secret heart. . . . She wanted to see the wild animals move about in their wild unconsciousness" (172–73). She wants to discover in "the core of the Rockies," in other words, what's missing at the core of her own being—authentic, uninhibited bodily and emotional expression. Like Bertie, however, her search for self in the other—in the mountains and in Romero—is ultimately overwhelmed by her own inner deficiency, by a paralyzing shame and fear. Desire thus turns into dread and repulsion. Described from her perspective, the mountains are "massive, gruesome, repellent" (181) and the wilderness is "squalid": "The strange squalor of the primitive forest pervaded the place, the squalor of animals and their droppings, the squalor of the wild. The Princess knew the peculiar repulsiveness of it" (184).

Dollie feels "hypnotised," furthermore, by a distant bobcat's eyes, by its "demonish watching," which makes her shiver "with cold and fear. She knew well enough the dread and repulsiveness of the wild" (185–86). She knew well enough, in other words, the dread and repulsiveness—the deep shame—of self-exposure. For Dollie, the spontaneous, "wild" expression of one's being, particularly the expression of one's passionate, erotic physicality, is demonic and dreadful.

The same external projection of inner shame is repeated in relation to Romero. Having made camp, they lie down to sleep and she dreams of being buried alive in the snow: "She was growing colder and colder, the snow was weighing down on her. The snow was going to absorb her" (187). Here again is the familiar Lawrencian lapse into white, frozen death. A part of Dollie, however, struggles against such schizoid numbness and retreat—"she was so cold, so shivering, and her heart could not beat. Oh, would not someone help her heart to beat?"—and she calls to Romero to make her warm. The result is a variation of the barn scene between Bertie and Maurice:

> As soon as he had lifted her in his arms, she wanted to scream to him not to touch her. She stiffened herself. Yet she was dumb.
>   And he was warm, but with a terrible animal warmth that seemed to annihilate her. He panted like an animal with desire. And she was given over to this thing. (188)

Although Bertie in "The Blind Man" is not, like Dollie, literally raped, the outcome is figuratively the same: both feel assailed and annihilated by the overpowering, animal, and erotic presence of the other. Yet both Bertie and Dollie feel an irrisistible inner compulsion to submit to this presence in the first place. The narrator states repeatedly that Dollie "had *willed* that it should happen to her" (italics his, 188). We are back to Ghent's notion of masochism as a distorted bid for recognition. The desire to surrender up to the other the defenses that have been preventing authentic self-experience is so intense it transforms into a manner of passionate submission. With both Dollie and Bertie, however, the terrors of such erotic submission—the threat of total invasion and annihilation of the self—are equally intense.

For Dollie, sexuality is bound up with her "demonic" core experience of self—with the narcissistic shame and rage associated with a passionate "letting go"—and thus she dreads what she also craves. The story reflects one of the most primitive unconscious fantasies involved with shame—the fantasy, in Wurmser's words, that "My body and mental self are filled with dangerous, demonic forces evoking severe disgust" (193). Sex with Romero is agonizing "Because, in some peculiar way, he had got hold of her, some unrealised part of her which she never wished to realise" (193). Intimacy reactivates shame; it is experienced as an intrusion, making the self vulnerable to the original trauma of rejection. Though Dollie's father had loved her as a "doll" or selfobject—an extension or projection of the self (Kohut xiv)—he had utterly denied her as a feeling, desiring, fully embodied subject in her own right.

The narrative also gives us Romero's point of view, and his experience of Dollie's rejection replays the profound narcissistic wounding—the rejection "in one's inmost area" (Wurmser 63)—at the experiential heart of the story. When Dollie tells him that she had not liked their sexual encounter—"'I don't care for that kind of thing'" (190), Romero is stunned: "A blank sort of wonder spread over his face, at these words, followed immediately by a black look of anger, and then a stony, sinister despair" (190). Lawrence is a master at tracking the silent, internal progression of affects in any given relational moment. Romero experiences Dollie's rejection as an acute narcissistic blow: shock, anger, and finally, "sinister despair" follow. Such despair leads to sadistic, controlling behavior—he destroys Dollie's clothes and holds her captive—and ultimately to his death. Romero shoots at the approaching Forest Service officers and is killed by their return fire.

Even before Romero's death, however, the narrator declares that both he and Dollie "were two people who had died" (193). Lawrence understood well the psychic death that results from the rejection of one's being at its affective, bodily core. Dollie tells the officers that Romero "had gone out of his mind" (195), and the narrator reports that Dollie "too was now a little mad" (196). Years later she refers to the episode as follows: "Since my accident in the mountains, when a man went mad and shot my horse from under me, and my guide had to shoot him dead, I have never felt quite myself" (196). As I will discuss later in relation to *The Rainbow*, horses always represent a primal sensuality in Lawrence's fiction, and they can provoke both desire and dread. Dollie cannot tolerate this level of sensual, bodily experience because of the original rejection and consequent shame she suffered. For her, relaxing her mental defenses means mental disintegration—madness—and death. Romero and the horse are connected in her mind, and both must be denied.

Lawrence's Mexico-set "The Woman Who Rode Away" has proved the most controversial of all his short stories. Written ten years after "The Prussian Officer," the tale is equally sadomasochistic: it dramatizes the same erotic ambivalence and splitting, the same intersubjective collapse into the polarity of domination and submission as the earlier story. The reason for the critical fuss, however, is that in this case the character in the masochistic position—the object of the male sadism—is a woman.[6] Kate Millett calls this story about an educated white woman who rides off into the mountains and finds herself the sacrificial victim in a barbaric Indian religious rite, "Lawrence's most impassioned statement of the doctrine of male supremacy and the penis as deity . . . a pornographic dream" (403).

Although Millett claims the story devotes equal attention to the masochistic and the sadistic, she perceives "a peculiar relish . . . a wallowing in the power of the Indian male, his beauty and indifference and cruelty, exerted not only on the silly woman, his victim, but on Lawrence too. It is the author himself standing fascinated before this silent and darkly beautiful killer, enthralled, aroused, awaiting the sacrificial rape" (405). True enough, but Millett does not pursue the implications of this insight in her wholesale indictment of the story as a sadistic fantasy of male vengeance and humiliation of women. The authorial identification with the Woman makes for a profound ambivalence that, as with so many Lawrence stories, complicates the surface plot and accounts for an ambiguity of tone and attitude.

The ambiguity is evident in the widely divergent critical readings of the story. Like Millett, R. P. Draper sees much sadistic pleasure in the story's ending; he refers to the "'glittering eagerness, and awe, and craving'" attributed to the Indians as betraying Lawrence's own vindictiveness toward independent women. Peter Balbert, on the other hand, believes there is "ample evidence of an antagonistic attitude toward the primitive 'darkness' of the story" (116), and that the Woman's "evaluation of the Indians as dangerous creatures is shared by Lawrence, who is willing to choose the 'educated' antagonism of the Woman over the barbarism and coldness of the Chilchui" (121). The story indeed contains both attitudes toward the Indians—a pleasureful identification with their power and savagery *and* a resistant terror of it. David Cavitch is most on the mark when he notes that "none of the story's portended violence occurs . . . even the sacrificial thrust is arrested, in a conditional verb—'Then the old man would strike'—. . . . The allegory is evidently about a state of ambivalence so intense that neither the desire for a demonic sexual experience nor the anxiety over its destructiveness can be dramatized by conclusive actions" (166).

Interpretations that stress only the devaluation and objectification of the Woman—the perspective of the Indians—miss the Woman's own perspective, the perspective from which the major part of the story is indeed told. Although the Indians deny her personal being, her personal feelings and sensations are acutely rendered by the narrative as the experience unfolds. Despite the fact that she is nameless (as are other characters in Lawrence's short stories), she is not a mere abstraction; she is granted an inner life or soul, even if it is the typically suppressed or deadened soul that Lawrence sees as endemic to modern civilization. Like Dollie in relation to her father, or Juliet before her sunbaths, the Woman, we are told, has been living an empty existence in dumb subjection to a husband who "had never become real to her, neither mentally nor physically" (547). Without a "real" other to confer her own reality, she feels herself, like Colin Urquhart's wife, shriveling into nothingness.

The Woman's expedition to the mountains to find the "mysterious, marvellous Indians" is a last-ditch effort, like Dollie's, to discover that real otherness and her own reality. As usual in Lawrence's work, however, the self-affirmative desire for surrender, for yielding up the false self in hopes of recognition of one's true or authentic being, becomes distorted by the deficiency and shame out of which it springs. Self-affirmative surrender to an external other becomes self-destructive submission to an idealized, tyrannical other. Although there is authorial identification with both the sadistic and the masochistic in this story, I would, like Millett in her initial insight, give greater weight to the latter. The story is less a vengeful celebration of the Woman's subjection than a disturbing enactment of the psychological dilemma inherent in masochistic fantasy.[7]

In *The Bonds of Love*, Benjamin analyzes Pauline Réage's sadomasochistic tale *Story of O* as a reflection of intersubjective breakdown and "the struggle to the death for recognition" (55). Millett independently points out the similarity between Réage's pornographic story and Lawrence's; Benjamin's analysis of O can thus shed light on "The Woman Who Rode Away" as well. In O, for instance, Benjamin observes that O's masters "must perform their violation rationally and ritually in order to maintain their boundaries and to make her will—not only her body—the object of their will" (57–58). Similarly, the Indians treat the Woman in an utterly impersonal, ritualistic manner that ensures distance and denies commonality. Just as O is told by her masters that she is being flogged "'to teach you that you are totally dedicated to something outside yourself'" (56), so the Woman is told her sacrifice will "serve the gods of the Chilchui," will reclaim the potency of the sun and empower the Indians once more. As Benjamin says of O, "her sacrifice actually creates the master's power, produces his coherent self, in which she can take refuge. Thus in losing her own self, she is gaining access, however circumscribed, to a more powerful one" (61).

The Indians' sadism differs in one important respect from that of the Captain in "The Prussian Officer." The Captain's sadism is desperately personal; the Indians', on the other hand, is profoundly disinterested. From the Woman's perspective, that absence of personal interest offers a fantasy of protection and containment. Because the Indians have objectified her and do not need her personally (as the Captain needs the orderly, Maurice needs Bertie, or Romero needs Dollie), the Woman is reassured of their strength since it is not dependent on her own fragile selfhood. The masochistic fantasy is consequently played out much more fully in this story than in the others. As Benjamin notes, the protective power of the sadist's disinterestedness "constitutes the all-important aspect of authority, without which the fantasy is not satisfying" (64). The Woman not only gains access to the Indians' greater power by giving up her own, she can also lose herself and "let go" (like Juliet in "Sun") without fear of destroying the other through the full expressive force of her erotic being (the fearful fantasy behind "Shadow in the Rose Garden"). Michael Bader elucidates this argument in a discussion of female masochism:

A script that calls for her partner ruthlessly to dominate her reassures her that the other—in this discussion, the man—will not be hurt by her excitement, thus permitting her to unleash it without worry or guilt. She identifies with his strength and then not only vicariously contacts and participates in his forbidden sexual agency—power by proxy, you might say—but also experiences him as a safe container for the expression of her own intrinsic sexual forcefulness and vitality. She therefore experiences herself privately as powerful. (283)

The scene in which the Woman is oiled and massaged in preparation for her sacrifice is highly erotic, even orgiastic. The description again emphasizes the Indians' remote, impersonal power, a power on which the pleasure of the masochistic fantasy depends:

> Their dark hands were incredibly powerful, yet soft with a watery softness she could not understand. . . . They were so impersonal, absorbed in something that was beyond her. They never saw her as a personal woman . . . the eyes were fixed with an unchanging, steadfast gleam, . . . the fixity of revenge, and the nascent exultance of those that are going to triumph—these things she could read in their faces, as she lay and was rubbed into a misty glow by their uncanny dark hands. Her limbs, her flesh, her very bones at last seemed to be diffusing into a roseate sort of mist, in which her consciousness hovered like some sun-gleam in a flushed cloud. . . . She knew she was a victim; that all this elaborate work upon her was the work of victimising her. But she did not mind. She wanted it. (577)

The Woman is paradoxically willing to risk annihilation of her self in search of her self, which is the masochistic predicament. The pleasureable aspects of her experience are nevertheless equally mixed with fear and ambivalence in the story as a whole, evident in the narrative emphasis on the Indians' "cruel," "sinister," and "inhuman" nature, and as Cavitch notes, in the hesitancy of the ending, in the failure to actualize the violence.

As in *Story of O*, a father-son recognition dynamic is also prominent in this story. Benjamin describes the young man René's delivery of O to the older Sir Stephen as "a way of surrendering himself sexually to the more powerful man . . . the desire for recognition by the father wholly overtakes the love of the mother; it becomes another motive for domination" (59). In Lawrence's story, a young Indian forms a bond with the Woman—"He came and sat with her a good deal—sometimes more than she wished—as if he wanted to be near her." He is described as "gentle and apparently submissive with . . . black hair streaming maidenly over his shoulders" (567). His femaleness and identification with the Woman, in other words, are both affirmed and ultimately repudiated in his alliance with the father.

The young Indian, who is being groomed to become the next chief, accompanies the Woman in her meetings with the old chief and serves as translator. As the old man runs his fingers over the Woman's naked body, "the young Indian had a strange look of ecstasy on his face" (564). Associated with both the Woman and the young Indian is the fantasy of being ravished by the ideal, omnipotent father, and the story plays out the petrifying ambivalence that so often accompanies such fantasy for Lawrence.

Finally, eye imagery in this story is also conspicuous. The Indian chief's power, in particular, is specifically located in his black, fixed eyes: "the old chief looked at her as if from the far, far dead, seeing something that was never to be seen" (563); "She was fascinated by the black, glass-like, intent eyes of the old cacique, that watched her without blinking, like a basilisk's, overpowering her" (573); "Only the eyes of the oldest man were not anxious. Black and fixed, and as if sightless, they watched the sun, seeing beyond the sun. And in their black, empty concentration there was power, power intensely abstract and remote, but deep, deep to the heart of the earth, and the heart of the sun" (581).

The fixation on eyes again signals the Lawrencian obsession with being seen, known, recognized deep to the heart of the self. The Indian chief/father's eyes hold that power, the penetrating, dark power of Juliet's sun to "know" the self and bring it into full erotic being. The Woman, as Benjamin says of O, is "the lost soul who can only be restored to grace by putting herself in the hands of the ideal, omnipotent other . . . [her] great longing is to be known, and in this respect she is like any lover, for the secret of love is to be known as oneself" (60). Only a real other, however, not an idealized projection, can provide such recognition. The narrator is aware of the Woman's "foolish romanticism" in seeking the Indians in the first place. Nevertheless, it is her masochistic fantasy as a derailed bid for recognition that is the story's prevailing fantasy, and it is one with which Lawrence deeply identified.

The assertion of male dominion in the story's final lines—"Then the old man would strike, and strike home, accomplish the sacrifice and achieve the power. The mastery that man must hold, and that passes from race to race" (581)—and the rigid gender polarity on which the story rides reflect a defensive splitting apparent throughout Lawrence's writing, a splitting that is especially blatant in many of his essays and letters. In the fiction, however, the polarity is frequently undermined by Lawrence's capacious, flexible imagination that includes a strong female identification and an equally firm, intuitive grasp of the importance of the other's independent subjectivity to the realization of one's own. The recognition the self craves, the stories make clear, can come only from an other who is recognized as a whole, independent subject in her or his own right. The fiction often dramatizes the consequences of collapsed intersubjectivity—a collapse Benjamin sees as historically embedded in our culture. Lawrence's stories explore this problem with great imaginative force and insight even if they fail to solve it.

"THE HORSE-DEALER'S DAUGHTER": CONFRONTING SHAME AND THE STRUGGLE TO LOVE

Like "The Princess," "The Horse-Dealer's Daughter" (originally titled "The Miracle") concerns two characters who surrender their mental defenses and encounter one another on a primal level beneath the rational surface of their lives. Here too the characters are confronted with their own deep sense of shame—externalized again in the natural imagery—but in this story, unlike "The Princess," both characters struggle to love in the face of their shame. In this case the sense of dread and repulsiveness associated with one's inmost self is not projected and denied but owned and acknowledged. The possibility that one can yet be loved at the core of one's shame (which is felt to be at the core of one's being) is the "miracle" the story movingly conveys.

Like Miriam in *Sons and Lovers*, Mabel Pervin is forced to live under the oppressive rule of her sensual but shallow brothers, who alternately neglect and ridicule her. "They had talked at her and round her for so many years," the narrator states, "that she hardly heard them at all" (139). Lawrence once again displays an unusual sensitivity to the pain and humiliation of being female in a brutal, male-dominated world. The Pervin brothers, however, are themselves in a demeaning state of loss and disgrace as the story opens. Their widowed father has died, leaving the family's horse-dealing business in severe debt. The horses are being sold, and the family is dispersing. For one brother, Joe, "The horses were almost like his own body to him. He felt he was done for now" (138). Joe is engaged to be married, and the narrator adds, "He would marry and go into harness. His life was over, he would be a subject animal now" (138). The other brother, Fred Henry, "was master of any horse. . . . But he was not master of the situations of life" (138).

The story thus begins with a state of loss and shameful self-diminishment, and that state, as usual, is connected with the loss or suppression of bodily, sensual life (represented by the customary horse symbolism). Though Mabel has lived on the horse farm amidst her horsey brothers, their scorn and rejection have served to close her off long ago from that primal level of experience. Having lost contact with her sensual, feeling life, Mabel, like so many Lawrence characters, has erected a psychic wall of proud reserve. "So long as there was money," the narrator states, "the girl felt herself established, and brutally proud, reserved" (142). Money and the memory of her mother "who had died when she was fourteen, and whom she had loved" (142) had provided her only sense of self-worth, her sole reasons for living. Now that the money was gone, only the memory of the dead mother remains, and Mabel devotes herself to tending to her mother's grave. The narrator describes how, when visiting the grave, "she seemed in a sort of ecstasy to be coming nearer to her fulfilment, her own glorification, approaching her dead mother, who was glorified" (143).

Wurmser discusses the "drives for union" frequently associated with shame (115). Mabel's desire to merge with her "glorified" dead mother is indeed rooted in her painful sense of loss and self-degradation; the narrative also associates her visits to the churchyard grave with fear of self-exposure and a schizoid-like retreat:

> There she always felt secure, as if no one could see her, although as a matter of fact she was exposed to the stare of everyone who passed along under the churchyard wall. Nevertheless, once under the shadow of the great looming church, among the graves, she felt immune from the world, reserved within the thick churchyard wall as in another country. (143)

For Mabel, as for Dollie, the retreat from affective life, along with regressive, merging fantasies, defend against the underlying pain of rejection and humiliation. Their lives, as a result, are marked by a subjective sense of emptiness and inauthenticity. "The life she [Mabel] followed here in the world," the narrator remarks, "was far less real than the world of death she inherited from her mother" (143).

Mabel's retreat into the world of death is interrupted, however, by the country doctor, Jack Fergusson. The doctor too is a divided soul, alienated from his innermost being. He is initially described as having "tired" eyes and as being "muffled up" in overcoat, scarf, and a cap that "was pulled down on his head" and "which he did not remove" (140). As Mabel has erected a dense wall of emotional reserve, the doctor has muffled and suppressed his sensual, feeling life beneath the protective garb of his professional identity. Nevertheless, he continues to feel the tug toward revived contact with affective life, apparent in his "craving" for contact with the "rough, inarticulate, powerfully emotional" working people:

> Nothing but work, drudgery, constant hastening from dwelling to dwelling among the colliers and the iron-workers. It wore him out, but at the same time he had a craving for it. It was a stimulant to him to be in the homes of the working people, moving, as it were, through the

innermost body of their life. His nerves were excited and gratified. . . .
He grumbled, he said he hated the hellish hole. But as a matter of fact
it excited him, the contact with the rough, strongly-feeling people was
a stimulant applied direct to his nerves. (144)

One afternoon, Fergusson spies Mabel walking "slowly and delib-
erately" toward the center of a pond, ultimately disappearing into its
depths. He hastens down the path to rescue her. The description of Fergusson's descent into the water emphasizes the pond's deathlike nature,
and particularly its "foul," "hideous," and "repellent" aspects:

> He slowly ventured into the pond. The bottom was deep, soft clay; he
> sank in, and the water clasped dead cold round his legs. As he stirred
> he could smell the cold, rotten clay that fouled up into the water. It was
> objectionable in his lungs. Still, repelled and yet not heeding, he moved
> deeper into the pond. The cold water rose over his thighs, over his
> loins, upon his abdomen. The lower part of his body was all sunk in
> the hideous cold element. And the bottom was so deeply soft and
> uncertain, he was afraid of pitching with his mouth underneath. (145)

At one point when reaching for Mabel's body, the doctor loses his balance and goes under, "horribly, suffocating in the foul, earthy water."
At last he succeeds in lifting her and staggering on to the bank, "out of
the horror of wet grey clay" (146).

Clyde de L. Ryals argues from a Jungian perspective that this scene
"is a careful working out of the rebirth archetype, embodying the rite of
baptism, the purification and revivication by water" (155). The foul,
slimy, and repugnant aspects of the pond, he maintains, are "symbolic
of the repressed contents of the mind of neurotic persons" (155). Quoting Jung, he adds that the image of "'slime out of the depths' . . . contains not only 'objectionable animal tendencies, but also germs of new
possibilities of life'" (156). Questions remain, however, as to what
exactly has been "repressed" and why "animal tendencies" should be so
"objectionable," especially since renewed contact with one's animal
nature is precisely what the story affirms; it is indeed what makes rebirth
possible. The Jungian interpretation misses, I believe, the rich particu-
larity of the symbolic imagery and the tension of unresolved ambivalence that drives the story throughout.

The doctor's hesitant descent into the "foul, earthy water" certainly
reflects, as Ryals notes, the characteristic Lawrencian horror of regressive merging or refusion. In order to understand the peculiar repulsiveness of the imagery, however,—the emphasis on the rotton smell, and
the repetition of the words "cold" and "foul"—we need to consider the
symbolic presence of shame. The swamp imagery recalls the repugnant,
foul-smelling marsh images associated in Lawrence's letters, and in *The*

Rainbow, with homosexual love. The imagery suggests not only a fear of refusion or absorption, but an unrestrained anality and profound self-contempt buried beneath the surface defenses.

If the infant's physical, sensual self-expression was originally met with coldness and rejection, then that internalized response will continue to define the self's experience of its own sensuality and bodily processes. Letting go of one's mental restraints means bodily release and thus exposing one's "objectionable," smelly, bodily products. The horrible "wet grey clay" of the pond reflects the anal imagery that is one of the most frequent symbolic manifestations of unconscious shame.

Mabel and the doctor had both abandoned their mental defenses, sunk "in overhead," and surrendered to their shameful bodily selves. When Mabel regains consciousness, she asks him, "Was I out of my mind?" and he replies that perhaps she was for a moment. The threat of madness, of losing all mental control, scares them both. Stronger than that fear, however, is the powerful, vitalizing magnetism they feel toward one another. For Fergusson, "It was as if she had the life of his body in her hands, and he could not extricate himself. Or perhaps he did not want to" (147–48). When Mabel discovers that he had undressed her—thus having had the life of *her* body in *his* hands—she asks directly, "'Do you love me then?'" She falls to passionately embracing him, "indiscriminately kissing his knees, his legs, as if unaware of everything," and "yearning and triumphant and confident," she murmers, "'You love me. I know you love me, I know'" (148).

To be seen in one's true nakedness—in one's undefended bodily being—is to be recognized, affirmed, indeed loved. For both Mabel and the doctor, however, shame and fear compete with their emerging faith in self and other and in the possibility of real intimacy. Fergusson

> looked down at the tangled wet hair, the wild, bare, animal shoulders. He was amazed, bewildered, and afraid. . . . It was horrible to have her there embracing his knees. It was horrible. He revolted from it violently. And yet—and yet—he had not the power to break away. (148)

We are told repeatedly that he had "no intention of loving her," that he had rescued her out of professional duty, and that he is "horrified" by this "personal element" (148–49). As in "The Princess," intimacy reactivates shame, threatening the terror of rejection, loss of control, and utter powerlessness. The doctor "had a horror of yielding to her," yet "something in him ached also. . . . He wanted to remain like that for ever, with his heart hurting him in a pain that was also life to him" (149). By warding off the deep pain of rejection and insulating themselves from all feeling, Mabel and the doctor had each been living a mechanical, nonauthentic existence. To reexperience pain is thus to reexperience life.

Shame remains, however, an unrelenting threat. In the midst of their embrace, Fergusson looks down at Mabel's damp hair: "Then, as it were suddenly, he smelt the horrid stagnant smell of that water" (149). Mabel pulls away from him with "terrible wistful, unfathomable" eyes. The doctor feels "ripped open," and thinks, "'How they would all jeer if they knew!'" (150). The story indeed concludes with the consciousness of acute shame. As Fergusson kisses her, Mabel murmers, "'My hair smells so horrible. . . . And I'm so awful, I'm so awful! Oh, no, I'm too awful,' and she broke into bitter, heart-broken sobbing. 'You can't want to love me, I'm horrible'" (152).

The story's final lines express the profound ambivalence that loving inevitably entails for Lawrence's characters:

> "I feel awful. I feel awful. I feel I'm horrible to you."
>
> "No, I want you, I want you," was all he answered, blindly, with that terrible intonation which frightened her almost more than her horror lest he should not want her. (152)

Like Dollie, Mabel is terrified of being destroyed by the very expression of animal desire she craves. The hope for Mabel and the doctor, though, lies in their willingness to open themselves to the painful consciousness of their shame, to tolerate their wrenching ambivalence, and to trust blindly that one might yet be loved in all one's "horrible" animality. That same hope continually nourished Lawrence's imagination.

CHAPTER 4

The Rainbow

TOM AND LYDIA: SUSTAINING THE MATERNAL IDENTIFICATION AND THE DEVELOPMENT OF FAITH

In 1913 Lawrence began work on a novel originally titled "The Sisters," later changed to "The Wedding Ring," and after several more revisions and drafts, was finally published as *The Rainbow* in 1915. The novel is a stylistic departure from the traditional realism of *Sons and Lovers*. Critics generally refer to Lawrence's well-known letter to Edward Garnett (5 June 1914) to explain the transition. In the letter Lawrence proclaims that he is no longer interested in "the old stable ego" of character. He is concerned not with the social self or surface manners but with a more elemental, invisible "carbon" of character. Ben-Ephraim claims that the novel achieves a "carbon-narrative" in which there is no interfering narrator or teller but "a seamless web wherein form is suited to content as both work toward the revelation of unknown facets of life" (130).

Along with the emphasis, both stylistic and thematic, on the fluid life beneath the ego or social self, the novel also highlights, as many critics have observed, the contradictions and oppositions inherent in this dynamic life beneath the surface. "Lawrence's character exposition," Ben-Ephraim asserts, "is based on contradictions" (143). Harold Bloom calls *The Rainbow*, as well as *Women in Love*, "visionary prose poems, inhabited by giant forms acting out the civil wars of the psyche" (*"The Rainbow"* 18). Just as ambivalence and contradictions in *Sons and Lovers* are enacted but not resolved, so too *The Rainbow* displays the negative capability of allowing oppositions and conflicts to stand without either deciding or dissolving them.[1] "From the first page to last page," Alan Friedman claims, "the organization of *The Rainbow* is planned to provide, inevitably, for the absence of any conclusion" (21). An intersubjective perspective can provide an effective lens through which to view the novel's unresolved oppositions and creative tensions.

The early chapters of *The Rainbow* focus on the relationship between Tom Brangwen and his Polish wife, Lydia. Tom's consciousness is foregrounded, and it is tangled in the typical Lawrencian dilemma. Tom is driven by an "innate desire to find in a woman the embodiment of all his inarticulate, powerful religious impulses" while simultaneously he feels terrified, indeed paralyzed, by the whole "business of love" (21). He would drink himself into a "kindled state of oneness with all the world . . . obliterating his own individuality" (28). Hungry for love but petrified by the potentially destructive and self-destroying intensity of his own hunger, Tom inhabits that characteristically schizoid state in which life in general is felt to be empty and unreal. With his first sight of Lydia, however, his subjective state shifts. He feels certain he has made contact with this strange, foreign woman; we are told repeatedly how they "exchanged recognition" (29–30). Most importantly, it is the woman's very foreignness—her impenetrable otherness—that restores a sense of reality for Tom:

> It was to him a profound satisfaction that she was a foreigner. A swift change had taken place on the earth for him, as if a new creation were fulfilled, in which he had real existence. Things had all been stark, unreal, barren, mere nullities before. Now they were actualities that he could handle. (32)

As Benjamin has argued, the self's sense of its own subjective reality is contingent on recognition of the other's separate subjectivity, on the other's "not-me" existence. Lydia's foreignness accentuates her separateness, assuring the reality of a world outside the self. As usual in Lawrence's fiction, however, the relationship with the woman here captures the multileveled, often contradictory nature of psychic and relational life. The female other's separate subjectivity can temper narcissistic fantasies if it is recognized and accepted; the fact of her separateness, however, can equally inflame narcissistic anxieties. The key task is to tolerate the tension of opposing self-states, a task that the text accomplishes even when Tom does not.

Ambivalence is inescapable. Lydia's alien quality, her remoteness, is at once a source of attraction and frustration. Her otherness is enforced not only by her being from a strange culture, but also by her withdrawn and reserved nature. Lydia keeps to herself and is emotionally distant. On the one hand Tom feels that "It was rather splendid, to be so ignored by her, whilst she lay against him, and he lifted her with his breathing, and felt her weight upon his living, so he had a completeness and an inviolable power. He did not interfere with her. He did not even know her" (46). On the other,

> They were such strangers, they must forever be such strangers, that his passion was a clanging torment to him. Such intimacy of embrace, and such utter foreignness of contact! It was unbearable. He could not bear to be near her, and know the utter foreignness between them, know how entirely they were strangers to each other. (48)

At the same time that Tom celebrates the "wonderful remoteness" (46) about Lydia, he is equally tormented by it. Her emotional absence insures her status as an object of desire: "he was ever drawn to her, drawn after her, with ever-raging, ever-unsatisfied desire. . . . [H]e could never quite reach her, he could never quite be satisfied, never be at peace, because she might go away" (58). He is driven to drink again "to escape the madness of sitting next to her when she did not belong to him" (61). Nevertheless, he recognizes that her separateness and integrity—her suffering that does not include him—must be respected, even honored: "He must not try to tear her into recognition of himself, and agreement with himself. It were disastrous, impious" (62).

Lydia's depression, as Tom is aware, stems from a history of heartrending loss. She has endured the deaths of her husband and her children. Her grief, Tom understands, "was sacred to her, and he must not violate her with his comfort" (63). As in *Sons and Lovers*, empathy and respect for the woman's inner pain—a compassionate awareness of the *causes* of her coldness and emotional reserve—stand in tension with the bitter rage that is also directed at her. It is perhaps not coincidental either that this depressed, remote character, the matriarch of the novel's succeeding generations, shares the name of Lawrence's own mother, Lydia. The relationship between Tom and Lydia is emotionally charged with a child's acutely conflicting feelings toward a withdrawn, affectively nonattuned mother. The unconscious mother-child scenario is perhaps nowhere more creatively played out than in the scene in which Tom cares for Lydia's four-year-old daughter, Anna, as Lydia lies in childbirth.

Lydia is upstairs in labor while Tom is downstairs with the panic-stricken child. Anna is screaming in terror for her mother, and Tom responds with irritation and mounting anger. Anna's feeling "cut off and lost in a horror of desolation" (72), as the narrator explains, mirrors Tom's own feelings toward Lydia. His angry exasperation with the child reflects a rising fury toward his own subjective experience of maternal nonresponsiveness and abandonment, as well as contempt for his own inner helplessness and rage. He tries to undress the resistant child, and as he lifts up her rigid body, "Its stiff blindness made a flash of rage go through him. He would like to break it" (74). The narrator uses the same terms to describe the behavior of both the child and the man: "blind," "automatic," "mechanical." Anna "had become a little, mechanical thing of fixed will," while Tom "too was blind, and intent, irritated into mechanical action" (73). Both are caught up in a rigidly defensive—hence mechanical—mode. Suddenly, however, Tom experiences a shift in consciousness:

> A new degree of anger came over him. What did it all matter? What
> did it matter if the mother talked Polish and cried in labour, if this
> child were stiff with resistance, and crying? Why take it to heart? Let
> the mother cry in labour, let the child cry in resistance, since they
> would do so. Why should he fight against it, why resist? Let it be, if it
> were so. Let them be as they were, if they insisted. (74)

Tom stops fighting, in other words, against the separate subjectivity
of both the mother and the child. He can allow the woman to be her separate self, in her suffering which excludes him, and he can allow the
child her anger without having to destroy it. He can simply "let them
be." Tom sits in a "daze" for a time as Anna continues to cry. When he
finally turns to look at her again, "He was shocked by her little, wet,
blinded face" (74). It is as if she has all at once become real to him—distinct from himself, unentangled from his projected relationship with his
own pain—and he is shocked by this recognition of her stark reality.
Tom's shift out of a mechanically defensive mode, the collapse of a
habitual pattern or framework, permits what psychoanalyst Robert
Langan calls "the emergence of the present" (638–42). The present
emerges in the vivid shock of Anna's face and in the brilliant scene in the
barn that follows.

With the shift in Tom's consciousness comes a changed manner and
attitude toward the child. His voice becomes "queer and distant and
calm" (74). He gently wraps Anna in a shawl that once belonged to his
mother and carries her out to the barn. There he continues to hold her
in one arm while, calmly and methodically, he prepares food for the
cows with the other. "They were in another world now," we are told:
"Outside there was the driving rain, inside, the softly-illuminated stillness and calmness of the barn" (75). Anna is soothed—"A new being
was created in her for the new conditions" (75). The description of this
scene in the barn is luminous in its senuous detail, in its evocation of an
exquistely real, yet profoundly dreamlike state:

> In a sort of dream, his heart sunk to the bottom, leaving the sur-
> face of him still, quite still, he rose with the panful of food, carefully
> balancing the child on one arm, the pan in the other hand. The silky
> fringe of the shawl swayed softly, grains and hay trickled to the floor;
> he went along a dimly-lit passage behind the mangers, where the horns
> of the cows pricked out of the obscurity. The child shrank, he balanced
> stiffly, rested the pan on the manger wall, and tipped out the food, half
> to this cow, half to the next. There was a noise of chains running, as
> the cows lifted or dropped their heads sharply; then a contented, sooth-
> ing sound, a long snuffing as the beast ate in silence.
>   The journey had to be performed several times. There was the
> rhythmic sound of the shovel in the barn, then the man returned, walk-

ing stiffly between the two weights, the face of the child peering out from the shawl. Then the next time, as he stooped, she freed her arm and put it round his neck, clinging soft and warm, making all easier. (75–76)

The present emerges here in the intensity and sharpness of the concrete detail, in the vibrant "thereness" of the description. While the scene in the barn conveys a vivid actuality and realness, it simultaneously represents an inner fantasy, a dream of prenatal harmony and fulfillment. The characters are enveloped in a rhythmic, warm and secure space, a place of animal satiation and mindless, bodily contentment. External and internal, reality and fantasy, as Winnicott has argued, are not mutually exclusive realms but are interrelated in highly complex, often paradoxical ways. Once Tom stops fighting against the woman's separate subjectivity, her reality apart from himself, he is paradoxically able to experience a deep, internal identification with her; he discovers the maternal within himself and assumes the role of tender, soothing nurturer. This new-found identification creates fresh possiblities in his relationship with the child and with his own anger and aggression. The phallic threat of the cows' horns pricking out of the obscurity in the barn, for instance, is acknowledged and contained.

With this reconfiguring of his inner world, Tom is able to recognize Anna in her real suffering while still identifying with her as a projection of his own child-self. He can feel empathy rather than contempt for his own inner sense of helplessness, anger, and loss. After Anna falls asleep in his arms, he takes her back to the house and puts her to bed in the room in which he spent his youth: "It was familiar. He remembered what it was to be a young man, untouched" (77). He then visits his wife in childbirth. As he beholds her suffering, he again experiences a "dread of her as she lay there. What had she to do with him? She was other than himself" (77). The narrator tells us, however, that "something made him go and touch her fingers." At the touch, Lydia opens her eyes and looks at him, and her look convinces Tom that she indeed "knew" him, knew him in a deep, primal, though impersonal way. No longer in dread of the woman, Tom feels a "great, scalding peace" come over him (77). The chapter ends with Tom back outdoors: he "lifted his face to the rain, and felt the darkness striking unseen and steadily upon him. The swift, unseen threshing of the night upon him silenced him and he was overcome. He turned away indoors, humbly. There was the infinite world, eternal, unchanging, as well as the world of life" (77).

Destructiveness and uncertainty, both within and without, can now be tolerated. The darkness need not be conquered—it can be survived. As in the final scene of *Sons and Lovers*, Lawrence's religious sensibility, his faith in an infinite, eternal world beyond the self, is born out of a laborious struggle within the self. Such faith, again, derives not from having forged a masculine ideal, a defensive paternal identification that combats or protects against the omnipotent mother. Rather, it comes from sustaining an identification with the mother in her nurturing, soothing, and protective function. Discovery of the "good" mother within is paradoxically dependent on discovery of the mother without—on recognition of her separate existence. When Tom is able finally to let the woman "be" in her singleness and otherness, he finds the maternal within himself and is liberated rather than threatened by it.

The battles of the inner world, however, are never absolutely won. The struggle to maintain the tension between narcissistic demands and intersubjective awareness remains constant. After the barn episode, Tom finds himself, once again, angry with Lydia and jealous of the new baby: "She sat close and impregnable with the child. And he was jealous of the child" (79). In the midst of an argument, however, he experiences another abrupt shift in consciousness: "Suddenly, in a flash, he saw she might be lonely, isolated, unsure. She had seemed to him the utterly certain, satisfied, absolute, excluding him. Could she need anything?" (88–89). Such intersubjective recognition continually competes with the omnipotent fantasies in Lawrence's fiction; it is again the tension between these two modes that so distinguishes his work. The self's need for recognition by and of a separate other, moreover, is not confined to Lawrence's male characters. Lydia, echoing Clara in relation to Paul, complains that Tom comes to her "as if I was nothing there," to which he retorts: "'You make me feel as if *I* was nothing" (89).

Nevertheless, Tom and Lydia have their moments of mutual recognition when their lovemaking becomes a meeting of selves rather than a matter of domination and submission. "She waited for him to meet her, not to bow before her, and serve her. She wanted his active participation, not his submission" (90). At first Tom resists, but ultimately "he let go his hold on himself, he relinquished himself, and knew the subterranean force of his desire to come to her, to be with her, to mingle with her, losing himself to find her, to find himself in her" (90). In my view the description here does not depict a pathological fantasy of merging. Rather, it suggests that Tom has developed enough trust in both the woman and himself to let himself go, to relinquish his defenses and love without restraint, without fearing that either self or other will be destroyed. He can lose himself with the faith that he will find himself and the other in the process. Tom and Lydia's love is described with one of Lawrence's favorite metaphors—that of calling and answering: "When she called, he answered, when he asked, her response came at once, or at length" (91). Faith in the female other's presence and responsiveness is restored; her response may not come "at once," but, Tom is confident, it *will* come. Tom and Lydia's relationship reaches a state of ideal mutuality and responsiveness that is always sought but rarely realized in Lawrence's fiction. Their love, represented by the utopian image of a rainbow's completed arch, creates the conditions for the child Anna to become freely and fully herself: she "was no more called upon to uphold with her childish might the broken end of the arch. Her father and her mother now met to the span of the heavens, and she, the child, was free to play in the space beneath, between" (91).

An ideal state of balance in a love relationship can be reached but it is difficult to sustain. As Benjamin has discussed, psychic and relational life are dynamic, not static, characterized even in health by the alternating movements of breakdown and repair. Such is the rhythm of Lawrence's art as well. Tom's death by drowning later in *The Rainbow* admittedly suggests breakdown. Drowning is psychologically resonant and bears considerable symbolic weight. The image of Tom's unconscious body "washed along in the black, swirling darkness, passively" (229) implies that "letting go" and losing oneself in love may indeed be disastrous.[2] The threat of annihilation through passive refusion with the mother is a narcissistic fantasy never totally eradicated in Lawrence's work. That fantasy, however, does not diminish or negate the alternate conceptions of m/other and self that also run throughout his texts. Tom's relationship with Lydia is not, as some critics have argued, merely that of a regressed, undifferentiated infant.[3] Lawrence never writes as schematically as we critics like to think. Howe's and Ben-Ephraim's ego psychological interpretations of the novel that see the succeeding Brangwen generations in terms of increasing individuation and linear development neglect the nuances and complex, mutable quality of Lawrence's characterizations. Tom's experience in the barn, for instance, represents a highly developed psychological achievement: the paradox of the m/other as both external and internal, separate yet deeply identified with the self, is powerfully (even if only momentarily) upheld. The image of Tom lifting his face to the "striking" darkness at the conclusion of the scene implies significant ego strength and a mature faith in self and other. Such faith is always a trembling potential in Lawrence's art even if it is not consistently or steadily maintained.

ANNA AND WILL:
DEFICIENCY, SHAME, AND THE WILL TO DOMINATE

The story of the second-generation Brangwens, Anna and Will, further elaborates the difficulties involved in maintaining a dialectical balance between self-assertion and mutual recognition and in achieving a state of intersubjectivity in the love relationship. Despite the joyous image of Anna playing freely in the space beneath the rainbow of her parents' marriage, Anna's inner world is not without deep inhibitions, uncertainty, and intense narcissistic anxieties. Once the narrative enters her consciousness, familiar psychological complexities emerge. Anna is uneasy and constrained in the world outside her home:

> She mistrusted herself, she mistrusted the outer world. She did not want to go on, she did not want to go out into it. . . . The people she met outside seemed to begrudge her her very existence. They seemed to want to belittle her also She was exceedingly reluctant to go amongst them. She depended upon her mother and her father. And she wanted to go out. (94–95)

We are repeatedly told how Anna felt "belittled" by the outside world as well as "diminished" and "degraded." Her sense of shame and injury, her horror of "crampedness," her feeling "as if never, never could she stretch her length and stride her stride" (99), betray a familiar Lawrencian condition. Anna is infuriated, furthermore, by what she perceives as her mother's "triumphant power" (98). As we saw in *Sons and Lovers*, Lawrence's female characters can suffer the same narcissistic binds as his men; they too must often contend with a deeply ambivalent state of dependency and an inner experience of deficiency and self-endangerment. Like Miriam in *Sons and Lovers*, Anna is haughty yet insecure, harboring ideal images of herself as a princess (95) while wrestling with a latent sense of inadequacy.

Will Brangwen's character, however, even more than Anna's, is determined by such inner deficiency and shame. The relationship between Anna and Will, as a result, collapses into a desperate power struggle in which each seeks only to dominate the other. Their honeymoon in a cottage "remote from the world," in which they "lay close together, complete and beyond the touch of time or change" (135) is blissful only briefly. "Gradually they began to wake up," the narrator reports, "the noises outside became more real" (135). Reality inevitably shatters the dream of an exclusive union with the other, in which the other's attention is focused solely and absolutely on the self.

Anna begins to assert her own subjectivity. At first she simply declares her hunger for food, but then she expresses an appetite for life outside the cottage, apart from her relationship with Will. Will's response is precisely that of a narcissistically enraged child—a child furious at the mother for her interests outside or beyond himself. He experiences Anna's turning away as abandonment, and the piercing sense of shame and anger that result give rise to a paradigmatic Lawrencian state:

Dread and desire for her to stay with him and shame at his own dependence on her drove him to anger. He began to lose his head. . . . All the
love, the magnificent new order was going to be lost, she would forfeit
it all for the outside things. . . . He began to hate this in her. Driven by
fear of her departure into a state of helplessness, almost of imbecility,
he wandered about the house. (141)

Anna too, however, is narcissistically enraged by Will's failure to
recognize *her*, by his intense self-absorption: "It was negative insensi-
tiveness to her that she could not bear, something clayey and ugly. His
intelligence was self-absorbed. . . . Nothing could touch him—he could
only absorb things into his own self" (143). She resents his intense passion for cathedrals and the mystic transports he achieves in the contem-
plation of them: "She wanted his eyes to come to her, to know her. And
they would not" (151). Lawrence, as usual in his best fiction, allows
equal expression of both sides of this conflict. As Kinkead-Weekes
points out in his discussion of the Anna-Will relationship, "there can be
no taking sides for Lawrence. Both lovers have half a truth; but their
conflict is not creative, for they do not marry their oppositions and go
through, beyond. They seek to impose themselves upon each other,
destructively" ("Marriage of Opposites" 30)

From my perspective, the narrative position again displays an intersubjective orientation that grants legitimacy to each character's separate
voice even as the characters themselves seek to stifle the voice of the other
out of their own overbearing narcissistic demands. Anna feels her subjectivity negated and denied by Will's "mindless" pursuit of "his own dark-
souled desires, following his own tunnelling nose. She felt often she must
suffocate. And she fought him off" (161). The narrator then comments
how Will "fought madly back again, frantic in sensual fear. He did foolish
things. He asserted himself on his rights, he arrogated the old position of
master of the house" (161). Such arrogation of male mastery is a strand in
Lawrence's writing (and a feature of his relationship with Frieda) for which
the author is, alas, well known. In this passage from *The Rainbow*, however, the narrator announces explicitly how "foolish" this sort of insistence
on male mastery really is. The scene reveals, furthermore, the motivational
source of this tendency in a "frantic" sense of self-deficiency and shame.

The narrator repeatedly expounds on Will's narcissistic insufficiency
in relation to Anna as the most compelling factor in his "willful" need
to dominate and control:

He wanted her to come to him, to complete him, to stand before him
so that his eyes did not, should not meet the naked darkness. Nothing
mattered to him but that she should come and complete him. For he
was ridden by the awful sense of his own limitation. (166)

For try as he might, he could not escape. She was everything to him, she was his life and his derivation. He depended on her. If she were taken away, he would collapse as a house from which the central pillar is removed. (172–73)

He felt as if he were suspended in space, held there by the grip of his will. If he relaxed his will he would fall, fall through endless space, into the bottomless pit, always falling, will-less, helpless, non-existent, just dropping to extinction, falling till the fire of friction had burned out, like a falling star, then nothing, nothing, complete nothing. (175)

Will's *will* indeed defines his very identity; it is the only thing defending against disintegration and utter nullity. Will's inner void, his lack of a coherent or authentic experience of self, dooms the possibility for mutual recognition in his relationship with Anna. He cannot be really *there* or present for her. She is thus furious at his psychological absence and emotional dependency on her, which she experiences as suffocating and oppressive: "she hated him, because he depended on her so utterly. He was horrible to her. She wanted to thrust him off, to set him apart. It was horrible that should cleave to her, so close, like a leopard that had leapt on her, and fastened" (173). Because of the breakdown of mutual recognition, self-assertion for both Anna and Will takes the form of aggressive domination. Anna's dancing in her pregnancy becomes something more than simply pride in her body or joyful self-expression: "She would dance his [Will's] nullification, she would dance to her unseen Lord. She was exalted over him, . . . dancing his non-existence, dancing herself to the Lord, to exultation" (170–71).

Anna and Will's power struggle is a precursor to that of Gudrun and Gerald in *Women in Love*. The sadomasochistic dynamic is a product of intersubjective breakdown; it represents a collapse into the terrifying narcissistic dramas of the inner world. Omnipotent fantasies of devouring and being devoured thus prevail. Anna realizes that she "was sinking under the silent grip of his physical will. He wanted her in his power. He wanted to devour her at leisure, to have her" (172). Will's sadism, however, is not only directed at his wife. He pursues the town girl Gertie and is aroused by her childlike vulnerability: "She would be small, almost like a child, and pretty. Her childishness whetted him keenly. She would be helpless between his hands. . . . He did not care about her, except that he wanted to overcome her resistance, to have her in his power, fully and exhaustively to enjoy her" (211–13). The relational dynamics here again look forward to Gerald's perverse relationship with Pussum in *Women in Love*.

As Tom had briefly wanted to "break" Anna's resistant four-year-old body before his transformation at the start of the barn scene, Will's eroticized domination of the helpless, childish Gertie betrays an enraged need to conquer his own helplessness and childlike dependency. This dynamic is even more disturbingly explicit in his relationship with his own child, Ursula. The narrator describes how Ursula's crying as a baby "echoed" directly to something deep within Will: "his soul answered its madness. It filled him with terror, almost with frenzy" (196). He would look at the baby in her mother's lap and "he was sick, it was so utterly helpless and vulnerable and extraneous" (196–97). Unlike Tom in relation to Anna, however, Will is unable to respond to Ursula as a suffering subject in her own right; she is to him only a narcissistic projection of his own infantile dependency, of his own intolerable vulnerability and helplessness.

Entangled in the violent drama of his inner world, Will develops a sadistic attitude toward the child—"He would smash into her sensitive child's world destructively" (207). Her very sensitivity and fragility enrage him, just as Paul in Sons and Lovers is driven to sadistic behavior toward Miriam whenever her vulnerability is most apparent. Will screams at Ursula excessively for small infractions. He feels impelled to test her ability to survive. "He had a curious craving to frighten her, to see what she would do with him" (208). He challenges her, for instance, to ride on his back as he leaps off a canal bridge into the dark water below (208–9). Or again, he takes her on the swingboat at the fair, pushing it perilously higher and higher until the "jerk at the top had almost shaken them both out" (210). Such sadism arises out of an enraged response to fragility in both the other and the self. Indeed, the lack of distinction between self and other—the other's fragility is the self's— makes aggression a form of self-destruction as well. Sadomasochism flourishes in the absence of a real other.

URSULA AND OTHERS:
INTERSUBJECTIVITY AND THE
QUEST FOR AUTHENTICITY

Ursula may be insufficiently real to Will, but to the reader she stands as one of Lawrence's most complex and supremely realized characters. The empathic rendering of her inner world is extraordinarily rich and subtle. While she will at times express a fearsome destructiveness reflective, as Ruderman and other feminist critics argue, of Lawrence's fear of female dominance, we see that destructiveness as rooted in the desperation that springs from intersubjective collapse. Ursula's struggle to discover her own reality or sense of authentic being is inextricably bound up with her struggle to discover the reality of the other. The others in her life, however, repeatedly fail her; they cannot withstand her fierce self-assertion. The failure of the other to survive the ruthless assertion of self is an unconscious fantasy also central, as we saw in *Sons and Lovers*, to Paul Morel's character. Lawrence again invests a female character with the intense conflicts and strivings of his own complicated subjectivity. He intuitively understood that the need to recognize and be recognized by a real, separate other is not essentially gendered, it is essentially human. As Benjamin explains, however, the assertion-recognition drama inevitably unfolds in gendered terms because of the gendered constructions of family and culture, a fact that Lawrence's fiction indeed makes clear.

The portrayal of Ursula's relationship with her father is a moving and psychologically astute account of a child's relationship with a narcissistic parent. The narrator describes, for instance, how Ursula attempts one afternoon to help Will plant potatoes in the field. "The responsibility excited her like a string tying her up" (206). The simile captures the complex, conflicting emotions—the sense of constriction and fear as well as deep, excited pleasure—that the responsibility of helping her father, of being close and connected with him, evokes. His insensitivity and utter lack of empathy, however, prove shattering. As a result, the child develops profound feelings of inadequacy. When Will brusquely rearranges Ursula's plantings,

> She stood by with the painful terrified helplessness of childhood. He was so unseeing and confident, she wanted to do the thing and yet she could not. . . . Then he went down the row, relentlessly, turning the potatoes in with his sharp spade cuts. He took no notice of her, only worked on. He had another world from hers.
> She stood helplessly, stranded on his world. . . . She knew she could not help him. A litle bit forlorn, at last she turned away, and ran down the garden, away from him, as fast as she could go away from him, to forget him and his work. (206)

Benjamin has discussed the importance for both males and females of identificatory love of the father. To be recognized by the father, to feel *like* the father, supports the child's sense of herself as a subject of desire. To be thwarted in that love is to feel one's very selfhood or subjectivity thwarted. A father's failures of empathic attunement can be every bit as narcissistically wounding as a mother's. Lawrence displays a searing awareness of the psychic and emotional consequences of such a wound to the child's nascent self: a defensive hardness, a retreat from feeling, and a subjective sense of unreality and emptiness. The narrator describes Ursula's reaction to Will's furiously shouting at her after she accidently walks over his seed beds:

> She stood dazzled with pain and shame and unreality. Her soul, her consciousness seemed to die away. She became shut off and senseless, a little fixed creature whose soul had gone hard and unresponsive. The sense of her own unreality hardened her like a frost. She cared no longer. (207)

We have arrived at that most characteristically Lawrencian state of the "shut off and senseless" soul—the hard-shell, schizoid condition. While Ursula's consciousness is generally foregrounded, at times the narrative perspective provides a dual focus in this child-parent battle, demonstrating an empathic understanding of the inner worlds of both combatants. We are told that Will "loved Ursula, therefore he always had a sense of shame, almost of betrayal, when he turned on her. So he turned fiercely and scathingly and with a wholesale brutality that made Ursula go white, mute, and numb" (329). Lawrence understood equally the mentality of the oppressor and the oppressed; he knew the unbearable shame that motivates them both.

Ursula's relationship with her mother is marked by her resentment and abhorrence of maternal physicality. She shudders at a Rubens picture depicting "storms of naked babies" and is repulsed by "the heat and welter of fecundity . . . she was against her mother, passionately against her mother; she craved for some spirituality and stateliness" (246). Ursula shares with many Lawrence characters a terror of the helpless, infantile state—a state that is distinguished above all by a stormy, passionate physicality. At the same time, however, his art tirelessly seeks to recover that state, to restore the sense of wild and spontaneous bodily life that was experienced as denied. The intense ambivalence toward uninhibited sensuality is a point I will return to again in the discussion of Ursula's confrontation with the horses at the end of the novel.

Ursula's narcissistic wound—the lack of recognition she experiences in relation to both her parents—results in a form of psychic splitting and paranoia that the narrative describes with canny precision:

> [S]he felt strong powers that would not recognise her. There was upon her always a fear and a dislike of authority . . . and the authorised Powers. But if she gave herself away, she would be lost, destroyed. There was always the menace against her . . . the grudging power of the mob lying in wait for her. . . . Wherever she was, at school, among friends, in the street, in the train, she instinctively abated herself, made herself smaller, feigned to be less than she was, for fear that her undiscovered self should be seen, pounced upon, attacked by the brutish resentment of the commonplace, the average Self. (252)

Lack of recognition is projected onto the world at large: the world and its "authorised Powers" fail to recognize her true worth. Her envious, destructive rage is also projected outward in the paranoiac fantasy of an angry "mob" lying in wait, ready to destroy her out of furious envy. The superior, grandiose sense of self she secretly harbors is a defensive response to narcissistic injury, to an even deeper sense of deficiency and shame.[4] The general misanthropy expressed here and elsewhere in Lawrence's work (Birkin utters similar sentiments in *Women in Love*) surfaces out of the rubble of relational collapse, in which the support the self needs from its relationships with its primary others is missing. It reflects a fundamental lack of trust in both self and other.

The narrative perspective simultaneously reveals, however, an awareness of the problematic nature of Ursula's misanthropic vision and its roots in a profound self-mistrust:

> She was at this time a nuisance on the face of the earth, . . . deep at the bottom of her, was a childish antagonism of mistrust. She thought she loved everybody and believed in everybody. But because she could not love herself nor believe in herself, she mistrusted everybody with the mistrust of a serpent or a captured bird. Her starts of revulsion and hatred were more inevitable than her impulses to love. (267–68)

Such deep-seated mistrust afflicts numerous Lawrence characters, male as well as female. The strugggle to overcome it, to learn to love both self and other (as Lawrence understood, one is always contingent on the other), forms a basic, underlying motivation for all of his fiction.

The relational dynamics of Ursula's early life are replayed in her feverish love-hate relationship with Anton Skrebensky. Her initial attraction to him follows a common Lawrencian pattern. Skrebensky appears to her as a "distinct, self-contained, self-supporting" other in contradistinction to her sense of her own unanchored and amorphous self. "He was irrevocable in his isolation. . . . He was in possession of himself. . . . Other people could not really give him anything nor take anything from him. His soul stood alone" (271). This perspective looks forward to Gudrun's view of Gerald swimming alone in the pond, "immune" and exulting in his isolation. The irony, of course, is that the seeming autonomy and self-containment of both Skrebensky and Gerald represent only a false appearance, a surface defense; both are shielding against the intense anxiety of an excessively dependent, disintegrating self.

Ursula at first believes that Skrebensky is an impervious, resilient "other" against whom she can assert her "maximum self" without fear of destroying him: "She could limit and define herself against him, the male, she could be her maximum self, female, oh female, triumphant for one moment in exquisite assertion against the male, in supreme con-tradistinction to the male" (281). Such exhilarating self-assertion, however, turns into furious destructiveness once the other proves indefinite and unresilient after all. We are told repeatedly how Skrebensky felt "as if he were losing himself" in his relationship with Ursula, that he was "becoming all vague, undefined, inchoate" (286–87). In Winnicott's terms, Skrebensky "fails to survive" Ursula's savage self-assertion. As discussed in relation to the broken doll episode in *Sons and Lovers*, sadism can emerge as a breakdown product of failed object use. This phenomenon can also illuminate the two vividly rendered scenes in the novel in which Ursula, identified with a callous, cruelly triumphant moon, psychically annihilates her lover.

In the first scene the language describing Ursula's communion with the moon suggests her need for an "other" against whom she can throw herself with wild, indeed violent, physical and emotional abandon: "Patiently she sat, under the cloak, with Skrebensky holding her hand. But her naked self was away there beating upon the moonlight, dashing the moonlight with her breasts and her belly and her thighs and her knees, in meeting, in communion" (296). The assaultive verbs—the "beating" and "dashing"—convey the urgent, aggressive nature of this clamorous need to assert herself *against* the other as a form of meeting or communion *with* the other. The enumeration of body parts—breasts, belly, thighs, knees—stresses again the essential bodily nature of this primal need. Psychologist Michael Bader discusses the importance of precisely this type of dynamic in any fulfilling erotic relationship:

> Full expression of one's erotic desire depends . . . on the ability of the subject to take the other for granted, to feel secure that the partner will survive if one turns inward to experience maximally one's own selfish excitement even if that excitement is harnessed to an aggressive "collision" with the object. In order for true sexual mutuality to occur, each self has to be sufficiently able to be completely alone and self-centered and secure enough about the object's durability to hurl oneself into it with abandon. (286)

Unlike the moon, however, Skrebensky cannot withstand Ursula's excited self-abandonment; he experiences it only as an abandonment of himself, and he feels utterly annihilated by it. His defense, as usual, is to *will* her submission, to attempt to control and compel her:

> His will was set and straining with all its tension to encompass her and compel her. If he could only compel her. He seemed to be annihilated. She was cold and hard and compact of brilliance as the moon itself, and beyond him as the moonlight was beyond him, never to be grasped or known. If he could only set a bond round her and compel her! (297)

For Ursula, Skrebensky's annihilation, his failure to survive, turns her self-assertive fury to sadistic hate. She becomes "fierce, corrosive,

seething with his destruction. . . . So she held him there, the victim, consumed, annihilated. She had triumphed: he was not any more" (299).
Here again, sadism, as Ghent argues, emerges as a perverted form of
object usage. Lawrence understands, however, that Ursula's "triumph"
over Skrebensky is hollow, as terrifying for her as for him. Ursula's realization that "she had broken him" fills her with an "overpowering fear
of herself" (299). In asserting herself she has destroyed the other; there
are then no limits to her own terrible destructiveness. She thus wants to
deny that it ever happened: "She was seized with a frenzied desire that
what had been should never be remembered, never be thought of, never
be for one moment allowed possible" (299). She longs to return to "her
ordinary warm self" and become "his servant, his adoring slave" (299).
We see, yet again, the recourse to the domination-submission polarity
once the balanced tension of intersubjectivity collapses.

At the end of the "First Love" chapter on her relationship with
Skrebensky, Ursula asks herself, "But who was he, and where did he
exist? In her own desire only" (309). The beloved other remains unreal.
Having failed to discover his externality, she is trapped in her own internal world, prey to her narcissistic fantasies. She thus feels "cold, apa-
thetic," not fully alive. The sight of an old beggar woman shouting
insults at her in the street fills her with violent dread: "Whenever she
thought of the red-eyed old woman, a sort of madness ran in inflamma-
tion over her flesh and her brain, she almost wanted to kill herself"
(309). The beggar woman is a projection, I suggest, of her own most
feared and dreaded image of herself: enraged, "bad," impoverished, and
isolated. Ursula's inner sense of "badness," her enraged destructiveness,
has indeed proved omnipotent, witchlike. Lawrence thus allows us to
see Ursula's triumph over Skrebensky, her devouring female omnipotence, not only as a fantasy projected onto the woman as hated object,
but also as emanating from the woman's own injured subjectivity. As
such, it is a form of imprisonment as agonizing for the woman as it is
for the man.

Critics have noted this fact before but have not had a theoretical
context in which to understand it.[5] Ben-Ephraim, for instance,
describes the struggle between Ursula and Skrebensky as representing
"two opposed negative forces: insufficient self and exaggerated self, her
egoism of light and his nothingness of darkness. . . . Looking to the
moon for 'consummation' she expresses a self-love that encloses her;
her universe is an impoverished one of mere self-reflection" (160). An
intersubjective framework permits us to see her narcissism or "exaggerated self" as directly related, indeed intertwined with, his insufficiency or lack of self. Intersubjective breakdown leads to the prison of
narcissism. Both Ursula and Skrebensky suffer from a deeply injured

selfhood against which Ursula's grandiosity—her inflated self—is a defensive response.

The narcissism of both characters prevents either from fully recognizing the other. When Ursula and Skrebensky attempt to revive their relationship later in the novel, the narrator tells us, "He was never aware of the separate being of her. She was like his own eyes and his own heart beating to him" (421). Because he cannot recognize her separate subjectivity, he experiences her absence only as a narcissistic wound, as an intolerable loss to the self: "Her absence was worse than pain to him. It destroyed his being" (423). For Ursula, his failure to recognize or acknowledge her leaves her equally wounded and enraged: "She thought she loved Anton Skrebensky. But she did not forgive him that he had not been strong enough to acknowledge her. He had denied her" (382). In the second moon scene, Ursula feels herself "melt into the white glare" of the moon as Skrebensky again "felt himself fusing down to nothingness" (443). Her failure to "discover" his reality and otherness turns, once more, to sadistic domination: "she clinched hold of him, hard, as if suddenly she had the strength of destruction, she fastened her arms round him and tightened him in her grip, whilst her mouth sought his in a hard, rending, ever-increasing kiss, till his body was powerless in her grip, . . . she seemed to be pressing in her beaked mouth till she had the heart of him" (444).

Ursula's self-abandonment, her reckless letting go, proves ultimately destructive and deadening for them both. The descriptive imagery objectifies her as a "fixed" and "rigid" statue, eternal yet lifeless: a "horrible figure that lay stretched in the moonlight on the sands with the tears gathering and travelling on the motionless, eternal face" (445). The familiar contours of a general cultural misogyny are apparent here as well. Woman has become objectified into a sphinx-like figure—powerful, eternal, and threateningly alien. She represents for Skrebensky "the darkness, the challenge, the horror" (447). Yet the imagery also captures Ursula's subjective pain. Her tears, fluid and alive, contrast with the lifeless rigidity of her statue-like face. The image of a single tear in particular, which slowly gathered and "shook with glittering moonlight, then, surcharged, brimmed over and ran trickling . . . with its burden of moonlight, into the darkness, to fall in the sand" (445) lyrically conveys Ursula's welling despair. The narrator asserts that "all within her was cold, dead, inert" (445). Without mutual recognition, both Ursula and Skrebensky succumb to a death-in-life existence. Skrebensky turns to the "dead reality" (419) of the false social self and the empty social world. He marries his Colonel's daughter and assumes a "puppet" existence. Ursula persists, however, in fighting inner deadness and in striving to recover an authentic experience of self.

The chapter entitled "Shame," which follows the first moon scene with Skrebensky, focuses on Ursula's relationship with her school mistress, Winifred Inger. Ursula is attracted to her teacher for precisely the same reason she was initially drawn to Skrebensky: both at first present an image of an ideal self that is autonomous, unconstrained, and fearlessly self-confident. At the beginning of the chapter the narrator reports that Ursula's life at this time was "unformed . . . essentially shrinking from all touch. . . . [S]he was never herself, since she *had* no self. . . . [S]he shrank violently from people, ashamed she was not as they were, fixed, emphatic, but a wavering, undefined sensibility only, without form or being" (311). Ursula sees in Winifred Inger exactly that defined and emphatic individuality that she herself lacks. Miss Inger possesses a "fine, upright, athletic bearing" and an "indomitably proud nature" (312). She is "free" and "easy" in her movements; her "whole body was defined, firm and magnificent" (314).

Winifred conducts a swimming class, and Ursula's view of her mistress flinging herself into the water with careless abandon and swimming with strong, sure strokes again looks ahead to Gudrun's view of Gerald's solitary swim in the "Diver" chapter of *Women in Love*. Water always represents a voluptuous sensuality and a relaxing of mental control in Lawrence's world. At the same time, however, it equally threatens total loss of control and dissolution of self—a drowning or merging in the fluid element. The image of a strong swimmer thus suggests a self comfortable with the body and with sensuality, and a self strong and assertive enough to resist the pull of passive refusion. As with Skrebensky and Gerald, however, Winifred's strength and self-possession are illusory; the idealized self she initially projects ultimately proves hollow.

From the beginning, Ursula craves recognition from this idealized other. After watching Winifred swim for a while, she dives in herself "and swam by herself, deliciously, yet with a craving of unsatisfaction. She wanted to touch the other, to touch her, to feel her. . . . She turned to see the face of her mistress looking at her, to her. She was acknowledged" (313). To be realized by this magnificent other is to realize her own magnificence. "Ah, if she did not so despise her own thin, dusky fragment of a body, if only she too were fearless and capable" (314). When Winifred grabs Ursula and holds her for a moment in the water, the homoerotic factor becomes obvious: "The bodies of the two women touched, heaved against each other for a moment, then were separate" (314).

The homosexual strains in Lawrence's fiction, whether between two men or two women, spring from the same motivational source—the desire to merge with an other who is an idealized version of the self. Lawrence intuitively understood the narcissistic nature of this dynamic in which the other is only an idealized projection, and it is, I believe, what finally repulsed him about the homosexual bond. This is not to say that a homosexual relationship is inherently narcissistic—two people of the same gender can certainly love one another in a non-narcissistic mode—only that for Lawrence it assumed that meaning. (See also note 7 to the introduction.) For him, the same-sexed other can never be a real *other*, which thus condemns the self to a suffocating solipsism.

The flip side of narcissistic idealization is self-contempt, and both sides repeatedly come into play in the intense same-sex relationships in Lawrence's work. This psychological pattern can help account for the association of swamps and marshes with homosexual love in both Lawrence's letters and fiction. As Ursula becomes intimate with Winifred, "their lives suddenly seemed to fuse into one, inseparable" (316), and soon Ursula begins to feel "a sort of nausea . . . a heavy, clogged sense of deadness began to gather upon her, from the other woman's contact. . . . She wanted some fine intensity, instead of this heavy cleaving of moist clay, that cleaves because it has no life of its own" (319). Ursula's relationship with Winfred again enacts a failure of otherness and a shriveling into the state of shame and self-degradation that underlies the narcissistic condition.

In *The Rainbow*, as in much of his other fiction, Lawrence displays a keen awareness of how the larger social world exacerbates a woman's narcissistically wounded state. The chapter entitled "The Man's World" chronicles Ursula's struggles as a schoolteacher in a male-dominated, institutional world. She is forced to confront the "hard, stark reality" of "the world of work and of man's convention" (377), a reality in which life becomes "a condition of hard, malevolent system" (350) and people are commodified and dehumanized. "She had brought her feelings and her generosity to where neither generosity nor emotion were wanted. And already she felt rebuffed. . . . She was nobody, there was no reality in herself, the reality was all outside of her, and she must apply herself to it" (347). Even the children "were not children. They were a squadron. She could not speak as she would to a child, because they were not individual children, they were a collective inhuman thing" (350). She is forced to retreat back into the hard-shell defense she had developed as a child in relation to her father, a mode of being in which she denied her emotions and "put away her personal self" (356). In order to survive, she becomes part of the system she deplores: "her face grew more and more shut, and over her flayed, exposed soul of a young girl who had gone open and warm to give herself to the children, there set a hard, insentient thing, that worked mechanically according to a system imposed" (367). Nevertheless, Ursula remains "in revolt" (377); she continues to struggle "against the confines of her life" (382), the confines of both the social world without and the psychic world within.

The climactic scene of the novel, and one of the most widely discussed in all of Lawrence's fiction, involves Ursula's confrontation with a herd of horses. The circumstances leading up to the scene are relevant. Pregnant with Skrebensky's child, she has decided she will marry him and become a good wife and mother. Yet "her soul was sick" at the thought, as she realizes that to do so would mean the "nullity" of her true self. She is prepared, however, to sacrifice this self: "What did the self, the form of life, matter?" (448). She is ready to submit to her mother's world, to "a bondaged sort of peace" (449). As the narrator informs us, however, "She was aware . . . of a gathering restiveness, a tumult impending within her" (450). The horses "looming in the rain" and ultimately "bursting" before her present a symbolic manifestation of that inner tumult.

Most critics agree that the horses represent, in Robert Langbaum's words, "externalized internal presences" (323). There seems to be no critical consensus, however, over the precise nature of those internal presences and the meaning of Ursula's symbolic encounter. Does the scene represent, as Stephen Miko asserts, a "purgation of the flesh" (182), or, as Langbaum and Colin Clarke maintain, a confrontation with positive anarchic and demonic energies? Keith Sagar, among others, points to the scene's connection to a passage in Lawrence's *Fantasia of the Unconscious* that refers to a man's "persistent passionate fear-dream about horses." Lawrence relates the dream "to some arrest in the deepest sensual activity in the male. . . . The spontaneous self is secretly yearning for the liberation and fulfilment of the deepest and most powerful sensual nature" (*Fantasia* 199–200). Some critics thus see the horses as symbolizing a specifically male sensual principle that Ursula had tried to conquer in Skrebensky, while others argue that the confrontation with the horses is precisely what prevents Ursula from denying that principle in herself.[6]

To my mind one of the most intriguing aspects of the horse scene lies in the dynamic oppositions enforced by the descriptive language, particularly the verbs. On the one hand the horses embody a state of extreme suppression and constraint:

> She was aware of their breasts gripped, clenched narrow in a hold that never relaxed, she was aware of their red nostrils flaming with long endurance, and of their haunches, so rounded, so massive, pressing, pressing, pressing to burst the grip upon their breasts, pressing forever till they went mad, running against the walls of time and never bursting free. . . . But the darkness and wetness of the rain could not put out the hard, urgent, massive fire that was locked within these flanks, never, never. . . . They had gathered under an oak-tree, knotting their awful, blind, triumphing flanks together. (452)

Words such as "gripped," "clenched," "pressing," "locked," and the oft-repeated "knotting" convey a profound restraint and repression. Contrarily, the verb "burst"—"The horses had burst before her"—is echoed five times on the same page. Suppression and release, tight control and chaotic discharge, are suggested at once in the description of the horse herd. The horses indeed represent an externalization of that sensual, bodily expressiveness that is always both desired and dreaded in Lawrence's world, and it is most often associated with a specifically masculine sexuality. In this scene, however, the gender element seems less pronounced. Here the craving for release—for uninhibited sensual and sexual expression—is simply so intense it is threatening: the self fears it will be destroyed by the ferocious intensity of the desire itself. The fantasy, enacted here and elsewhere in Lawrence's fiction, is that the self will be overpowered and enslaved by the very wildness it craves. The vital animality the self lacks internally is experienced as wholly external. All power, in other words, is dangerously outside the self.

> That concentrated, knitted flank of the horse-group had conquered. It stirred uneasily, awaiting her, knowing its triumph. . . . Her heart was gone, her limbs were dissolved, she was dissolved like water. All the hardness and looming power was in the massive body of the horse group. (453)

The consuming sense of shame that such an experience of self-dissolution and powerlessness evokes results in the habitual "hard-shell" defense—the total retreat from emotional and relational life. Ursula wants only to "extricate" herself from everything: "if she could but disengage herself from feeling, from her body, from all the vast encumbrance of the world that was in contact with her, from her father, and her mother, and her lover, and all her acquaintance" (456).

Lawrence does not, however, leave Ursula in this state. After the delirium and illness that follow her experience with the horses, she comes to reflect again on her relationship with Skrebensky. Her introspection yields some important and bracing psychological insights. She understands that Skrebensky "had never become finally real. In the weeks of passionate ecstasy he had been with her in her desire, she had created him for the time being. But in the end he had failed and broken down" (457). The other had never become real; intersubjectivity had failed; and Lawrence and his heroine are aware of the perils these circumstances can create. The self wants limits:

> Who was she to have a man according to her own desire? It was not for her to create, but to recognise a man created by God. . . . She was glad she could not create her man. She was glad she had nothing to do with his creation. (457)

Ursula is relieved, in other words, that there are limits to her own omnipotent fantasies and desires. If the other is only an extension or projection of herself—created out of her own desire—she will be trapped in her own inner world and its nightmare fantasies. What Ursula wants—what Benjamin claims we all want—is recognition from and of a real other, along with the liberation that springs from discovery of a reality outside ourselves, a reality our fantasies cannot destroy.

An earlier scene in the novel, in which Ursula visits her grandmother Lydia, offers a similar affirmation of limits in which boundaries or restrictions on one's own omnipotence are welcomed. This scene too expresses the profound relief of discovering a world outside one's own creation. Lydia tells Ursula about her first husband who had died bitterly because he had taken too much upon himself and had failed. He had assumed too much responsibility for her, his wife, presuming that her whole existence depended upon him. Lydia explains how she should have told him,

> "You are not the beginning and the end." But I was too young, he had never let me become myself, I thought he was truly the beginning and the end. So I let him take all upon himself. Yet all did not depend on him. Life must go on, and I must marry your grandfather, and have your uncle Tom, and your uncle Fred. We cannot take so much upon ourselves. (241)

Assuming such utter responsibility for others robs them of their independent agency; it is a form of narcissistic control, and it springs from lack of boundaries and lack of faith in the other's separateness and resilience.[7] Lydia is here asserting her separate subjectivity and her ability to survive, and this is deeply comforting to her granddaughter Ursula, as such recognition always is for Lawrence's characters.

In a passage that echoes Tom's experience at the end of the barn scene, Ursula looks out from the "peace and security" of her grandmother's room: "the door opened on to the greater space, the past, which was so big, that all it contained seemed tiny, loves and births and deaths, tiny units and features within a vast horizon. That was a great relief, to know the tiny importance of the individual, within the great past" (242). To recognize a vast and infinite world beyond the self, to know one's "tiny importance" in relation to a greater reality, is experienced not as a narcissistic wound but as a profound relief. It means that the self is *not* everything, that there is a secure, external realm in which the self is *contained* rather than submerged or annihilated.

At the end of the novel Ursula's narcissism is also relieved by her recognition that she is not alone in her suffering, that others too have created hard shells, "husks," to shield themselves from the pain of existence. As she watches the working people go by in the street, she feels that they, like herself, are "waiting in pain for the new liberation" (458). Sometimes "great terror possessed her. . . . [S]he could only know the old horror of the husk which bound in her and all mankind. They were all in prison, they were all going mad" (458). The final lines of the novel, however, express faith and optimism:

> She knew that the sordid people who crept hard-scaled and separate on the face of the world's corruption were living still, that the rainbow was arched in their blood and would quiver to life in their spirit, that they would cast off their horny covering of disintegration, that new, clean, naked bodies would issue to a new germination, to a new growth, rising to the light and the wind and the clean rain of heaven. She saw in the rainbow the earth's new architecture, the old brittle corruption of houses and factories swept away, the world built up in a living fabric of Truth, fitting to the over-arching heaven. (459)

Critics disagree over whether the optimism here is convincing or justified.[8] From a psychological perspective, Ursula's faith, her belief in the potential goodness and vitality both within the self and without, does seem earned. She has, to use a phrase Lawrence applied to his relationship with Frieda, "come through." She has endured relational failures and her own frightening destructiveness, and yet she has survived. The self beneath the hard shell has proved less fragile, less easily annihilated, than was unconsciously feared. Ursula did not, in the end, have to sacrifice what Winnicott would call her "true self"—her sense of authentic being—to a life of inauthentic social conformity. Genuine faith in self, relational theorists teach, always implies faith in other as well. Ursula's social optimism can thus be understood as stemming from real psychological growth in which an isolating narcissism, at least temporarily, is overcome. The final image of "the world built up in a living fabric of Truth, fitting to the over-arching heaven" suggests a basic mutuality, a "fitting" or attunement, between two living presences. All dualities—earth and heaven, body and spirit, self and other—can exist harmoniously in a state of dynamic, dialectical balance. Though Lawrence's characters rarely achieve this balance in their lives, it represents an ideal state toward which they strive and one that his fiction continually seeks to replicate.

CHAPTER 5

Women in Love

GERALD AND GUDRUN:
THE SADOMASOCHISTIC SCENARIO

Between the completion of *The Rainbow* and publication of *Women in Love*, Lawrence endured "the nightmare years," as Paul Delany has called them—a period of time that encompassed his growing anger and despair over the First World War, an increasingly embattled marriage with Frieda, and the suppression of *The Rainbow*. Although Ursula's story continues in *Women in Love*, in terms of tone and style, the novel does not read as an extension of or sequel to *The Rainbow*. Stylistically *Women in Love* is less incantatory and gothic, more sober and disjointed than its predecessor.[1] The continuity of succeeding generations that structures *The Rainbow* gives way to a more radical discontinuity in plot and character development. In *Women in Love* character is revealed in what Robert Langbaum aptly describes as "discontinuous explosive self-objectifications" (334). The optimism and hope that Ursula experiences at the end of *The Rainbow* have not survived the transition. Faith in self and other must be rediscovered in *Women in Love*, and the novel works toward that discovery in its own unique terms.

Like *The Rainbow*, *Women in Love* is built on oppositions and contradictory states. Here, however, argument—extensive and elaborate debate—distinguishes the discourse, and paradoxical tensions are even more densely woven throughout the text. In Bakhtinian terms, the novel is Lawrence's most dialogic work. Bakhtin's contention about a Dostoyevsky novel holds equally true for *Women in Love*: it "is constructed not as the whole of a single consciousness, absorbing other consciousnesses as objects into itself, but as a whole formed by the interaction of several consciousnesses, none of which entirely becomes an object for the other" (18). Although Birkin is most closely identified with Lawrence and articulates his views in many of the novel's arguments, he is not, as David Lodge maintains, "allowed to win these arguments. There are no winners. *Women in Love* is not a *roman à thèse*. It has not got a single *thèse*, but several, of which Lawrence's treatment is remarkably even-

handed. . . . A fluid, flexible handling of point of view was always characteristic of Lawrence's writing, but it was not always so impartial"
(63–64). Numerous critics have written about the self-opposing or self-
correcting aspect of the novel, particularly in regard to the Birkin-Ursula
relationship.[2] Bloom drolly remarks, "Since Lawrence is both Birkin and
Ursula, he has the curious trait, for a novelist, of perpetually infuriating
himself" (*Rainbow* 15).

The novel's portrayal of simultaneous conflicting states of consciousness supports a current emphasis in psychoanalytic relational theory on the multiple and discontinuous dimension of psychic experience.
Philip Bromberg suggests that psychic life is characterized by shifting,
discontinuous states of consciousness in an ongoing dialectic with a
sense of linear or unitary selfhood. The key to health, he argues, is "the
ability to stand in the spaces between realities without losing any of
them—the capacity to feel like one self while being many" (166).
Women in Love exemplifies that ability as it plays out a multitude of
competing voices, identities, and stories without any one voice, identity
or story subsuming the others. The continual obstructing of one position
by another, the checking or contradicting of one voice by another, can
indeed make for a frustrating reading experience.[3] Gamini Salgado notes
that even the argumentative mode, so crucial to the tenor and fabric of
the novel, is itself "persistently devalued—summarised, parodied, dismissed, interrupted and trivialised" (139). For Salgado, the novel is so
shot through with paradoxes and contradictions that the reader is left
with "the sense that its 'message' or 'messages' are snares and delusions:
the final effect is the typically 'modern' one of having the experience and
missing the meaning" (143). Yet Salgado goes on to assert that "the tension between the 'messages' vivifies the novel" (143). I agree, and would
even push the point further by claiming that the tension finally *is* the
message or meaning, at least on a psychological level.

Salgado also observes that at times "Characters are described in ways
which seem to make their inner lives interchangeable" (143). All three
major erotic relationships in the novel—Gerald and Gudrun, Gerald and
Birkin, and Birkin and Ursula—do in fact share underlying fantasies in
common as they enact the obsessional themes of the central authorial consciousness. The three relationships nevertheless present variations and per-
mutations on those themes. There is both sameness and difference in the
representation of the characters' identities and relationships, a simultaneous sameness and difference that again marks an intersubjective mode of
consciousness. The identities of the individual characters also seem to
change significantly with the relational context. Gudrun, for instance, can
seem to be a monstrous magna mater with Gerald, while with Ursula she
can appear as a troubled, insecure outsider.

Shifts between projection of omnipotent, narcissistic fantasy and empathic awareness of the other's vulnerable, limited subjectivity, as I have been arguing throughout this study, characterize Lawrence's fiction in general. These shifts are most dramatic and pronounced, however, in *Women in Love*. Whereas in *Sons and Lovers* Mrs. Morel is the central object of those projective fantasies, in *Women in Love* it is Gerald who occupies that pivotal psychic position. I agree with David Cavitch that Gerald is the novel's "dominant erotic presence" (65). He is at once god-like—the embodiment of a dreadful and desirable power—and yet also deeply wounded; like Mrs. Morel, he is psychologically brittle, his self-structure exceedingly frail. Joyce Carol Oates has remarked on the fluctuating, mutable quality of Gerald's identity: "As Gudrun's frenzied lover, as Birkin's elusive beloved, he seems a substantially different person from the Gerald Crich who is a ruthless god of the machine" (93). Oates goes on to argue that Gerald is "Lawrence's only tragic figure." He represents, she believes, the author "in his deepest, most aggrieved, most nihilistic soul" (93).

Several critics consider Gerald a tragic hero and his condition as emblematic of the tragic malaise of modern civilization.[4] Lydia Blanchard ("*Women in Love*") diagnoses that condition explicitly as one of pathological narcissism. She views the whole novel as a statement about both cultural and personal narcissism, with Gerald as the most "representative of the novel's narcissistic personalities" (108). Of all of the characters, he suffers most from an inner void and must seek "for a means to stop up the terrible gap of insufficiency" (108).[5] He is also provided with the most extensive family history in the novel, and that background, Blanchard suggests, can help us understand the roots of his condition. She compares Gerald's cold aloofness (and his imagistic association with crystals of ice) with the same cold detachment in his mother. "Lawrence makes abundantly clear," Blanchard asserts, "that Mrs. Crich's disorders have a fatal influence on her son" (108). Her disorders, however, are a direct result of the sexual repression and psychological subjugation she suffers at the hands of her husband (and the patriarchy he represents).

We are back to the same problem dramatized in *Sons and Lovers*, in which the mother's impaired subjectivity has dire consequences for her son. Gerald asks Birkin whether he thinks his (Gerald's) mother is "abnormal," to which Birkin replies, "'No! I think she only wanted something more, or other than the common run of life. And not getting it, she has gone wrong, perhaps.'" Gerald then "gloomily" responds, "'After producing a brood of wrong children'" (208). A mother whose own desires—whose own agentic expression—has been thwarted has again produced a brood of "wrong," "wanting" or deficient children.

The mother is less a real subject than an idealized object, a victim once more of her husband's (and the culture's) split narcissistic projections. She represents darkness, dread and destruction—"the dread was his wife, the destroyer, and it was the pain, the destruction, a darkness which was one and both" (214)—as well as a white, pure virginity—"he thought of her as pure, chaste, the white flame which was known to him alone, the flame of her sex, was a white flower of snow to his mind" (218). Enthralled by his wife's emotional and sexual power, the husband must keep her in thrall; because she rules his inner psychic world, he must dominate her in the outer social world:

> like a hawk in a cage, she had sunk into silence. By force of circum-
> stance, because all the world combined to make the cage unbreakable,
> he had been too strong for her, he had kept her prisoner. And because
> she was his prisoner, his passion for her had always remained keen as
> death. He had always loved her, loved her with intensity. Within the
> cage, she was denied nothing, she was given all licence. (215)

Gerald is the product of his mother's diminished subjectivity and the "relation of utter interdestruction" (217) between his parents. Both mother and father have proved radically unreliable, leaving the child/self's inner state equally unstable. Without a secure relational foundation, Gerald's inner world, the narrator tells us repeatedly, is dangerously chaotic, always on the verge of a terrifying disintegration. As his father lies dying, "Gerald found himself left exposed and unready before the storm of living, like the mutinous first mate of a ship that has lost its captain, and who sees only a terrible chaos in front of him" (221). The sense of inner deficiency and the fear of shameful self-exposure, a condition common to so many Lawrence characters, is epitomized in Gerald. Accompanying this condition, as always, is a wild, destructive rage. With the death of his father, Gerald feels that "now, with something of the terror of a destructive child, he saw himself on the point of inheriting his own destruction" (221).

Terror of one's own unlimited destructiveness is another common thread we have been following in the psychology of Lawrence's characters. Such fear can either inhibit erotic expression completely, or it can lead to love relationships structured in polarized, sadomasochistic terms. As discussed previously, if one experiences the collapse of one's primary love objects—in Winnicott's terms, if they have failed to survive a healthy destructiveness and assertion of self—then one's own destructiveness will seem perilously without boundaries. The self fails to discover a real other and an external world that can safely limit and contain the self's terrifying omnipotent fantasies. Characterological destructiveness or sadism can result. As Benjamin explains, "When the child experiences the parent as caving in, he continues to attack, in fantasy or reality, seeking a boundary for his reactive rage" (*Bonds* 70). The fearful fantasy that one's inner destructive rage can destroy the other—is in fact omnipotent—plays a significant role in the characterization of Gerald. The narrator confirms that Gerald "had all his life been tortured by a furious and destructive demon, which possessed him sometimes like an insanity" (229). We are told that as a child he accidently shot and killed his brother. Although Gerald himself never refers to this incident, nor do we hear him thinking or brooding about it, it is presented as an important fact in his history. A child's fantasy of destruction—playing with guns—has indeed proved to have a real, catastrophic effect.

Catastrophe erupts again when Gerald's sister and her lover drown, and the placement of this event in the narrative is significant. It follows immediately upon a passage that describes Gerald's fantasy of totally abandoning himself, of "letting go" and "lapsing out" as he sits in the boat with Gudrun:

> His mind was almost submerged, he was almost transfused, lapsed out for the first time in his life, into the things about him. For he always kept such a keen attentiveness, concentrated and unyielding in himself. Now he had let go, imperceptibly he was melting into oneness with the whole. It was like pure, perfect sleep, his first great sleep of life. He had been so insistent, so guarded, all his life. But here was sleep, and peace, and perfect lapsing out. (178)

Like Mrs. Morel lapsing out into the lilies, such letting go or releasing of one's rigid mental defenses is experienced as a profound relief; it represents a supreme state of peace. The most common critical view of such lapsing and merging scenes, of course, is that they symbolize a regressive desire for refusion with the mother. Again, however, that desire may stem from an even deeper one—the desire for authentic self-experience, for a dropping of the guard that has been preventing a genuine experience of self. It is the desire for what Emmanuel Ghent calls "surrender, in the sense of yielding, of false self" ("Masochism" 109).

One of the dangers of such a "lapsing" fantasy, however, is the attendant fantasy that if one actually "lets go" and drops the defenses protecting against destructive rage, then chaos and catastrophe will inevitably ensue. "'Wasn't this *bound* to happen?'" Gudrun bitterly remarks, as shouting and confusion erupt on the water at the discovery of the drowning. Fear of an uncontained inner destructiveness constitutes, then, another factor in understanding the annihilation anxieties that so often accompany the fantasies of erotic merging in Lawrence's fiction. As Gerald responds to the sudden cries around him, his old defensive self-structure snaps immediately back into place: "He was looking fixedly into the darkness, very keen and alert and single in himself, instrumental. . . . It was as if he belonged naturally to dread and catastrophe, as if he were himself again" (179). For Gerald, "letting go" indeed leads naturally to disaster.

The water imagery associated with Gerald, in both its fluid and its icy, crystalline state, reflects the psychological chemistry of his character—the inner dissolution and the outer, defensive rigidity. He is like the psychotic patients Michael Eigen describes, who are "falling apart, yet hard as steel" (*Psychotic* 18). When Gerald looks in the mirror at one point, the falseness, the utter inauthenticity of his self-experience, is vividly conveyed:

> He looked at his own face. There it was, shapely and healthy and the same as ever, yet somehow, it was not real, it was a mask. He dared not touch it, for fear it should prove to be only a composition mask. His eyes were blue and keen as ever, and as firm in their sockets. Yet he was not sure that they were not blue false bubbles that would burst in a moment and leave clear annihilation. . . . His mind was very active. But it was like a bubble floating in the darkness. At any moment it might burst and leave him in chaos. . . . It was as if his centres of feeling were drying up. (232)

The defensive self-structure protecting against such inner emptiness and dissolution is precisely what Lawrence equates with the "mechanical principle"—the willful domination of matter/mater that Gerald embodies: "He had to fight with Matter, with the earth and the coal it enclosed. This was the sole idea, to turn upon the inanimate matter of the underground, and reduce it to his will" (227). If Gerald's principle of mechanical domination is also symbolic of a predominant force in modern industrial society—the domination of nature/mother/woman—then Lawrence's characterization of Gerald anticipates an argument of contemporary psychoanalytic feminist theory, the view that cultural misogyny is psychologically rooted in the unconscious defense against the omnipotent fantasies of infantile narcissism, particularly the fantasy of the omnipotent mother.[6]

With the death of his father, Gerald's defensive fortifications threaten to collapse: he "knew he would have to find reinforcements, otherwise he would collapse inwards upon the great dark void which circled at the centre of his soul" (322). He turns to Gudrun to fill the void. He comes to her out of a raging narcissistic neediness that Gudrun ultimately finds repellent. She, however, is as deficient and as narcissistically impaired as he. Each finally represents only a mirror and projection—in Kohut's terms, a "selfobject"—for the other, and thus their relationship is characterized by the domination-submission polarity

Benjamin describes. Although our significant human relationships always involve some degree of unconscious projection and selfobject functioning, such narcissistic relating, as Benjamin insists, must be balanced by an equally felt awareness of the other's separate subjectivity. Intersubjective mutuality is impossible in a love relationship when neither lover is real—when neither is a fully realized external subject—for the other.

Gudrun's character, like Gerald's, presents a hard surface that protects against a crumbling inner state. She too suffers from feelings of deficiency, shame, and isolation, and she will urgently turn to others to fill the void and defend against disintegration. In the "Water-Party" chapter, for instance, the empathic narrator enters her consciousness and reveals her suffering. As Gudrun sits listening to Ursula's singing, we hear her desolation:

> Ursula seemed so peaceful and sufficient unto herself, sitting there unconsciously crooning her song, strong and unquestioned at the centre of her own universe. And Gudrun felt herself outside. Always this desolating, agonised feeling, that she was outside of life, an onlooker, whilst Ursula was a partaker, caused Gudrun to suffer from a sense of her own negation, and made her, that she must always demand the other to be aware of her, to be in connection with her. (165)

There is thus a bullying aspect to Gudrun's relations with others, as there is with Gerald and with Hermione (another character who harbors "a terrible void, a lack, a deficiency of being within her" 16). Gudrun's need for domination and control are manifested in her small sculptures and her fondness, as Ursula notes, for little things—"she must always work small things, that one can put between one's hands, birds, and tiny animals. She likes to look through the wrong end of the opera glasses, and see the world that way" (39). By reducing others, as Benjamin has discussed in relation to sadism, the self attempts to establish its own identity: the self's "effort to gain control over the other actually represents an effort to separate, to achieve its own autonomy" (*Like Subjects* 187).

Gudrun is initially attracted to Gerald because he projects an ideal image of autonomy. As she watches him swim in the "Diver" chapter, the narrative description emphasizes his invulnerable self-sufficiency: "He was alone now, alone and immune in the middle of the waters, which he had all to himself. He exulted in his isolation in the new element, unquestioned and unconditioned. He was happy, thrusting with his legs and all his body, without bond or connection anywhere, just himself in the watery world" (47). The narrator then adds, "Gudrun envied him almost painfully."

The masochistic element in Gudrun's relationship with Gerald stems from this representation of him as an ideal—an idealized other who reflects an image of an ideal self. As such, he will also be the object of envy, anger and fear; the deficient self (as discussed in relation to the sadomasochistic fantasies in the short stories) both desires the power of the idealized other and dreads being overwhelmed by it. Cavitch argues that if one considers the canceled prologue to *Women in Love*, in which Birkin expresses an explicit homoerotic attraction to Gerald, then one needs to understand Gudrun as the "vehicle of feelings that he [Lawrence] originally understood to be homoerotic; and that her responses give evidence of Lawrence's shame and anxiety over such desires" (67). This seems true, though the shame and anxiety, I submit, arise less over homosexuality per se than out of the problems involved in a narcissistic relationship with an idealized other.

Benjamin discusses how, for both boys and girls, the father's lack of recognition and the failure to establish an identificatory bond with him can lead to "masochistic fantasies of surrendering to the ideal man's power" ("Father and Daughter" 289). Those fantasies comprise one dimension of Gudrun's relationship with Gerald. They are exemplified perhaps most strikingly in the scene in which Gudrun watches with hypnotic fascination as Gerald savagely lashes his mare while it balks in terror at the railroad tracks:

> He bit himself down on the mare like a keen edge biting home, and *forced* her round. She reared as she breathed, her nostrils were two wide, hot holes, her mouth was apart, her eyes frenzied. It was a repulsive sight. But he held on her unrelaxed, with an almost mechanical relentlessness, keen as a sword pressing in to her. Both man and horse were sweating with violence. Yet he seemed calm as a ray of cold sunshine. (111)

The violent eroticism of the scene—the body of the mare is penetrated and dominated by the cold, impersonal power of the man—is typical of the sadomasochistic fantasies that play throughout Lawrence's fiction. Gudrun betrays a masochistic desire similar to that expressed in "The Woman Who Rode Away"—the desire to submit to a ruthless, unyielding masculine control:

> Gudrun was as if numbed in her mind by the sense of indomitable soft weight of the man, bearing down into the living body of the horse: the strong, indomitable thighs of the blond man clenching the palpitating body of the mare into pure control; a sort of soft white magnetic domination from the loins and thighs and calves, enclosing and encompassing the mare heavily into unutterable subordination, soft blood-subordination, terrible. (113)

The imagery also conveys the paradoxical nature of the fantasy: it presents a terrible violation at the same time as it suggests a form of protection and containment—an inviolable masculine strength "enclosing and encompassing" the bodily self. Once again, the frustrated psychological need to "surrender," in Ghent's sense, to the beloved other and to be recognized in one's bodily, passionate being has mutated into a fantasy of passionate submission to an overpowering, idealized other.

The fear of destroying the fragile mother out of one's own passionate intensity, along with the failure to establish a secure, identificatory bond with the father, together figure into the psychodynamics of Lawrence's sadomasochistic fantasies. Perhaps because he is less overtly identified with Gudrun, Lawrence is able with her character to play out, to a much greater extent than he does with Birkin's, the full ambivalence involved in the desire to be ravished by the ideal, masculine other. Gudrun's "thick, hot attraction" to the degraded life of the miners in the colliery district of Beldover reveals the same dynamic: "It seemed to envelop Gudrun in a laborer's caress, there was in the whole atmosphere a resonance of physical men, a glamourous thickness of labour and maleness surcharged in the air" (115). She is intoxicated by it, overcome by "a nostalgia for the place," and yet, "She hated it, she knew how utterly cut off it was, how hideous and how sickeningly mindless" (116).[7]

The "nostalgia" Gudrun feels for the place, a word used repeatedly in the description of her state of mind here, suggests a longing for a past state of being or self-experience that has been lost. It perhaps refers to what Winnicott calls the "true self"—a self-state characterized by the spontaneous expression of impulse. Such "true" self-experience for Lawrence is also associated with a ruthless, masculine self-assertion free from anxiety over the welfare of the other. Thus the masculine underworld awakens in Gudrun "a fatal desire, and a fatal callousness" (116). Because that state was originally associated with rejection and repression, however, it has equally come to represent a site of deep shame and "badness" in the self. The intense longing to let go, to unleash one's erotic and aggressive impulses and to be *recognized* and affirmed in that authentic expression of self, forms one of the wellsprings of Lawrence's creative work. The severe ambivalence bound up with that state, however, helps determine the complex, conflictual nature of his imaginative vision. Gudrun is terrified of the "demoniacal" nature of the maleness she craves, and she also fears being utterly absorbed and annihilated by it: In Beldover, "Sometimes Gudrun would . . . see how she was sinking in. And then she was filled with a fury of contempt and anger. She felt she was sinking into one mass with the rest—all so close and intermingled and breathless" (118). Merging fantasies in Lawrence's fiction are as associated with the powerful, idealized father as they are with the omnipotent mother. As Benjamin has argued about the oedipal phase in our culture, narcissism or omnipotence has simply been displaced or transferred.

The masochistic dimension of Gudrun's relation to maleness and to Gerald is echoed in the sadomasochistic relationship of Pussum and Gerald. Pussum "was so profane, so slave-like, watching him, absorbed by him. . . . [S]he was absorbed by his self-revelation, by *him*, she wanted the secret of him, the experience of his male being" (67). Gudrun's hypnotic dance before the cattle, "her throat exposed as in some voluptuous ecstasy before them" (167), expresses a similar desire: "it was as if she had the electric pulse from their breasts running into her hands. Soon she would touch them, actually touch them. A terrible shiver of fear and pleasure went through her" (168).

Perhaps the novel's most potent symbol of masochistic desire, shame, and fear in relation to a powerful, bestial masculinity is Loerke's statue of the naked girl, "her face in her hands, as if in shame and grief, in a little abandon" sitting astride the "massive, magnificent stallion, rigid with pent up power" (429). Gudrun indeed recognizes herself in the piece: "Gudrun went pale, and a darkness came over her eyes, like shame, she looked up with a certain supplication, almost slave-like" (429). The naked girl in the statue is described as childish and pathetic, still "a mere bud," her sexuality unrealized. Gudrun identifies with the girl (as, I believe, does Lawrence), and the image of her expresses, above all, a sense of excruciating self-exposure and deep shame: "her feet folded one over the other, as if to hide. But there was no hiding. There she was exposed naked on the naked flank of the horse" (429). The statue recalls the scene with Ursula and the horse herd at the end of *The Rainbow*, where Ursula's feelings of exposure, powerlessness, and dread in relation to the horses (which are also described as rigid with pent-up power) are equally paramount. The sadomasochistic fantasy of submitting to a brute male sexuality exerted a powerful hold on Lawrence's imagination throughout his life. Ultimately, however, *Women in Love* rejects that fantasy, just as Ursula rejects the statue and its unrealistic representation of the horse as "stock and stupid and brutal" (430)—as only a distorted fantasy reflecting a distorted subjectivity cut off from real life.

Gudrun and Gerald share both masochistic and sadistic tendencies; they indeed mirror one another—"they were of the same kind, he and she, a sort of diabolic freemasonry subsisted between them" (122). This is most dramatically illustrated in the scene with Bismarck the rabbit. Gudrun and Gerald each exhibit the same seething, irrational rage at the "bestial stupidity" of the "demoniacal" animal as it struggles to break free of their hold. Both perhaps are responding with fury to their own suppressed animal, bodily life. After Gerald brutally strikes the rabbit, they share a "mutual hellish recognition" (242). Both feel torn, rent, like the red gash down Gudrun's forearm, which Gerald experiences as a rip "torn across his own brain" (242). The scene, like many others in this novel, is so strange, contradictory, and symbolically rich that it defies any single rational explanation. Is it the rabbit's demonic power or its desperation or lack of power that is so infuriating for Gudrun and Gerald? Sadism and masochism seem to blend into each other, and it is difficult to determine who really is wielding the power in this scene: "Gudrun looked at Gerald with strange, darkened eyes, strained with underworld knowledge, almost supplicating, like those of a creature which is at his mercy, yet which is his ultimate victor" (242). And Gerald "had the power of lightening in his nerves, she seemed like a soft recipient of his magical, hideous white fire. He was unconfident, he had qualms of fear" (242).

Throughout the relationship between Gerald and Gudrun, the sadistic and masochistic roles alternate between them. As the narrator states, "Sometimes it was he who seemed strongest, whilst she was almost gone, creeping near the earth like a spent wind; sometimes it was the reverse. But always it was this eternal see-saw, one destroyed that the other might exist, one ratified because the other was nulled" (445). This dynamic, again, is inevitable in a relationship in which each subject is only a narcissistic object for the other. As much as Gerald represents an idealized projection for Gudrun, so Gudrun represents an idealized projection for him: "she was the all-desirable, the all-beautiful. He wanted only to come to her, nothing more. He was only this, this being that should come to her, and be given to her" (239). Just as Gudrun wants to be "filled" with the "precious knowledge" of Gerald (332), so Gerald "seemed to be gathering her into himself, her warmth, her softness, her adorable weight, drinking in the suffusion of her physical being, avidly. He lifted her, and seemed to pour her into himself, like wine into a cup" (331).

Gerald's inner life is as consumed by shame as Gudrun's. When Gerald visits his father's grave, his shame is characteristically objectified in the anal imagery of soft, revolting clay: "He felt the clay beneath, and shrank, it was so horribly cold and sticky. He stood away in revulsion" (338). At this point in the narrative, Gerald feels he is falling into an "infinite void," and that "If he fell, he would be gone for ever. He must withdraw, he must seek reinforcements" (337). He turns to Gudrun for that reinforcement, breaking into her bedroom, his boots still packed with the sticky clay. Although the clay imagery here ties this passage with "The Horse-Dealer's Daughter," the scene differs significantly from the short story: unlike Mabel and Jack, Gudrun and Gerald have not both sunk into the smelly, cold element and re-emerged together, confronting and recognizing each other in their mutual shame. Rather, Gerald turns to Gudrun to escape from the clay and the void, to submerge himself in her maternal "soft effluence": "she was the great bath of life, he worshipped her. Mother and substance of all life she was. And he, child and man, received of her and was made whole" (344).

As the narrative perspective enters Gudrun's consciousness, however, we are reminded that she is no mere "bath," but a complex subjectivity who resists such objectification. As Gerald lapses into unconsciousness after their lovemaking, Gudrun lies awake, envious and resentful of his very ability to lapse and escape: "Ah, she could shriek with torment, he was so far off, and perfected, in another world . . . that he should lie so perfect and immune, in another world, whilst she was tormented with violent wakefulness, cast out in the outer darkness" (346). The alternating dynamic of fusion and exclusion indeed comes to define the final progression of Gerald and Gudrun's relationship as it moves toward its crisis in the Tyrol. The Alps setting perfectly symbolizes this dynamic as it represents at once a womblike return—"the centre, the knot, the navel of the world" (401)—and a cold, deathly disconnection from life and relationships. It embodies the tragic irony of narcissistic desire that drives both Gerald and Gudrun.

The Alpine environment also suggests a place of "letting go" and release. As Gudrun states, "It is impossible really to let go, in England, of that I am assured" (394), and so Lawrence takes his characters out of England, away from the repressions and inhibitions of their ordinary, quotidian life. As we have come to understand, however, such letting go often means disaster for Lawrence's characters since instinctual release is unconsciously bound up with a terrifying destructiveness. Like the tragic heroes of classical drama, Gerald is fated from the beginning of this novel; the destiny of his character is clear from the time he was a child playing with a gun and it shattered his world. The boundaries between fantasy and reality collapsed for Gerald then, and they collapse for him again at the novel's end.

As the drama of Gerald and Gudrun approaches its climax, the fantasies of fusion and exclusion intensify. Gudrun, for instance, gazes at the snow-covered peaks and experiences a profound sense of rejection and isolation: "She could *see* it, she knew it, but she was not of it. She was divorced, debarred, a soul shut out" (403). Like Gerald, she yearns for a regressive retreat—a oneness—that is nevertheless associated with frigidity and death: "If she could but come there, alone, and pass into the infolded navel of eternal snow and of uprising, immortal peaks of snow and rock, she would be a oneness with all, she would be herself the eternal, infinite silence, the sleeping, timeless, frozen centre of All" (410). Gudrun momentarily experiences such fusion in the scene in which she rides the toboggan with Gerald: "she fused like one molten, dancing globule, rushed through a white intensity" (420). At the bottom of the slope, "Utter oblivion came over her, as she lay for a few moments abandoned against him," and she proclaims, "It was the complete moment of my life" (420–21).

Gudrun ultimately resists abandoning herself to Gerald, however, out of "fear of his power over her, which she must always counterfoil" (443). Yet, paradoxically, it is also her experience of his weakness and deficiency, his infantile neediness, that equally prevents real surrender and erotic mutuality in their relationship: "Perhaps this was what he was always dogging her for, like a child that is famished, crying for the breast. . . . Had she asked for a child, whom she must nurse through the nights, for her lover? She despised him. . . . An infant crying in the night, this Don Juan. She would murder it gladly" (466). Gerald and Gudrun's relationship is characterized not only by the polarity of domination and submission, but also by that of grandiosity and contempt, of idealization and repudiation—the seesaw of narcissistic experiencing.

Gudrun dismisses Gerald and abandons herself instead to Loerke's degraded, self-enclosed world. Loerke represents a total surrender to inner experience and to a world of fantasy and art that is absolute in itself, untempered by reality or connection with the outside. Loerke is described as "detached from everything" and "absolute in himself" (452). He lectures Ursula on how she "*must not* confuse the relative world of action, with the absolute world of art" (431). Lawrence was himself deeply opposed to this conception of art as disconnected from the real world because it represented for him the same perilous slide into solipsism as did homosexuality (thus Loerke's characterization as overtly homosexual). Lawrence returns again and again in his writing to the conviction that without connection to real otherness, the self inevitably withers within. Loerke is therefore portrayed as shrunken and distorted; Birkin describes him as "a gnawing little negation, gnawing at the roots of life" (428). Yet Gudrun's attraction to Loerke's world reflects an inclination or temptation that Lawrence understood well; it is an attraction, his fiction makes clear, against which he had to battle persistently.

Gerald's experience in the Alps, even more than Gudrun's, is characterized by exclusion and abandonment. Gudrun's rejection of him replays an original trauma of maternal coldness and betrayal. He is infuriated by Gudrun's relationship with Loerke as well as by her ecstatic surrender to the mountain peaks: "Why did she betray the two of them so terribly, in embracing the glow of the evening? Why did she leave him standing there, with the ice-wind blowing through his heart, like death, to gratify herself among the rosy snow-tips?" (447). Ultimately Gerald's masochism, not his sadism, triumphs in relation to Gudrun's maternal and sexual power. He tells Birkin that his experience of her "withers my consciousness, somehow, it burns the pith of my mind. . . . It blasts your soul's eye . . . and leaves you sightless. Yet you *want* to be sightless, you *want* to be blasted" (439–40).

This desire to be "blasted" recalls Ghent's description of the desire underlying masochistic submission—the wish to have one's defensive protections stripped away, "to 'come clean,' as part of an even more general longing to be known, recognized" ("Masochism" 110). The imagery with which the narrator later describes Gerald's inner state underscores such longing:

> A strange rent had been torn in him; like a victim that is torn open and given to the heavens, so he had been torn apart and given to Gudrun. How should he close again? This wound, this strange, infinitely-sensi-tive opening of his soul, where he was exposed, like an open flower, to all the universe, and in which he was given to his complement, the other, the unknown, this wound, this disclosure, this unfolding of his own covering, leaving him incomplete, limited, unfinished, like an open flower under the sky, this was his cruelest joy. Why then should he forego it. Why should he close up and become impervious, immune, like a partial thing in a sheath, when he had broken forth, like a seed that has germinated, to issue forth in being, embracing the unrealised heavens. (445–46)

Even if such self-exposure ultimately means self-destruction, it is still preferable, this passage suggests, to a death-in-life existence of impervi-ous immunity and exhausting, relentless control. It is the same para-dox—the urge for life that becomes a drive toward death—that fuels the masochism of "The Woman Who Rode Away."

Though Gerald comes close to realizing a sadistic fantasy of mur-dering Gudrun—"he could feel the slippery chords of her life. And this he crushed, this he could crush. What bliss! Oh, what bliss, at last, what satisfaction, at last!" (471)—the passion dissipates in a "revulsion of contempt and disgust" and a final wave of narcissistic despair (472). As Gerald stumbles toward his death in the snow, the narrator discloses these curious thoughts: "Somebody was going to murder him. He had a great dread of being murdered. But it was a dread which stood outside him, like his own ghost" (473). Inner destructiveness, once again, is pro-jected onto the external world, and, once more, its real, devastating power is confirmed—Gerald is in fact destroyed. "It was bound to hap-pen. To be murdered!" (473). In a sense, he is murdered by his own ghost since boundaries have dissolved and he is trapped in a persecutory

world of his own omnipotent projections. Gerald's death in the snow is
another of those symbolically resonant Lawrencian scenes that hold conflicting associations. His drifting asleep in the "hollow basin of snow"
suggests a blissful fantasy of regressive merging while the scene as a
whole equally communicates a terrible sense of isolation, emotional
frigidity, numbness, and despair.

Gerald's tragedy, as Blanchard has argued, is the tragedy of narcissism. If otherness is not discovered, there are then no limits on one's own
destructive fantasies, no escape from one's own worst nightmares. The
Gerald-Gudrun relationship enacts a characteristic Lawrencian scenario,
but in this novel it is only one scenario among others. Though their relationship reflects a breakdown of intersubjective tension, the *story* of
their relationship is held in tension with other relational stories, particularly that of Birkin and Ursula. The novel juggles competing, alterna-
tive versions of self and other; it manages the "trembling instability of
the balance" that Gerald and Gudrun cannot.

BIRKIN AND GERALD:
SEEKING THE NARCISSISTIC IDEAL

A number of critics have pointed to the canceled prologue to *Women in
Love* as evidence of an explicit homosexual attraction between Birkin
and Gerald that, for various reasons, Lawrence was unable to deal with
directly in the novel.[8] I do not believe *Women in Love* attempts to dis-
guise homosexual love as much as it attempts to explore it in more art-
ful and productive ways than the prologue seemed to allow. Birkin's
strong feelings for Gerald are certainly quite explicit in the novel, and
they are no less symbolically sexual than the male attraction described
in the prologue. Latent or repressed homosexuality in itself cannot
explain those feelings or account for the conflicts they arouse. As I have
argued at various points in this study, the homoerotic story in
Lawrence's work is part of a larger psychodynamic story involving self-
deficiency, merging, and idealization. In the prologue's description of
the two types of men toward whom Birkin is drawn, such narcissistic
dynamics are again apparent. Birkin craves the idealized autonomy and
icy impenetrability of the "white-skinned northmen," and he equally
yearns to merge and lose himself in the warm fluidity of the "dark-
skinned" men:

> these white-skinned, keen-limbed men with eyes like blue-flashing ice
> and hair like crystals of winter sunshine, the northmen, inhuman as
> sharp-crying gulls, distinct like splinters of ice, like crystals, isolated,
> individual; and then the men with dark eyes that one can enter and

plunge into, bathe in, as in a liquid darkness, dark-skinned, supple, night-smelling men, who are the living substance of the viscous, universal, heavy darkness. (Appendix III, *Women in Love* 513–14)

Birkin's problems, in other words, are not simply those of an unacknowledged or disavowed homosexuality; they are the problems of narcissism. James Cowan ("Blutbrüderschaft") makes this argument quite convincingly within the context of Kohut's self-psychology. "Birkin's conflict," he asserts, "derives from motives that are not aimed primarily at sexual gratification but at preservation of the self" (200). Kohut theorizes that healthy self-development demands successful maternal mirroring and paternal idealizing relationships in early life, and Cowan believes Lawrence's psychological history reveals deficits in both relational modes. Lawrence's father was unavailable for idealization, and his mother, Cowan speculates, "provided excessive mirroring at times and used him for her own selfobject needs but . . . was unable to respond appropriately to his actual needs for separation-individuation and autonomy. It is in this early developmental context in relation to both parental imagos that the homoerotic feelings that emerged from time to time are to be understood" (199–200).

Psychoanalyst Otto Kernberg has also written about the unconscious narcissistic aims that underlie sexual relationships: "both men and women may wish to enact a homosexual relationship or to reverse the sex roles in an ultimate attempt to overcome the boundaries between the sexes that unavoidably limit narcissistic gratification in sexual intimacy; both long for complete fusion with the loved object, with oedipal and preoedipal implications which can never be fulfilled" (58). Narcissistic fantasy is indeed always bound up to some degree in erotic life. In Birkin's relationship with Gerald, Lawrence explores the human need for ideal experiencing in a less destructive or pathological light than he does in the Gudrun-Gerald relationship. With Birkin, Gerald is allowed to maintain more consistently his status as a separate, ideal other. He does not collapse, as he does with Gudrun, into the needy, dependent infant. Gerald is the object of Birkin's idealized, narcissistic projections, but he does not dissolve, as he does for Gudrun, into a mere projection or reflection of the self. He ultimately resists Birkin's need to fuse with or incorporate him as a selfobject. Gerald's detachment is a source of torment for Birkin, but it is also what keeps Birkin's passion alive and, along with Ursula, helps save him from narcissistic despair.

In the novel as a whole, there are relatively few pages devoted exclusively to Birkin's relationship with Gerald, even though its psychological significance is equivalent to that of his relationship with Ursula. The "Man to Man" and "Gladiatorial" chapters contain the most extended scenes between them. "Man to Man" opens with Birkin in a sick, irritable state over his relationship with Ursula. "He knew his life rested with her," but he is repulsed by the suffocating, constricted life that conventional marriage to him represents: "The hot narrow intimacy between man and wife was abhorrent" (199). This leads into his famous rant on the Magna Mater—"the Great Mother of everything, out of whom proceeded everything and to whom everything must finally be rendered up. . . . He had a horror of the Magna Mater, she was detestable" (200). While Birkin is in this feverish state, Gerald pays him a visit. His entrance at this point in the narrative certainly seems to confirm the view of Ruderman, Storch, and others that the powerful Lawrencian male essentially represents a refuge from the horrible "merging, the clutching, the mingling" (200) of maternal/female love. Gerald, we are told, "was protective, offering the warm shelter of his physical strength" (202). The two men converse about death, about what Birkin calls "mystic, universal degeneration"—a process of "degradation" that precedes death and continues after it (204). The narrator informs us that Gerald possesses a deeper, more "direct and personal" knowledge of this process than Birkin, "But he was not going to give himself away. . . . Gerald would be a dark horse to the end" (204).

For Birkin, Gerald embodies a powerful physicality that holds an enviable "mystic" sensual knowledge. Gerald's aloofness, however, insures that he will remain for Birkin a mysterious, "dark-horse" other. At this point in the narrative, Birkin realizes that he loves Gerald, "that it had been a necessity inside himself all his life—to love a man purely and fully. Of course he had been loving Gerald all along, and all along denying it" (206). He now wants "love and eternal conjunction" with a man as well as a woman. He proposes the Blutbrüderschaft, that they "swear to be true to each other . . . to love each other . . . implicitly and perfectly, finally, without any possibility of going back on it" (206–7). Birkin's proposal that the two men be indissolubly bound by this pact, "of one blood," as it were, reflects a narcissistic ideal of perfect union or oneness. It suggests precisely the sort of "mingling" that Birkin so dreads with a woman. From such merging or oneness, narcissistic fears of enslavement and annihilation inevitably arise; and as we have seen, those fears can threaten homosexual as well as heterosexual relationships in Lawrence's fiction. At the end of the "Man to Man" chapter, the power dynamic shifts, and Birkin is granted an inner force or strength that Gerald lacks. Birkin "looked at Gerald with clear, happy eyes of discovery," while "Gerald looked down at him, attracted, so deeply bondaged in fascinated attraction, that he was mistrustful, resenting the bondage, hating the attraction" (207). This is the same dynamic we have observed so often in Lawrence's work, whether it be between Miriam and

Paul in *Sons and Lovers* or Bertie and Maurice in "The Blind Man."

The celebrated nude wrestling scene in the "Gladitorial" chapter enacts a highly erotic fantasy in which Birkin penetrates and fuses with Gerald's powerful physicality while, most importantly, still controlling and dominating it:

> He seemed to penetrate into Gerald's more solid, more diffuse bulk, to interfuse his body through the body of the other, as if to bring it subtly into subjection, always seizing with some rapid necromantic fore-knowledge every motion of the other flesh, converting and counteracting it, playing upon the limbs and trunk of Gerald like some hard wind. It was as if Birkin's whole physical intelligence interpenetrated into Gerald's body, as if his fine, sublimated energy entered into the flesh of the fuller man, like some potency, casting a fine net, a prison, through the muscles into the very depths of Gerald's physical being. (270)

As Cowan concludes from this passage, "Birkin's attachment to Gerald is the expression not of an object-instinctive drive but of the longing for merger in an idealized selfobject relationship" ("Blutbrüderschaft" 203). In this fantasy, Lawrence allows Birkin to maintain his dominance and control despite his absorption into Gerald's more powerful physical being. That fact prevents the fantasy from collapsing into the annihilation anxiety that usually accompanies such fusion with the other, whether the other be male or female.

Interestingly, the wrestling scene, with its repeated emphasis on the "oneness" of the two bodies clinched in struggle, is followed by a discussion of the real *differences* between the two men. The dialogue reveals that Gerald likes to eat before bed; Birkin doesn't. "There you are, we are not alike," Birkin announces. Birkin also notices Gerald's fine, expensive clothes and thinks, "This was another of the differences between them" (273). These reflections lead to thoughts of Ursula—"it was the woman who was gaining ascendance over Birkin's being, at this moment. Gerald was becoming dim again, lapsing out of him" (274). In other words, as Birkin becomes aware of Gerald's otherness, of his distinct, separate subjectivity, his fantasy fades. Ursula is associated with reality, with real otherness, and his desire for her returns. In this chapter and elsewhere, the dialectic of narcissistic fantasy and intersubjective recognition defines a continual tension in Birkin's relational life—a dialectic fundamental to the novel as a whole.

BIRKIN AND URSULA: MAINTAINING THE VITAL TENSION

Blanchard maintains that although Ursula and Birkin, "aware of the 'river of dissolution,' share several qualities of narcissism . . . especially in their desire to break both with other people and with their responsibilities to society, it is nevertheless through them that Lawrence explores alternatives to Gudrun and Gerald" ("*Women in Love*" 112). I would like to examine those alternatives in more psychological detail than the scope of Blanchard's essay allows. A distinction, first of all, needs to be made between the sort of dissolution Birkin seeks and the potential disintegration of self that underlies pathological narcissism. As Birkin explains to Ursula, "'You've got to lapse out before you can know what sensual reality is, lapse into unknowingness, and give up your volition. You've got to do it. You've got to learn not-to-be, before you can come into being" (44). In a discussion of Winnicott's work, Eigen makes a distinction between "disintegration" and "unintegration" that is useful in thinking about Birkin's notion here:

> For Winnicott, *disintegration* means one would hold on to something if one could, but a process one cannot control is spinning one out of existence. . . . *Unintegration*, by contrast, is a "purer" state. The subject dips into creative formlessness. He lives between the lines of his built-up personality. He gets to where he was before defensive encapsulation took over. . . . Unintegration refers to the chaos of experiencing before it congeals into psychic formations that can be used defensively. It refers to a time or dimension of experiencing before the ability to split off and oppose aspects of the self to one another (particularly mind-body, thinking-feeling). (*Psychotic* 334)

For Birkin (and Lawrence) this mode of being is associated with a specifically sensual, bodily state and a ruthless, "demonic" energy. It is "the deluge," Birkin tells Ursula, in which "the mind and the known world is drowned in darkness.—Everything must go. . . . Then you find yourself a palpable body of darkness, a demon" (43). As Eigen explains, "unintegration can be menacing as well as renewing" (337), and it often "oscillates with and gives way to fragmentation and disintegration" (342). Birkin does a better job of negotiating the line between unintegration and disintegration than many of Lawrence's other characters. He understands that passionate, authentic life resides in our continued contact with a primitive, unintegrated realm, but that connection must be balanced by an equally durable contact with external reality, with otherness.

Birkin is motivated by the same yearning for surrender, for the lapsing or release of psychic defenses that drives so many Lawrence characters. Unlike Gerald or Gudrun, however, Birkin realizes this process must not occur in isolation nor in relation to an other who is only an idealized projection of self. As he tells Ursula, "I deliver *myself* over to the unknown, in coming to you, I am without reserves or defences, stripped entirely into the unkown. Only there needs the pledge between us, that we will both cast off everything, cast off ourselves even, and cease to be, so that that which is perfectly ourselves can take place in us" (147). Dissolution of self must take place *in relation* to another self who has undergone the same process in order for the transformation to occur. Ursula does not quite understand him. She asks if "it is because you love me, that you want me?" And Birkin replies, "No it isn't. It is because I believe in you—if I *do* believe in you. . . . Yes, I must believe in you, or else I shouldn't be here saying this" (147). *Belief* in the other is indeed more fundamental than love; it is a prerequisite for mature love. It implies faith in the other's reality and integrity, faith that when all of the defenses do come down, the other will still be there. Although Birkin reveals some shakiness—such belief in the female other is always an exceedingly difficult task for Lawrence's characters—he ultimately makes the leap and affirms his faith. When the social conventions, the masks and defenses are shed and the "demonic" self emerges, the essential Ursula, he believes, will survive. She will not retaliate, withdraw, or collapse but will be there to recognize him, just as he will be there to recognize her in her authentic being and demonic assertion of self.

Many critics stress the defensive nature of Birkin's oft discussed metaphor of the star balance: "'What I want is a strange conjunction with you . . . not meeting and mingling . . . but an equilibrium, a pure balance of two single beings:—as the stars balance each other" (148). While this vision certainly does protect against the dreaded merger with the woman, it represents more than merely a defensive fantasy. The metaphor equally accentuates a profound reciprocity, a recognition that self and other are mutually bound and interdependent. The imagery of separate stars may reflect a defensive response to the female other's devouring power, but it simultaneously promotes her strength and singularity, and it reaffirms connection with her. Nor does the fact that Ursula mocks such talk of stars and mystical conjunction necessarily undermine the credibility of Birkin's metaphor; in fact, her mockery only confirms it. In constantly challenging him, Ursula is asserting herself and upholding the balance between them. "'I think you are very silly,'" she tells him. "'I think you want to tell me you love me, and you go all this way round to do it'" (148).

Ursula does not completely understand Birkin, but he does not completely understand her, either. Their failures of understanding ironically help to keep their relationship creative and alive. Misunderstandings reinforce difference, reconfirming the irreducible duality of self and other, of two separate subjectivities. Neither subject can be completely known as a cognitively perceived object by the other. That sort of "knowing," as Lawrence demonstrates with Hermione's character, can indeed be a form of domination and control, an attempt at narcissistic absorption or possession of the other. Understanding or knowing the other is not the same thing as recognition of the other. Recognition has to do with a felt awareness, appreciation, or to use Lawrence's words, "belief in" the other's intrinsic selfhood. Mutual recognition, not necessarily understanding, is the essential factor for a relationship to flourish.

Not only do Birkin and Ursula fail to understand one another fully, they also each experience a violent hatred of the other. The hatred, however, is precisely what rouses them into passionate existence and relationship. After the drowning of Gerald's sister and their first desperate lovemaking, both Ursula and Birkin descend into a lethargic, deathly state—a condition, symptomatic of pathological narcissism, in which the self is engulfed by feelings of futility, emptiness, and despair. The "Sunday Evening" chapter begins, "the life-blood seemed to ebb away from Ursula, and within the emptiness a heavy despair gathered. Her passion seemed to bleed to death, and there was nothing. She sat suspended in a state of complete nullity, harder to bear than death" (191). After a visit with Birkin, however, she rages back into life, transfigured by hate:

> Her whole nature seemed sharpened and intensified into a pure dart of hate. . . . It merely took hold of her, the most poignant and ultimate hatred, pure and clear and beyond thought. She could not think of it at all, she was translated beyond herself. . . . He was the enemy, fine as a diamond, and as hard and jewel-like, the quintessence of all that was inimical.
>
> She thought of his face, white and purely wrought, and of his eyes that had such a dark, constant will of assertion, and she touched her own forehead, to feel if she were mad, she was so transfigured in white flame of essential hate.
>
> . . . It was as if he were a beam of essential enmity, a beam of light that did not only destroy her, but denied her altogether, revoked her whole world. She saw him as a clear stroke of uttermost contradiction, a strange gem-like being whose existence defined her own non-existence. (197–98)

Ursula is responding to Birkin's pure, obdurate otherness; his opposing "gem-like being" limits her self, her narcissism. This hatred of him ultimately liberates her and makes real love possible. Birkin and Ursula will each assert their self against the other's being and assertion of self, and each will withstand the assault. From the perspective of object relations theory, the ability to tolerate ambivalence, to experience hatred and love for the same object, marks a critical achievement in psychological development. In Kleinian terms, it heralds the transition from the omnipotence, idealization and splitting of the paranoid-schizoid position to the integration and containment of the depressive stage.

Lawrence intuitively understood this process. In "The Reality of Peace," he writes, "It is not of love that we are fulfilled, but of love in such intimate equipoise with hate that the transcendence takes place" (693).

Ursula's ability to hate so well, with such fierce, unthinking abandon, is exactly what makes her possible for Birkin; it allows him to love and hate her with equal ferocity. Following one of their arguments about love, Birkin thinks, "Here was one who would go the whole lengths of heaven or hell, whichever she had to go. And he mistrusted her, he was afraid of a woman capable of such abandon, such dangerous thoroughness of destructivity. Yet he chuckled within himself also" (154). Ursula's capacity for destructivity reassures him about his own inner destructiveness and her ability to survive. In the canceled prologue, the familiar Lawrencian fear of destroying the female other appears once again to be at at the root of heterosexual inhibition. Like Paul in relation to Miriam, Birkin feels that with Hermione,

> He could not take her and destroy her. He could not forget her. . . . He was too much aware of her, and of her fear, and of her writhing torment, as she lay in sacrifice. He had too much deference for her feeling. . . . He was always aware of *her* feelings, so that he had none of his own. Which made this last love-making between them an ignominious failure, very, very cruel to bear. (508)

Acute awareness of the female other's fragility, not her power, proves once more to be the obstacle to the spontaneous expression of passion and sexual release.

This brings me to the scene in "Moony" in which Birkin throws stones at the reflection of the moon, perhaps the most overanalyzed passage in Lawrence's entire oeuvre. I won't let that deter me, however, from offering yet another possible reading. Most analyses of the scene classify it as one more example of Birkin's rage against the possessive Great Mother, the "accursed Syria Dea" (246). The stoning, as Daleski contends, is an attack on the "self-assertive, sensual, devouring woman" (167).[9] That dynamic may be part of the psychology of the scene, but I do not think it is the whole meaning, or even the most important. For me the most intriguing line is Birkin's response to Ursula when, after the stoning, she asks, "'Why should you hate the moon? It hasn't done you any harm, has it?'" And he replies with the simple question: "'Was it hate?'" (248). The question is punctuated, the narrator reports, by a few minutes of silence. Birkin's question is a real one, enforced by the silence which follows it. He is not at all sure it was hate that he experienced, leaving the reader to wonder as well. Contributing to the ambiguity is the narrative perspective of the scene. As Peter Garrett remarks, "The description is from Ursula's point of view, but the intensity seems to reside in the moon itself" (43). The moon indeed seems to be endowed with a consciousness, a subjectivity, of its own:

> But at the centre, the heart of all, was still a vivid, incandescent quivering of a white moon not quite destroyed, a white body of fire writhing and striving and not even now broken open, not yet violated. It seemed to be drawing itself together with strange, violent pangs, in blind effort. It was getting stronger, it was re-asserting itself, the inviolable moon. And the rays were hastening in in thin lines of light, to return to the strengthened moon, that shook upon the water in triumphant reassumption.
>
> Birkin stood and watched, motionless, till the pond was almost calm, the moon was almost serene. Then, satisfied of so much, he looked for more stones. (247)

The identification with the moon in this passage makes its recovery, its "triumphant reassumption," seem satisfying and desirable. Although its restoration encourages Birkin to throw more stones, we are never told that he is feeling rage or hostility. "Like a madness," the narrator says, "he must go on" (247). What is going on here, I suggest, is less enraged hostility than a Winnicottian destructiveness, a compulsive *testing* of the female other's durability. Included in this sort of destructiveness, as Benjamin explains, is "the intention *to discover* if the other will survive. Winnicott's conception of destruction is innocent; it is best understood as a refusal, a negation, the mental experience of 'You do not exist for me,' whose favorable outcome is pleasure in the other's survival" (*Bonds* 38). Birkin must keep trying to obliterate the moon, but the moon's resilience, her triumph, is also his.

The metaphor of the moon's reflection as a rose also casts the moon's recovery in a positive, celebratory light: "the heart of the rose intertwining vigorously and blindly, calling back the scattered fragments, winning home the fragments, in a pulse and an effort of return" (247), or again, "a ragged rose, a distorted, frayed moon was shaking upon the waters again, re-asserted, renewed, trying to recover from its convulsion, to get over the disfigurement and the agitation, to be whole and composed, at peace" (248). For Lawrence the rose is often a symbol of the type of love he seeks, one that preserves the duality of oneness and separateness: "We are like a rose. In the pure passion for oneness, in the pure passion for distinctness and separateness, a dual passion of unutterable separation and lovely conjunction of the two, the new configuration takes place, the transcendence, the two in their perfect singleness, transported into one surpassing heaven of a rose-blossom" ("Love" 154). The moon's victorious reassertion in the wake of Birkin's unrelenting destructiveness is precisely what makes this kind of love or intersubjectivity possible; the other has not been destroyed by the self's passionate destructiveness but is there, inviolable and whole, to recognize and receive the self.

A similar dynamic of attack and recovery also precedes the pivotal moment in Ursula and Birkin's relationship when, in the "Excurse" chapter, they break through to a new "mystically-physically satisfying" (314) form of love. At the beginning of the chapter, Birkin and Ursula engage in a heated argument about Hermione. Ursula, in a state of fury, throws down the rings Birkin has given her and storms off. Birkin, now abandoned and alone, launches into another tirade against fusion and women: "Fusion, fusion, this horrible fusion of two beings, . . . was it not nauseous and horrible anyhow, whether it was a fusion of the spirit or of the emotional body? Hermione saw herself as the perfect Idea, to which all men must come: and Ursula was the perfect Womb, the bath of birth, to which all men must come! And both were horrible" (309).

The fact that Birkin's terror and rage over fusion erupt immediately following his abandonment by the woman suggests again that the merging fantasy is a reactive phenomenon, that it is, above all, a response to narcissistic injury. After venting his rage, Birkin spies the rings lying in the mud: "They were the little tokens of the reality of beauty, the reality of happiness in warm creation.—But he had made his hands all dirty and gritty" (309). The rings are a reminder of the goodness in self and other that exists along with the badness—with the rage and shame that are symbolically suggested by his dirty hands. Goodness can survive the rage, and with that realization, Birkin feels a sense of release, a healing dissolution: "There was a darkness over his mind. The terrible knot of consciousness that had persisted there like an obsession was broken, gone, his life was dissolved in darkness over his limbs and his body" (309). Birkin can now admit to his need for the woman—"He wanted her to come back" (310)—without feeling overwhelmed by that need. Ursula does come back, and Birkin experiences her return "as if asleep, at peace, slumbering and utterly relaxed" (310). The narrator states repeatedly that they were at peace together, "peace at last. The old, detestable world of tension had passed away at last" (310).

At this point Birkin and Ursula experience a strange new stillness, a stillness of simply "being" and of feeling acknowledged or recognized in that being. Stripped of its defensive structures, the self is highly vulnerable in this naked state. Ursula is afraid, just as Mabel and the doctor are afraid at the end of "Horse-Dealer's Daughter." Ursula "wished he were passionate, because in passion she was at home. But this was so still and frail, as space is more frightening than force" (311). For Lawrence's characters the most satisfying moments of coming together often follow a serious quarrel in which rage and destructiveness are

expressed and tolerated. Peace and stillness follow. Ursula's love, like
the moon's reflection, has survived Birkin's fury. His renewed faith in
her revives faith in himself as well, and it establishes the foundation for
a real relationship between them.

The nature of the lovemaking that follows later in this chapter has
provoked a good deal of critical controversy. Most commentators agree
that the descriptive language suggests anal intercourse, but there is little
consensus as to its meaning. Some view the anality in a negative, critical
light; they see it as a sublimation of or substitution for homosexual desire
and as simply another form of masculine control over the female. Others
celebrate it as a liberation or purgation.[10] Anality is always tied to shame
in Lawrence's work, and as we have seen repeatedly, the need to embrace
that shame, and to have it embraced by another, is considered crucial to
the experience of authentic selfhood. Anality is also tied to a "mystic"
sensuality and to dissolution and disintegration. These associations are
embodied in the West African statuette Birkin ponders: the image of the
woman with the beetle's face and "protuberant buttocks" suggests to him
"mindless progressive knowledge through the senses, knowledge arrested
and ending in the senses, mystic knowledge in disintegration and dissolution, knowledge such as the beetles have, which live purely within the
world of corruption and cold dissolution" (253). Homosexuality, as we
have seen (particularly in reference to the beetle imagery), is bound up
with these associations as well. Thus although descent into this realm of
anal sensuality and dissolution may be necessary for rebirth, as Colin
Clarke has argued, it does not in itself represent a positive or liberating
direction for Lawrence. For the descent to be emancipating, it must occur
in the context of relationship and otherness. Without the presence of a
real other, the lapse into this dissolute state becomes stifling and deathly,
a dead-end retreat into the nether regions of the self.

Birkin and Ursula, however, recognize one another in their shameful, bodily selves, and that mutual recognition is their salvation. As
Ursula caresses Birkin's thighs, "she seemed to touch the quick of the
mystery of darkness that was bodily him. . . . It was a perfect passing
away for both of them, and at the same time the most intolerable acces-
sion into being, the marvellous fulness of immediate gratification, overwhelming, outflooding from the Source of the deepest life-force, the
darkest, deepest, strangest life-source of the human body, at the back
and base of the loins" (314).[11] Ursula takes Birkin as he had taken her
earlier: "He had taken her at the roots of her darkness and shame—like
a demon, laughing over the fountain of mystic corruption which was
one of the sources of her being, laughing, shrugging, accepting, accepting finally" (304). Here is the creative inspiration for so much of
Lawrence's work—the drive to be accepted, accepted finally, at the roots

of one's being. For Lawrence, as for all of us, those roots lie in the powerful physicality of infant life, in our primal, bodily needs and passions as we experience them *in relation to the others* on whom we depend. The shame connected with bodily life for Lawrence had to be confronted over and over again; in order for the body to be reclaimed, the shame must be reclaimed and owned, too. This perspective can shed light on the anal emphasis in much of the tender lovemaking between Connie and Mellors in *Lady Chatterley's Lover* as well.

In the final pages of "Excurse," the image of darkness predominates—a good, holding and containing darkness that typically accompanies psychological discovery or transition in Lawrence's novels. Ursula "knew there was no leaving him, the darkness held them both and contained them, it was not to be surpassed. Besides she had a full mystic knowledge of his suave loins of darkness, dark-clad and suave, and in this knowledge there was some of the inevitability and the beauty of fate, fate which one asks for, which one accepts in full" (318). The acceptance of fate signals an acceptance of limits, of outside forces the self cannot control. The surrender to such forces can, paradoxically, be liberating in that it represents an escape from narcissistic self-imprisonment. "Excurse" concludes with a celebration of otherness:

> She had her desire of him, she touched, she received the maximums of unspeakable communication in touch, dark, subtle, positively silent, a magnificent gift and give again, a perfect acceptance and yielding, a mystery, the reality of that which can never be known, vital, sensual reality that can never be transmuted into mind content, but remains outside, living body of darkness and silence and subtlety, the mystic body of reality. She had her desire fulfilled, he had his desire fulfilled. For she was to him what he was to her, the immemorial magnificence of mystic, palpable, real otherness. (320)

As Winnicott understood, the discovery of an immutable external reality can be profoundly joyous as well as painful. The present but unknowable "mystic body of reality" that Birkin and Ursula each discover in the other also confirms the sense of their own "vital, sensual reality," and that discovery is transforming.

Women in Love ends famously in the midst of an argument. Distraught over Gerald's death, Birkin clings to a belief in the potential of the love he and Gerald had for one another; he refuses to abandon the possibility of "eternal union" with a man. Ursula dismisses that belief:

> "I don't believe it," she said. "It's an obstinacy, a theory, a perversity."
> "Well—" he said.
> "You can't have two kinds of love. Why should you!"

"It seems as if I can't," he said. "Yet I wanted it."
"You can't have it because it's false, impossible," she said.
"I don't believe that," he answered. (481)

If we consider Birkin's and Ursula's positions here as depicting two different psychic positions or modes of relating, then neither is absolutely
right or wrong. The unresolved argument itself presents the deepest psychological truth: either position alone can lead to deathliness and
despair, but together, each balanced by the active opposition of the
other, they hold the promise of a rich, fulfilling life.

Birkin's desire for Gerald represents a form of ideal, narcissistic
relating that, as we have seen, can spiral into madness, chaos, and
despair if not countered by contact with reality and otherness. Yet the
ideal realm is also a source of passion and creativity; to close it off completely, to lose contact with this intense, primal level of psychic experience, can be equally deadening. Eigen asserts that "Creativity thrives on
the interplay between ideal images in the mind and the hard facts of
life," and that "In optimal conditions one develops the capacity to be
able to flexibly undergo and process both 'ideal' and 'realistic' dimensions of experience in a rich, well-nigh unlimited variety of ways" (Electrified Tightrope 95, 102). Ursula is right to counter Birkin's belief, and
Birkin is right to hold on to it. In the dynamic, creative tension between
them lies the best hope for authentic living.

EPILOGUE

David Lodge believes that after *Women in Love*, Lawrence "forsakes the dialogic principle." In the leadership novels and in *Lady Chatterley's Lover*, Lodge argues, "there is one privileged ideological position for the heroine to occupy, and towards which a dominant authorial discourse inexorably guides her" (65). Although one can find moments that admit competing voices and opposing or paradoxical positions—the characterization of Kate's ambivalence at the end of *The Plumed Serpent*, for example—the tensions are not as consistently sustained as they are in much of Lawrence's earlier work. The narcissistic fantasies—evident in the idealized, authoritarian males, the repudiation of the maternal, and the elevation of the phallus to sacred object—are, for the most part, allowed to reign uncontested.[1]

Although such fantasies, as we have seen, play a significant role in the earlier fiction, they exist there in dialectical tension with an intersubjective mode of consciousness that recognizes and values the subjectivity of the other. Those works play with a dual consciousness. In "Apocalypse," Lawrence effectively describes these dual forms of consciousness: "Man has two supreme forms of consciousness, the consciousness that I AM, and that I am full of power; then the other way of consciousness, the awareness that IT IS, and that IT, which is the objective universe or the other person, has a separate existence from mine, even preponderant over mine" (168).[2] The goal in psychic and relational life, as Lawrence understood, is to balance the I AM (narcissistic mode) with the IT IS (intersubjective). As Benjamin has argued, however, our culture has made that balance exceedingly difficult to maintain because of the diminishment of maternal/female subjectivity. The self must struggle valiantly to realize the mother's separate subjectivity, her individual agency, in a culture that seeks to deny it.

Crucial to the discovery of the m/other's subjectivity, as I have stressed throughout this study, is the process of "destruction." According to Benjamin, the m/other must survive the self's ruthless self-assertion and "act of negation," for only an "other who survives can be seen in its alterity, as external—outside one's own control and yet able to have decisive impact on the self. . . . The self limited in its contact with externality remains in the thrall of idealization and repudiation, of iden-

131

tifications and projections that demand submission to an authority or redeemer" ("Shadow of the Other" 237). The mother's ability to survive depends upon her capacity for accepting and tolerating aggression, both her own and the child's. As psychologist Elsa First explains, a mother needs "to be on good terms with her own aggression, to feel where it has been constructive to her, to be able to identify with the child's aggression and play with it resiliently. . . . Resilience . . . requires acceptance of aggressivity and activity in oneself, as a part of one's own aliveness, rather than fearing that any assertion of one's own rights will be destructive to the other" (159). Our culture's profound discomfort with female assertiveness and aggression, however, serves to make such maternal resilience a difficult task indeed.

Lawrence's most interesting texts oscillate between faith in the mother's survival and externality, and disruption or loss of such faith. They fall into a rhythm of breakdown and repair. Such is the natural rhythm, Benjamin suggests, of psychic life: "The breakdown of tension between self and other in favor of relating as subject and object is a common fact of mental life. For that matter, breakdown is a common feature within intersubjective relatedness—what counts is the ability to restore or repair the relationship" ("Recogniton and Destruction" 58). The great Lawrence novels display a high degree of psychic flexibility; they move exhilaratingly between the poles of oneness and separateness, of omnipotent, narcissistic fantasy and recognition of otherness and limits. They allow us to experience the full force of those magnetic tensions that both energize and challenge our passionate human relationships.

NOTES

CHAPTER 1. INTRODUCTION

1. Faith Pullin rivals Millett in her all-out indictment of Lawrence. She contends that "Lawrence was not really interested in his woman characters, or only for as long as they supported and encouraged the male. Lawrence isn't concerned with women as themselves" (50). She argues that in *Sons and Lovers* "instead of examining the interactions of real men and women, what Lawrence actually wrote about was the relationship between man and a series of female stereotypes" (73)—a perspective with which I wholly disagree.

Hilary Simpson and Cornelia Nixon offer more judicious discussions of Lawrence's misogyny and antifeminism. Both tie his attitude to the larger social and cultural context—Simpson to his association with women in the suffrage movement and his fear of women's increasing social power, and Nixon to the stresses he suffered during the First World War, including the banning of *The Rainbow*, and to his mounting ambivalence about his homosexual urges. Sandra Gilbert and Susan Gubar also connect Lawrence's hostility toward independent women to a general cultural anxiety over women's enhanced social position after the war.

2. See, for instance, David Lodge's chapter on *Women in Love* in *After Bakhtin*, Avrom Fleishman's "Lawrence and Bakhtin" in Brown and Keynes, and Jack Stewart's "Linguistic Incantation and Parody in *Women in Love.*"

3. The schizoid diagnosis is one that Marguerite Beede Howe, Scott Sanders, Karyn Sproles, and John Turner have also explicitly made. John Worthen doesn't use the clinical term, but his emphasis on Lawrence's emotional detachment suggests the same conclusion. Worthen quotes from one of Lawrence's early letters: "'in the moments of deepest emotion myself has watched myself'" (*D. H. Lawrence* 146).

4. The lack of maternal subjectivity—the failure to conceive of the mother as a subject in her own right, with her own desires and bodily reality outside of the child's experience of her—is a problem that many feminist critics have found with traditional psychoanalytic and object relations theories. As Benjamin shows, however, the problem resides not only within psychoanalytic theory but within our culture at large. It is indeed the problem that she critiques and that Lawrence struggles with so passionately in his art.

5. See Winnicott's "The Use of an Object and Relating through Identifications" (*Playing and Reality* 86–94) for a discussion of this concept. The capacity to use an object, he explains, involves "the subject's placing of the object outside the area of the subject's omnipotent control; that is, the subject's perception

of the object as an external phenomenon, not as a projective entity, in fact recognition of it as an entity in its own right" (89).

6. A passage in Lawrence's *Psychoanalysis and the Unconscious* gives an especially evocative description of the joy in discovering otherness: "There is a tremendous great joy in exploring and discovering the beloved. For what is the beloved? She is that which I myself am not. Knowing the breach between us, the uncloseable gulf, I in the same breath realize her *features*. . . . This is objective knowledge, as distinct from objective emotion. It contains always the element of self-amplification, as if the self were amplified by knowledge in the beloved. It should also contain the knowledge of the *limits* of the self" (38).

Discovery of real otherness is indeed a discovery of one's own limits—a liberation from narcissism. Because such discovery was so problematic in Lawrence's early relational life, his work reflects an excessive emphasis on the breaches and differences between the sexes and, especially in his nonfiction writing, an insistence on a sometimes stereotypical gender polarity (a feature of the often irritating *Fantasia of the Unconscious*).

7. Jeffrey Meyers's biography accents Lawrence's intense ambivalence about homosexuality. Meyers quotes the letter to Bertrand Russell in which Lawrence describes his disgust after meeting the economist John Maynard Keynes and his Cambridge homosexual set: "'It is true Cambridge made me very black and down . . . I cannot bear its smell of rottenness, marsh-stagnancy. I get a melancholic malaria. How can so sick people rise up? They must die first'" (165). In a letter to David Garnett, Lawrence refers to the same group as arousing "'this horrible sense of frowstiness, so repulsive, as if it came from deep inward dirt—a sort of sewer,'" and he advises Garnett to sever his association with them. Lawrence concludes, "'I feel as if I should go mad, if I think of your set. . . . It makes me dream of beetles'" (166).

Brenda Maddox also sees Lawrence's revulsion to homosexuality as tied to his fear of an isolating narcissism: "Homosexuality, for Lawrence, threatened more than the criminality and social ostracism of the time. It meant being locked in the tomb of himself and his own sex, shut off from Woman, the unknown and the current of life" (203). Mark Kinkead-Weekes (*D. H. Lawrence*) makes a similar point. He quotes a letter to Henry Savage (II:115) in which Lawrence connects homosexuality with narcissistic self-reflection: "'I believe a man projects his own image on another man, like on a mirror. But from a woman he wants himself re-born, re-constructed. So he can always get satisfaction from a man, but it is the hardest thing in life to get one's soul and body satisfied from a woman, so that one is free from oneself'" (103).

8. In the paranoid-schizoid position, the primary maternal object is experienced as both good (a source of libidinal gratification) and bad (frustrating and withholding). In order to protect the good from the bad, the object remains split in unconscious fantasy—the bad is projected out, and good and bad remain separate and isolated. In the depressive position, the ego has developed enough strength to integrate the split and experience the mother as a single whole, both good and bad. The depressive position involves tolerance of ambivalence, guilt over one's own destructive fantasies, and desire for reparation. See, for instance, Melanie Klein, *Love, Guilt and Reparation*, 287–91,

and Hanna Segal, *Introduction to the Work of Melanie Klein*, 26–36, 75–83.

For a discussion of these positions as dialectical rather than strictly linear, see also Thomas Ogden, 29–30; Michael Eigen, *Psychotic Core*, 176–79; and Annie Sweetnam.

9. Lawrence's ability to hold in play a dynamic balance of opposites is also James Cowan's thesis in *D. H. Lawrence and the Trembling Balance.* Cowan analyzes the numerous forms such balance takes in Lawrence's work, from that between "homeostatic physiological forces" to the antithesis "between the known and the unknown, light and darkness, the moths of the mind and the 'honorable beasts' of the blood" (21). In addition, Cowan stresses the important concept of resilience in relation to Lawrence's writing—a process of falling apart and reintegrating, "a sequence of stability, instability, resilience, and creative change" (29). This concept is equally crucial to my thesis about the perpetual process of breakdown and repair in Lawrence's fiction, the alternating collapse into the rigid polarities of narcissistic fantasy and the re-establishment of the paradoxical tensions of intersubjectivity.

CHAPTER 2. *SONS AND LOVERS*

1. Lewiecki-Wilson and Nigel Kelsey also focus on Mrs. Morel as a victim of patriarchy and its social and political constraints. According to Kelsey, "The Morel household is conditioned by a complex web of economic and politico-ideological relations" (87). He points to scenes in which Mrs. Morel laughs "when her oppression boldly exposes its nakedness to her" and argues that such laughter is a recognition of "the absurdity of one's emotional and material dependence on the various forms that oppression may take" (91).

Lewiecki-Wilson similarly examines how Mrs. Morel is robbed of her independent identity by patriarchy: "Morel controls her identity, despite her education or former social level. . . . He has leased the home and has the paying job, even if she actually makes the home and judiciously distributes the money" (75).

2. Peter Balbert emphasizes the gender issue in this scene and believes it demonstrates Mrs. Morel's "nagging and neurotic sexual envy of the state of manhood itself" (95–96). The affective tone of the passage, however, does not convey envy but wrenching loss. Mrs. Morel, due to her constrained and emotionally impoverished life, is indeed overly invested in the child. When Mr. Morel claims the boy as belonging to the masculine world—the father's world outside the home—Mrs. Morel's devastation is understandable.

Critics seem to me more interested in blame than the text itself. Both parents exhibit harmful and destructive behavior towards their children in this novel, yet the narrative also demonstates an empathic awareness of the parents' individual plights. The novel portrays the complex web of conflicting relational needs and desires that, in infinitely various forms, characterize family life.

3. Dorothy Van Ghent sees the lilies and the white moonlight as representative of a "vast torrential force," a primal, nonhuman otherness associated with phallic power and eros (9); Harvey says the whiteness of the moonlight and the lilies symbolizes Mrs. Morel's "severe emotional chastity" (73); John Stoll

believes the phallic lilies serve as "an ironic commentary" on Mrs. Morel, who has lost her passional nature (85); for Storch, the lilies "reeling in the moonlight" confirm Mrs. Morel's "terrible female power" and "evoke the mother's prohibition of the son's oedipal desires, transformed into a mystical taboo" (189); Lewiecki-Wilson believes the scene "deconstructs the myth of fixed gender division as it renders a sexually charged physical world by intermixing male and female imagery" (90); and Michael Black emphasizes the multiple and competing symbolic possibilites of the scene which, he argues, resists any easy algebraic equations: "One can't just say that the moon 'stands for' a will-driven feminine dominance which is cold; nor that the lilies 'stand for' a remembered passion now passing away; nor that the pollen on her face, easily brushed off, is her own participation in that passion" (180).

4. See Gavriel Ben-Ephraim for a discussion of the moon as a symbol of maternal power and dominance throughout Lawrence's early novels.

5. According to Storch, "The body of the mother is, in fantasy, dismembered and destroyed, disintegrating in a flash of fiery consuming anger, and liquified into the wax and sweat of elemental fluids. . . . The scene is a vivid depiction of a child's sadistic fantasy against the mother" (99). Daniel Dervin believes the doll contains projections of both the bad mother and the badness within Paul himself: "Perhaps as Paul takes over the doll and decides its fate, it becomes a 'bad' self-representation that needs to be destroyed. . . . [I]t is from this point on that Paul ceases to be only a shadow-self" (114). Dervin views the scene in a more positive light than Storch, arguing that for Paul "the immolated doll marks the dawn of imaginative power" (151).

6. Weiss sees both Miriam and Clara as mother-surrogates in the oedipal conflict, with each representing one side of the madonna-whore split. For Ben-Ephraim, Miriam is just another link in a chain of possessive women because "Paul is a man who needs to be possessed" (110). For Mark Spilka, Miriam represents one of three "destructive forms of love" in the novel—"oedipal, spiritual, and 'unbalanced-possessive'" (*Love Ethic* 82). Pullin and Millett see her as one in a series of female stereotypes who exist exclusively to cater to Paul's needs. Miriam's role, according to Millett, is "to worship his talent in the role of disciple" (347).

7. Charles Rossman takes perhaps the most negative view of Clara. He emphasizes her "coldness and aloofness" and her "rigid, egocentric isolation which has cut her off from all warm contact with others" (266). These traits are in fact responsible, he believes, for provoking her husband's brutality.

8. Several critics share Weiss's view that the town is in "polar hostility to Gertrude, as the world of men" and that "In choosing the town Paul is accepting his father, an idealized image" and is thus embarked on a new, more positive direction (66–67). Other critics are more skeptical. Ben-Ephraim thinks "Paul Morel is too wounded and bereaved a young man to experience a beginning so hopeful and so new" (122). Black compares the last paragraph to "the dereliction, the despair, the sense of being pervious to death" that Ursula experiences toward the end of *The Rainbow*. Lawrence, Black argues, "wills his central characters into the effort to move towards the world, towards social human life" but much of the rest of his work shows them moving away from it

(186–87). I share the perspective of critics like Harvey and Murfin who stress "the superbly realistic ambivalence of the novel's conclusion," its "truthful ambiguity" (Harvey 78–79). The last paragraph, Murfin claims, is "as self-divided and self-conflicted as Lawrence's characters" (131).

9. Cowan ("Lawrence, Freud and Masturbation") also makes this point: "There is little quesion that despite the dangers of the devourment and engulfment posed by the symbiotic merger with his mother, the imago of the nurturant and supportive mother was well established in Lawrence's internal representational world" (94).

CHAPTER 3. THE SHORT STORIES

1. See also Linda Williams and Earl Ingersoll for discussions of looking and the gaze in terms of exhibitionistic-voyeuristic and sadomasochistic dynamics in Lawrence's fiction.

2. See Storch for a finely observed Kleinian analysis of the oral rage, envy, and splitting evident in Lawrence's work. David Willbern, in a superb essay on "The Man Who Loved Islands," also analyzes the imagery in that story in terms of "a failure of mutuality and positive reciprocity at the oral stage" (230).

3. R. E. Pritchard says the importance of the color blue in Lawrence's imagery in general "may be traced back to his mother's blue eyes" (25). The color is also central to "The Woman Who Rode Away." The Woman's eyes are blue and she is wrapped in a blue blanket at her sacrifice. The young Indian explains that blue is "the colour of the wind. It is the colour of what goes away and is never coming back, but which is always here, waiting like death among us . . . it is the colour that stands away off, looking at us from the distance, that cannot come near to us" (574). If blue is indeed associated with the mother, then the description here again suggests the experience of the mother as distant, withholding, and withdrawn. It evokes the absent presence characteristic of maternal depression.

4. Other psychoanalytic discussions of this story have focused on Maurice's infantile dependency. Ruderman emphasizes Isabel's emasculating maternalism, while Richard Wheeler notes the womblike imagery associated with Maurice's blood-consciousness. My intersubjective reading here elaborates on a brief discussion of the story in *Literature and the Relational Self* (73–74).

5. Though Dorothy Brett may have provided the model for this character, just as Mabel Luhan inspired the creation of the heroine in "The Woman Who Rode Away," my argument is that these characters reflect Lawrence's own internal identifications and conflicts far more than they reflect any actual characteristics of the real women.

My perspective on this story is also similar to Barbara Smalley's Horneyian analysis of it. Smalley too sees Dollie's essentially schizoid character structure as conditioned by her relationship with her "neurotic" father. "Her father taught her," Smalley concludes, "to have contempt for her real self and to believe that she is not acceptable when she acts in accordance with her real wishes and feelings. Consequently when she reacts naturally and authentically, she has feelings of worthlessness and fears of being rejected by others" (188–89).

6. Dervin suggests that a careful scrutiny of the catalogue of Lawrence's characters "might well indicate that Lawrence did not play favorites with his anger, that he did not structure it along lines of gender. But when his self-hatred is directed toward a female object, he risks being cast, rightly or wrongly, as antifeminist" (211).

7. From a non-psychoanalytic perspective, Kingsley Widmer also emphasizes Lawrence's identification with both the Woman and her masochism: "we can apply to the repeatedly heroine-identifying Lawrence, and to his heroine, one of Lawrence's own insights: in the 'civilized' person, 'cruelty lust is directed almost as much against himself as against his victim'" (33–34).

CHAPTER 4. *THE RAINBOW*

1. Several critics emphasize such oppositional tension as the most definitive aspect of the novel. Julian Moynahan draws on Lawrence's "The Crown" (*Studies in Classic American Literature*) to discuss Lawrence's philosophy of life as a "warring of opposites, of flesh and spirit, emotion and reason, organic instinct and spiritual insight" (46). He claims that "The characters of *The Rainbow* live in an extraordinary state of tension, both within themselves and through their connections with others. . . . [T]he tension is essential to their living experience and not by itself a sign of any shortcoming" (46). Scott Sanders focuses on the novel's oppositions between nature and culture, the natural self and the social self, the body and mind, and silence and language (63–90). Kinkead-Weekes ("The Marble and the Statue") uses Lawrence's "Study of Thomas Hardy" to understand the novel's oppositional structure, particularly the essential male-female opposition.

2. Sanders argues that "Loss of self-control recurs in the experience of every figure in the novel. People are possessed by demons, they lapse into spells, drown in floods; they are overcome by speechlessness, absorbed into fields of force, bewitched by the moods and motions of the natural world" (63).

3. According to Howe, the first generation Brangwens "symbolize the individual ego *in utero*, for they exist in blood-unity with a living matrix" (38). "Tom Brangwen," she claims, "is the infant," while Will represents "the child" and Ursula "the adolescent" (50). Ben-Ephraim shares this view, referring to "the barely individuated state of the Brangwen men" (133) and the fact that Tom "is not fully created" (138).

4. The best explication of these psychodynamics can be found in Heinz Kohut's landmark study of the narcissistic personality, *The Analysis of the Self*.

5. Critics have often drawn on Lawrence's own theories of gender opposition, particularly as articulated in his "Study of Thomas Hardy," to understand the breakdown of the Ursula-Skrebensky relationship. The "essential female" needs an "essential male," and thus Skrebensky's lack of a core maleness defeats them both. As Daleski writes, "In the end she 'annihilates' him because, as we have already been led to expect, he has no genuine male self to oppose to her; he is no sun but a 'shadow,' a 'darkness' which the moonlight destroys" (112). The tear rolling down Ursula's cheek in the second moon scene,

Daleski suggests, "is a tacit admission of the vanity of her victory" (120).

6. Spilka (*Love Ethic*), Langbaum, and Sagar relate the horses to the male sensual principle Ursula had tried to destroy, while Moynahan and Ben-Ephraim maintain that the confrontation with the horses ultimately prevents deathliness and destruction. Moynahan believes Ursula is "'saved' by being brought face to face with a truth about herself and about life, the denial of which could only lead to a kind of death-in-life" (68). Kinkead-Weekes ("Marriage of Opposites") comes closest to my view in his interpretation of the horses as representative of the "conflicting forces" in Ursula herself: "It is the opposed energies that make the horses what they are, give them their looming archetypal power. But the horses are also gripped, clenched, unfinished. Their oppositions are trying to get free" (36–37).

7. This is the same sort of excessive responsibility and narcissistic control that Juliet exerts over her son at the beginning of the story "Sun," and that March assumes in *The Fox*, only to realize how miserably she has failed:

> Verily, in her own small way, she had felt herself responsible for the well-being of the world. And this had been her great stimulant, this grand feeling that, in her own small sphere, she was responsible for the well-being of the world.
>
> And she had failed. She knew that, even in her small way, she had failed. She had failed to satisfy her own feeling of responsibility. . . . Poor March, in her goodwill and her responsibility, she had strained herself till it seemed to her that the whole of life and everything was only a horrible abyss of nothingness. (68–69)

8. F. R. Leavis, Graham Hough, Sagar, and Sanders all find Ursula's optimism at the end unpersuasive and outweighed by the heavy social criticism that precedes it. Spilka (*Love Ethic*), Langbaum, Daleski, and Ben-Ephraim, on the other hand, feel that the regenerative vision is prepared for in Ursula's progressive struggle towards self-realization and wholeness. "The vision of the rainbow at the end of the novel," Ben-Ephraim claims, "is painstakingly earned" (172).

CHAPTER 5. WOMEN IN LOVE

1. See Tony Pinkney for a provocative argument about the transition from *The Rainbow*'s "gothic modernism" to the "classic modernism" of *Women in Love*.

2. The view of Ursula as a corrective influence is most often propounded in response to feminist attacks on Birkin's misogyny—his rage at the Magna Mater and his perceived advocacy of male superiority. See, for instance, Lydia Blanchard ("Love and Power"); Peter Balbert ("Ursula Brangwen and 'The Essential Criticism'"); and Mark Spilka (*Renewing the Normative*).

3. Bryan Reddick makes this point as well: "The ironic texture of most of the narrative—balancing character against character, couple against couple, lover against lover, abruptly emphasizing contradictions in experience and in interrelationships, satirizing the man who most accurately describes the story

world—creates in the reader's relationship to the characters the same kind of ambivalence uniting and dividing the characters themselves" (170).

4. Leavis, for instance, states that in Gerald "we have peculiarly well exemplified the way in which, in Lawrence's art, the diagnosis of the malady of the individual psyche can become that of the malady of a civilization" (158). Pritchard also holds Gerald up as "the tragic hero of *Women in Love*, the epitome of his civilization, torn apart and destroyed by unrecognized contradictions within, and his death is the death of his civilization" (105).

5. Eric Levy has also discussed the importance of this void condition, particularly in relation to Gerald and Gudrun. Without the benefit of a theoretical framework, Levy nevertheless makes some astute psychological observations. He notes that "the fantasy of invulnerable isolation" and the need for control in the void characters compensate for their "overwhelming insecurity" (9); that the combination of shame and contempt [two poles of narcissism] distinguishes the psychology of these characters; and that "love between void characters leads only to disintegration" (19).

6. See in particular Dorothy Dinnerstein's *The Mermaid and the Minatour*, which ties both cultural misogyny and the ecological crisis of the contemporary West to the need to dominate and control the omnipotent mother of narcissistic fantasy. Benjamin criticizes Dinnerstein for basing the complex phenomenon of cultural misogyny on the single psychological fact of infantile dependency on the mother. Benjamin is less interested in determining an original cause for the omnipotent mother fantasy than in identifying the social and cultural conditions that intensify and sustain that fantasy. (See "The Omnipotent Mother.") As Benjamin shows, and as Lawrence's fiction makes painstakingly clear, the social suppression of women and the fantasy of maternal omnipotence feed on each other.

7. Pritchard also associates these passages in the "Coal-Dust" chapter with masochism and homosexuality: "The appeal is to the depths of the psyche, to submission to 'inhuman' forces within, . . . the response to this 'unnatural' energy is a perverse one, masochistic in Gudrun, equivalent of an unacceptable homosexual one in Lawrence" (88).

8. Scott Sanders, for instance, states bluntly, "Behind the notion of Blutbrüderschaft lurks the less mysterious reality of homosexual love which he [Lawrence] was unwilling or unable to acknowledge" (126). Jeffrey Meyers ("D. H. Lawrence and Homosexuality") believes that in *Women in Love*, Lawrence "never really moves beyond homosexuality. He merely substitutes anal marriage for homosexual love" (146). Charles Ross takes issue with both Sanders and Meyers, arguing that the novel presents the Blutbrüderschaft relationship as "a necessary, sustaining complement to heterosexual marriage," and that homoerotic feelings are in fact "openly discussed and potentially part of a new society" (181–82).

The idea of the Blutbrüderschaft as primarily a complement to heterosexual marriage is similar to Worthen's argument in *D. H. Lawrence and the Idea of the Novel*. Birkin's need for Gerald, Worthen believes, reflects "his need for more than a single intimacy" (96). George Donaldson straddles the fence, suggesting that Birkin (as well as Lawrence) is genuinely unclear and uncertain about what he wants from his relationship with Gerald. The novel, Donaldson says, presents an inconclusive, "tentative and self-exploratory" approach to love between men (66).

9. Other readings of this scene include Kinkead-Weekes's view ("Eros and Metaphor") that it represents a "way of salvation," a "disintegration back to opposing elements . . . that when it has taken its course, a new beauty and peace are born out of the terrible conflict" (111–12). Pritchard also sees the stoning as "an act of creative violence, destroying congealed stillness to create the vitality of the active interchange between light and dark, male and female, that produces momentary peace" (98). Langbaum agrees with Clarke that the scene shows the necessity of dissolution. Birkin is really attacking the female "separated ego" and "self-sufficiency"; the "fluidly 'ragged rose'" that emerges is a reflection of "the fluid, indefinitely outlined self Ursula must achieve, of an individuality open to connection" (344). Blanchard, in her article on the novel's narcissism, stresses the importance of the moon as a symbol of reflection, as a mirroring image or narcissistic projection: "the significance of the stoning is . . . that Birkin attempts to destroy a *reflection*—at the same time as he recognizes the dangers in withdrawing upon oneself" (116).

10. Meyers takes the critical view, as does Ben-Ephraim, who asserts that the sodomy scene attempts to "reverse . . . the obligation to the female, by bowing the magna mater to an enclosure, a containing organ, of the male. Specifically, the anus is substituted for the uterus as the controlling center, the arbiter of submission and domination" (232). Pritchard, although he too equates the anus with the womb, takes a more positive perspective. He highlights the process of rebirth: "The anus provides almost a new womb, from which his new self, or sense of it, can emerge" (69). Pritchard also shares my view of the importance of accepting shame: "It is only . . . through recognition and complete acceptance of one's physical organic condition in its totality (that includes the physical, corrupt and 'shameful' as well as the mental, spiritual and conventionally moral) that freedom and energy in the body and spirit can be achieved. Out of the mud rise the lotus and the swan" (25).

Spilka ("Lawrence Up-Tight") takes issue with the anal rebirth argument. He disagrees with Colin Clarke's thesis about dissolution and anal descent as life-renewing processes. Rather, Spilka stresses purgation, in which "anal terrors [are] worked off through equilibrated love, and in that sense incorporated, accepted, as the self is finally able to accept another without being overwhelmed or destroyed by its own deathly fears and urges" (256). Although I agree with that statement, Spilka embeds it in a developmental framework that seems too rigid. He sees the anal eroticism as similar to the homosexuality of the nude wrestling scene; Birkin, he believes, must "work through such impulses so as to get beyond them" (257). Conversely, I see the anality and the homoerotic idealizations as needing to be continually recovered, continually re-acknowledged as belonging to the self, not dismissed or "worked off" in order "to get beyond them." Birkin (as well as Lawrence) understands that his very vitality is bound up with his owning those impulses or self-experiences. They cannot, however, be allowed to engulf or consume the self; rather, they must be held in tension with other forms of self-in-relation.

11. Kinkead-Weekes (*D. H. Lawrence*) discusses how this passage is also influenced by Lawrence's reading in the occult, where he learned about the ancient Indian concept of kundalini, an energy force centered at the base of the spine (395).

EPILOGUE

1. Cowan offers an object relational analysis of Lawrence's preoccupation with the phallus. It reflects, he suggests, "a continued search for the father's penis as a part object that could substitute for the unavailable nurturant whole paternal imago that still could not be reliably established and stabilized in object constancy" ("Lawrence, Freud and Masturbation" 94).

2. Anne Fernihough also quotes this passage in her recent book on Lawrence's aesthetics. She demonstrates how a dialectical consciousness is crucial to Lawrence's art criticism and aesthetic philosophy. The dialectical dynamic, she believes, counters the imperialist tendencies and leadership politics in much of his other writing. The "art criticism emerges as an antidote to his own worst excesses in novels like *The Plumed Serpent*, where the 'metaphysic' (to use Lawrence's expression in 'Study of Thomas Hardy') threatens to destroy the work" (191). I have tried to show from a psychoanalytic perspective how such a dialectic also informs his best novels, and works equally as "an antidote to his own worst excesses."

WORKS CITED

Arcana, Judith. "I Remember Mama: Mother-Blaming in *Sons and Lovers* Criticism." *D. H. Lawrence Review* 20 (1989): 137–51.

Bader, Michael J. "Adaptive Sadomasochism and Psychological Growth." *Psychoanalytic Dialogues* 3 (1993): 279–300.

Bakhtin, Mikhail. *Problems of Dostoevsky's Poetics*. Ed. & Trans. Caryl Emerson. Introd. Wayne C. Booth. Minneapolis: U of Minnesota P, 1984.

Balbert, Peter. *D. H. Lawrence and the Phallic Imagination: Essays on Sexual Identity and Feminist Misreading*. New York: St. Martin's, 1989.

——. "Ursula Brangwen and 'The Essential Criticism': The Female Corrective in *Women in Love*." *Studies in the Novel* 17 (1985): 267–85.

Ben-Ephraim, Gavriel. *The Moon's Dominion: Narrative Dichotomy and Female Dominance in Lawrence's Earlier Novels*. East Brunswick & London: Associated UP, 1981.

Benjamin, Jessica. *The Bonds of Love: Psychoanalysis, Feminism, and the Problem of Domination*. New York: Pantheon, 1988.

——. "Father and Daughter: Identification with Difference—A Contribution to Gender Identity." *Psychoanalytic Dialogues* 1 (1991): 277–99.

——. *Like Subjects, Love Objects: Essays on Recognition and Sexual Difference*. New Haven: Yale UP, 1995.

——. "The Omnipotent Mother: A Psychoanalytic Study of Fantasy and Reality." *Representations of Motherhood*. Ed. Donna Bassin, Margaret Honey, and Meryle Mahrer Kaplan. New Haven: Yale UP, 1994. 129–46.

——. "Recognition and Destruction: An Outline of Intersubjectivity." Skolnick and Warshaw, *Relational Perspectives* 43–60.

——. "The Shadow of the Other (Subject): Intersubjectivity and Feminist Theory." *Constellations* 1 (1994): 231–54.

Berman, Jeffrey. *Narcissism and the Novel*. New York: New York UP, 1990.

Black, Michael. *D. H. Lawrence: The Early Fiction*. Cambridge, Cambridge UP, 1986.

Blanchard, Lydia. "Love and Power: A Reconsideration of Sexual Politics in D. H. Lawrence." *Modern Fiction Studies* 21 (1975): 431–43.

——. "*Women in Love*: Mourning Becomes Narcissism." *Mosaic* 15 (1982): 105–18.

Bloom, Harold, ed. *D. H. Lawrence's The Rainbow*. New York: Chelsea House, 1988.

——, ed. *Sons and Lovers*. New York: Chelsea House, 1988.

——, ed. *Women in Love*. New York, Chelsea House, 1988.

Bromberg, Philip. "Shadow and Substance: A Relational Perspective on Clinical Process." *Psychoanalytic Psychology* 10 (1993): 147–68.

Brown, Christopher. "The Eyes Have It: Vision in 'The Fox'." *Wascana Review* 15 (1980): 61–68.

Brown, Keith and Milton Keynes, eds. *Rethinking Lawrence*. Philadelphia: Open UP, 1990.

Carter, Angela. *Nothing Sacred*. London: Virago, 1982.

Cavitch, David. *D. H. Lawrence and the New World*. New York: Oxford UP, 1969.

Chodorow, Nancy. *The Reproduction of Mothering: Psychoanalysis and the Sociology of Gender*. Berkeley: U of California P, 1978.

Clarke, Colin. *River of Dissolution: D. H. Lawrence and English Romanticism*. New York: Barnes & Noble, 1969.

Clayton, John. *Gestures of Healing: Anxiety and the Modern Novel*. Amherst: U Mass P, 1991.

Cowan, James C. "Blutbrüderschaft and Self Psychology in D. H. Lawrence's Women in Love." *The Annual of Psychoanalysis*, vol. 20. Ed. Chicago Institute for Psychoanalysis. Hillsdale, NJ & London: Analytic P, 1992.

———. *D. H. Lawrence and the Trembling Balance*. University Park & London: Penn State UP, 1990.

———. "Lawrence, Freud and Masturbation." *Mosaic* 28 (1995): 64–98.

Cushman, Keith. *D. H. Lawrence at Work: The Emergence of the 'Prussian Officer' Stories*. Charlottesville: UP of Virginia, 1978.

Daleski, H. M. *The Forked Flame: A Study of D. H. Lawrence*. 1965. Madison: U of Wisconsin P, 1987.

Delany, Paul. *D. H. Lawrence's Nightmare: The Writer and His Circle in the Years of the Great War*. New York: Basic, 1978.

Dervin, Daniel. *A 'Strange Sapience': The Creative Imagination of D. H. Lawrence*. Amherst: U Mass P, 1984.

Dinnerstein, Dorothy. *The Mermaid and the Minataur*. New York: Harper & Row, 1976.

Dix, Carol. *D. H. Lawrence and Women*. Totowa, NJ: Rowman & Littlefield, 1980.

Donaldson, George. "'Men in Love'? D. H. Lawrence, Rupert Birkin and Gerald Crich." *D. H. Lawrence: Centenary Essays*. Ed. Mara Kalnins. Bristol: Bristol Classical P, 1986. 41–67.

Draper, R. P. "The Defeat of Feminism: D. H. Lawrence's 'The Fox' and 'The Woman Who Rode Away.'" *Critical Essays on D.H. Lawrence*. Ed. Dennis Jackson and Fleda Brown Jackson. Boston: G. K. Hall, 1988.

Eigen, Michael. *The Electrified Tightrope*. Ed. Adam Phillips. Northvale, NJ: Jason Aronson, 1993.

———. *The Psychotic Core*. Northvale, NJ: Jason Aronson, 1986.

Fast, Irene. *Gender Identity: A Differentiation Model*. Hillsdale, NJ: Analytic P, 1984.

Fernihough, Anne. *D. H. Lawrence: Aesthetics and Ideology*. Oxford: Clarendon, 1993.

First, Elsa. "Mothering, Hate, and Winnicott." Bassin et al., *Representations of Motherhood* 147–61.

Flax, Jane. *Thinking Fragments: Psychoanalysis, Feminism, and Postmodernism in the Contemporary West*. Berkeley: U of California P, 1990.

Fleishman, Avrom. "Lawrence and Bakhtin: Where Pluralism Ends and Dialogism Begins." Brown 109–19.

Friedman, Alan. "*The Rainbow*: A 'Developing Rejection of Old Forms.'" Bloom, *The Rainbow* 21–31.

Garrett, Peter. "The Revelation of the Unconscious." Bloom, *Women in Love* 35–45.

Ghent, Emmanuel. "Forward." Skolnick and Warshaw xiii–xxii.

———. "Masochism, Submission, Surrender." *Contemporary Psychoanalysis* 26 (1990): 108–36.

Gilbert, Sandra M. and Susan Gubar. *No Man's Land: The Place of the Woman Writer in the Twentieth Century*, vol. 1: *The War of the Words*. New Haven: Yale UP, 1987.

Greenberg, Jay. *Oedipus and Beyond: A Clinical Theory*. Cambridge: Harvard UP, 1991.

Guntrip, Harry. *Schizoid Phenomena, Object Relations, and the Self*. New York: International UP, 1969.

Harvey, Geoffrey. *Sons and Lovers*. Atlantic Highlands, NJ: Humanities P Int., 1987.

Hough, Graham. *The Dark Sun: A Study of D. H. Lawrence*. 1956. Rpt. New York: Octagon, 1973.

Howe, Marguerite Beede. *The Art of the Self in D. H. Lawrence*. Athens, Ohio: Ohio UP, 1977.

Ingersoll, Earl. "Staging the Gaze in D. H. Lawrence's *Women in Love*." *Studies in the Novel* 26 (1994): 268–80.

Kelsey, Nigel. *D. H. Lawrence: Sexual Crisis*. New York: St. Martin's, 1991.

Kernberg, Otto. "Aggression and Love in the Relationship of the Couple." *Journal of the American Psychoanalytic Association* 39 (1991): 45–70.

Kinkead-Weekes, Mark. *D. H. Lawrence: Triumph to Exile 1912–1922*. Cambridge: Cambridge UP, 1996.

———. "Eros and Metaphor: Sexual Relationship in the Fiction of Lawrence." Smith, *Lawrence and Women* 101–21.

———. "The Marble and the Statue." *Twentieth Century Interpretations of 'The Rainbow'*. Ed. Mark Kinkead-Weekes. Englewood Cliffs, NJ: Prentice Hall, 1971. 96–120.

———. "The Marriage of Opposites in *The Rainbow*." *D. H. Lawrence: Centenary Essays*. Ed. Mara Kalnins. Bristol: Bristol Classical P, 1986. 21–39.

Klein, Melanie. *Envy and Gratitude & Other Works, 1946–63*. New York: Delacorte/Seymour Lawrence, 1975.

———. *Love, Guilt and Reparation & Other Works, 1921–1945*. New York: Delacorte/Seymour Lawrence, 1975.

Kohut, Heinz. *The Analysis of the Self*. New York: International UP, 1971.

Langan, Robert. "The Depth of the Field." *Contemporary Psychoanalysis* 29 (1993): 628–44.

Langbaum, Robert. *The Mysteries of Identity: A Theme in Modern Literature*. New York: Oxford UP, 1977.

Lawrence, D. H. *Aaron's Rod*. Ed. Mara Kalnins. Cambridge: Cambridge UP, 1988.

———. "A Propos of *Lady Chatterley's Lover*." *Phoenix II* 487–515.

———. *Apocalypse and the Writings on Revelation*. Ed. Mara Kalnins. Cambridge: Cambridge UP, 1980.

———. "Art and Morality." *Phoenix* 521–26.

———. "The Blind Man." *England, My England* 46–63.

———. *The Complete Short Stories*. 3 vols. Harmondsworth, Middlesex: Penguin, 1976.

———. *England, My England and Other Stories*. Ed. Bruce Steele. Cambridge: Cambridge UP, 1990.

———. *The Fox, The Captain's Doll, The Ladybird*. Ed. Dieter Mehl. Cambridge: Cambridge UP, 1992.

———. "Glad Ghosts." *Complete Short Stories*. Vol. 3. 661–700.

———. "The Horse-Dealer's Daughter." *England, My England* 137–52.

———. *Kangaroo*. Ed. Bruce Steele. Cambridge: Cambridge UP, 1994.

———. *Lady Chatterley's Lover*. Ed. Michael Squires. Cambridge: Cambridge UP, 1993.

———. *The Letters of D. H. Lawrence*. Ed. James T. Boulton. 4 vols. Cambridge: Cambridge UP, 1979–87.

———. "Love." *Phoenix* 151–56.

———. *Love Among the Haystacks and Other Stories*. Ed John Worthen. Cambridge: Cambridge UP, 1987.

———. "Morality and the Novel." *Phoenix*. 527–32.

———. *Mr. Noon*. Ed. Lindeth Vasey. Cambridge: Cambridge UP, 1984.

———. "New Eve and Old Adam." *Love Among the Haystacks* 161–83.

———. "Odour of Chrysanthemums." *Prussian Officer* 181–99.

———. *Phoenix. The Posthumous Papers of D. H. Lawrence*. 1936. Ed. Edward D. McDonald. New York: Viking, 1972.

———. *Phoenix II: Uncollected, Unpublished and Other Prose Works by D. H. Lawrence*. 1968. Ed. Warren Roberts and Harry T. Moore. Harmondsworth, UK: Penguin, 1972.

———. *The Plumed Serpent*. Ed. L.D. Clark. Cambridge, Cambridge UP, 1987.

———. "The Princess." *St. Mawr* 157–96.

———. *The Prussian Officer and Other Stories*. Ed. John Worthen. Cambridge: Cambridge UP, 1983.

———. *Psychoanalysis of the Unconscious and Fantasia of the Unconscious*. Intro. Philip Rieff. New York: Viking, 1960.

———. *The Rainbow*. Ed. Mark Kinkead-Weeks. Cambridge: Cambridge UP, 1989.

———. "The Reality of Peace." *Phoenix* 669–94.

———. "The Shadow in the Rose Garden." *Prussian Officer* 121–32.

———. *St. Mawr and Other Stories*. Ed. Brian Finney. Cambridge: Cambridge UP, 1983.

———. *Sons and Lovers*. Ed. Helen Baron and Carl Baron. Cambridge: Cambridge UP, 1992.

———. *Studies in Classic American Literature*. New York: Viking, 1961.

———. "Sun." *Complete Short Stories.* Vol. 2. 528–45.

———. "We Need One Another." *Phoenix.* 188–95.

———. *The White Peacock.* Ed. Andrew Robertson. Cambridge: Cambridge UP, 1983.

———. "The Woman Who Rode Away." *Complete Short Stories.* Vol 2. 546–81.

———. *Women in Love.* Ed. David Farmer, Lindeth Vasey & John Worthen. Cambridge: Cambridge UP, 1987.

Leavis, F. R. *D. H. Lawrence: Novelist.* New York: Knopf, 1956.

Levy, Eric. "Lawrence's Psychology of Void and Center in *Women in Love.*" *D. H. Lawrence Review* 23 (1991): 5–19.

Lewiecki-Wilson, Cynthia. *Writing against the Family: Gender in Lawrence and Joyce.* Carbondale & Edwardsville: Southern Ill. UP, 1994.

Lodge, David. *After Bakhtin: Essays on Fiction and Criticism.* London & New York: Routledge, 1990.

Maddox, Brenda. *D. H. Lawrence: The Story of a Marriage.* New York: Simon & Schuster, 1994.

Mahler, Margaret, Fred Pine, and Anni Bergman. *The Psychological Birth of the Human Infant.* New York: Basic, 1975.

Mailer, Norman. *The Prisoner of Sex.* Boston: Little, Brown, 1971.

Martz, Louis. "Portrait of Miriam." Bloom, *Sons and Lovers* 47–69.

McDargh, John. *Psychoanalytic Object Relations Theory and The Study of Religion: On Faith and the Imaging of God.* Lanham, MD: UP of America, 1983.

Meyers, Jeffrey. *D. H. Lawrence: A Biography.* 1990. New York: Vintage, 1992.

———. "D. H. Lawrence and Homosexuality." *D H. Lawrence: Novelist, Poet, Prophet.* Ed. Stephen Spender. New York: Harper & Row, 1973. 135–46.

Miko, Stephen J. *Toward Women in Love: The Emergence of aLawrentian Aesthetic.* New Haven & London: Yale UP, 1971.

Millett, Kate. *Sexual Politics.* New York: Ballantine, 1969.

Mitchell, Stephen A. *Hope and Dread in Psychoanalysis.* New York: Basic, 1993.

———. *Relational Concepts in Psychoanalysis: An Integration.* Cambridge, MA: Harvard UP, 1988.

Morrison, Andrew. *Shame: The Underside of Narcissism.* Hillsdale, NJ: Analytic P, 1989.

Moynahan, Julian. *The Deed of Life: The Novels and Tales of D. H. Lawrence.* Princeton: Princeton UP, 1963.

Murfin, Ross C. *Sons and Lovers: A Novel of Division and Desire.* Boston: G. K. Hall, 1987.

Nin, Anaïs. *D. H. Lawrence: An Unprofessional Study.* 1932. Denver: Swallow P, 1946.

Nixon, Cornelia. *Lawrence's Leadership Politics and the Turn against Women.* Berkeley: U of Calif. P, 1986.

Ogden, Thomas H. *The Primitive Edge of Experience.* Northvale, NJ: Jason Aronson, 1989.

Pinkney, Tony. *D. H. Lawrence and Modernism.* Iowa City: U of Iowa P, 1990.

Pritchard. R. E. *D. H. Lawrence: Body of Darkness*. Pittsburgh: U of Pittsburgh P, 1971.

Pullin, Faith. "Lawrence's Treatment of Women in *Sons and Lovers*." Smith 49–74.

Reddick, Bryan D. "Point of View and Narrative Tone in *Women in Love*: The Portrayal of Interpsychic Space." *D. H. Lawrence Review* 7 (1974): 156–71.

Ross, Charles. "Homoerotic Feeling in *Women in Love*: Lawrence's 'Struggle for Verbal Consciousness' in the Manuscripts." *D. H. Lawrence: The Man Who Lived*. Ed. Robert B. Partlow Jr. and Harry T. Moore. Carbondale: Southern Illinois UP, 1980. 168–82.

Rossman, Charles. "You Are the Call and I Am the Answer." *D. H. Lawrence Review* 8 (1975): 255–324.

Ruderman, Judith. *D. H. Lawrence and the Devouring Mother: The Search for the Patriarchal Ideal of Leadership*. Durham, NC: Duke UP, 1984.

Ryals, Clyde de L. "D. H. Lawrence's 'The Horse-Dealer's Daughter': An Interpretation." *Critical Essays on D. H. Lawrence*. Ed. Dennis Jackson and Fleda Brown Jackson. Boston: G. K. Hall, 1988. 153–69.

Sagar, Keith. *The Art of D. H. Lawrence*. Cambridge: Cambridge UP, 1966.

Salgado, Gamini. "Taking the Nail for a Walk: On Reading Women in Love." *D. H. Lawrence*. Ed. Peter Widdowson. London & New York: Longman, 1992. 137–45.

Sanders, Scott. *D. H. Lawrence: The World of the Five Major Novels*. New York: Viking, 1973.

Schapiro, Barbara. *Literature and the Relational Self*. New York: New York UP, 1994.

Schorer, Mark. "Technique as Discovery." *Hudson Review* 1 (1948). Partial rpt. in *D. H. Lawrence and 'Sons and Lovers': Sources and Criticism*. Ed. E. W. Tedlock, Jr. New York: New York UP, 1965. 167–68.

Schwartz, Murray. "D. H. Lawrence and Psychoanalysis: An Introduction." *D. H. Lawrence Review* 10 (1977): 215–22.

Segal, Hanna. *Introduction to the Work of Melanie Klein*. 2nd ed. New York: Basic, 1974.

Siegel, Carol. *Lawrence among the Women: Wavering Boundaries in Women's Literary Traditions*. Charolottesville: UP of Virginia, 1991.

Simpson, Hilary. *D. H. Lawrence and Feminism*. London: Croom Helm, 1982.

Skolnick, Neil J. and Susan C. Warshaw, eds. *Relational Perspectives in Psychoanalysis*. Hillsdale, NJ: Analytic P, 1992.

Smalley, Barbara M. "Lawrence's 'The Princess' and Horney's 'Idealized Self.'" *Third Force Psychology and the Study of Literature*. Ed. Bernard J Paris. Rutherford, NJ: Fairleigh Dickinson UP, 1986. 179–90.

Smith, Anne, ed. *Lawrence and Women*. New York: Barnes & Noble, 1978.

Spezzano, Charles. *Affect in Psychoanalysis: A Clinical Synthesis*. Hillsdale, NJ: Analytic P, 1993.

Spilka, Mark. "Lawrence Up-Tight, or the Anal Phase Once Over." *Novel* 4 (1971): 252–67.

———. *The Love Ethic of D. H. Lawrence*. Bloomington: Indiana UP, 1955.

———. *Renewing the Normative D. H. Lawrence: A Personal Progress*. Columbia: U of Missouri P, 1992.

Sproles, Karyn Z. "D.H. Lawrence and the Schizoid State: Reading Sons and Lovers through *The White Peacock.*" *Paunch* 63–64 (1990): 39–70.

Stern, Daniel. *The Interpersonal World of the Infant.* New York: Basic, 1985.

Stewart, Jack. "Linguistic Incantation and Parody in *Women in Love.*" *Style* 30 (1996): 95–112.

Stoll, John. *The Novels of D. H. Lawrence: A Search for Integration.* Columbia: U of Missouri P, 1971.

Stolorow, Robert and George Atwood. *Contexts of Being: The Intersubjective Foundations of Psychological Life.* Hillsdale, NJ: Analytic P, 1992.

Storch, Margaret. *Sons and Adversaries: Women in William Blake and D. H. Lawrence.* Knoxville: U of Tennessee P, 1990.

Sweetnam, Annie. "The Changing Contexts of Gender between Fixed and Fluid Experience." *Psychoanalytic Dialogues* 6 (1996): 437–59.

Turner, John. "The Capacity to Be Alone and Its Failure in D. H. Lawrence's 'The Man Who Loved Islands.'" *D. H. Lawrence Review* 16 (1983): 259–89.

Van Ghent, Dorothy. "On *Sons and Lovers.*" Bloom, *Sons and Lovers* 5–22.

Weiss, Daniel. *Oedipus in Nottingham: D. H. Lawrence.* Seattle: U of Washington P, 1962.

Wheeler, Richard. "Intimacy and Irony in 'The Blind Man.'" *D. H. Lawrence Review* 9 (1976): 236–53.

Widdowson, Peter, ed. *D. H. Lawrence.* London & NY: Longman, 1992.

Widmer, Kingsley. *The Art of Perversity: D. H. Lawrence's Shorter Fictions.* Seattle: U of Washington P, 1962.

Willbern, David. "Malice in Paradise: Isolation and Projection in 'The Man Who Loved Islands.'" *D. H. Lawrence Review* 10 (1977): 223–39.

Williams, Linda Ruth. *Sex in the Head: Visions of Feminity and Film in D. H. Lawrence.* Detroit: Wayne State UP, 1993.

Winnicott, D. W. *The Maturational Processes and the Facilitating Environment: Studies in the Theory of Emotional Development.* New York: International UP, 1965.

———. *Playing and Reality.* London: Tavistock, 1971.

———. *Psychoanalytic Explorations.* Ed. Clare Winnicott, Ray Shepard, Madeleine Davis. Cambridge, MA: Harvard UP, 1989.

———. *Through Paediatrics to Psycho-Analysis.* New York: Basic, 1975.

Worthen, John. *D. H. Lawrence and the Idea of the Novel.* London: Macmillan, 1979.

———. *D. H. Lawrence: The Early Years 1885–1912.* Cambridge: Cambridge UP, 1991.

Wurmser, Léon. *The Mask of Shame.* Baltimore: Johns Hopkins UP, 1981.

INDEX

Anality, 62–63, 76, 113–114, 127, 128, 141 n.10
Analysis of the Self (Kohut), 138 n.4
Arcana, Judith, 22, 30–31
Art of the Self in D. H. Lawrence (Howe), 15
Atwood, George, 5–6

Bader, Michael, 70–71, 93
Bakhtin, Mikhail, 2, 103
Balbert, Peter, 69, 135 n.2, 139 n.2
Baron, Carl and Helen, 21
Beardsall, George, 11
Ben-Ephraim, Gavriel, 79, 85, 94, 136 n.4, n.6, n.8, 138 n.3, 139 n.6, n.8, 141 n.10
Benjamin, Jessica, 7–9, 16, 17, 36, 49, 70, 71, 72, 73, 80, 85, 90, 100, 106–107, 109, 110, 112, 125, 131–132, 133 n.4, 140 n.6
Berman, Jeffrey, 23, 30
Bernhardt, Sarah, 13–14
Black, Michael, 136 n.3, n.8
Blanchard, Lydia, 22, 23, 105, 117, 120–121, 139 n.2, 141 n.9
Bloom, Harold, 79, 104
"Blutbrüderschaft" (Cowan), 51, 118
Bonds of Love, The (Benjamin), 7–9, 70, 106–107, 125
Brett, Dorothy, 137 n.5
Bromberg, Philip, 104
Brown, Christopher, 58
Brown, Keith, 133 n.2

Carter, Angela, 47
Cavitch, David, 69, 71, 105, 110
Chambers, Jessie, 14, 15, 40, 44
Clarke, Colin, 98, 127, 141 n.9, n.10

Clayton, John, 16
Cowan, James, 51, 118, 135 n.9, 137 n.9, 142 n.1
Cushman, Keith, 57

Daleski, H. M., 21, 48, 124, 138–139 n.5, 139 n.8
Delany, Paul, 103
Dervin, Daniel, 16, 33, 136 n.5, 138 n.6
Dinnerstein, Dorothy, 140 n.6
Dix, Carol, 2
Donaldson, George, 140–141 n.8
Dostoyevsky, Fyodor, 103
Draper, R. P., 69

Eigen, Michael, 3, 5, 7, 33, 108, 121, 129, 135 n.8
Electrified Tightrope, The (Eigen), 129
Erikson, E., 15

False self, 4, 59, 69, 92, 95, 96, 98, 107, 108
Fast, Irene, 9–10
Father: ambivalent feelings toward, 10, 48–51, 71, 111; idealization of, 10, 16, 17, 51, 53, 72, 84, 111, 112, 118, 131; identification with, 12–13, 16, 49–51, 71–72, 84, 90–91, 110, 111, 118
"Father and Daughter" (Benjamin), 110
Fernihough, Anne, 142 n.2
First, Elsa, 132
Flax, Jane, 5
Fleishman, Avrom, 133 n.2
Freud, Sigmund, 1, 15, 47
Friedman, Alan, 79

Garnett, David, 134 n.7
Garnet, Edward, 79
Garrett, Peter, 124–125
Gender identity, 3, 9–10, 19, 47–48, 64, 99, 136 n.3
Gestures of Healing (Clayton), 16
Ghent, Emmanuel, 3, 34, 59, 67, 94, 107, 111, 116
Greenberg, Jay, 7
Guntrip, Harry, 24

Harvey, Geoffrey, 21, 26, 135 n.3, 137 n.8
Hegel, G. W. F., 8
Homosexuality, 13, 51, 61, 63, 65, 71–72, 76, 96–97, 110, 115, 117, 118, 119, 120, 127, 133 n.1, 134 n.7, 140 n.7, n.8, 141 n.10
Hope and Dread in Psychoanalysis (Mitchell), 4, 5, 7, 36
Hough, Graham, 139 n.8
Howe, Marguerite Beede, 15, 85, 133 n.3, 138 n.3

Idealization, 13, 16, 17, 18, 38, 43, 51, 53, 86, 96–97, 109, 110, 111, 113, 115, 117, 118, 119, 120, 123, 128, 129, 131, 136 n.8, 141 n.10. *See also* Narcissism
intersubjectivity: and attunement, 6, 18, 27, 28, 31–32, 46, 51, 58, 59, 90, 101; and breakdown, 8–10, 18–19, 43, 49, 55, 58–59, 61–73, 85, 87–89, 90, 93–95, 99, 101, 108, 113, 115, 117; and dialectical tension, 2–3, 7, 8–9, 17, 19, 22, 36, 44, 79, 80, 84, 85–86, 101, 104, 117, 120, 122, 128, 129, 131–132, 135 n.9, 142 n.2; and mutual recognition, 7, 8, 32, 46, 55–61, 65, 66, 72, 84, 85–86, 88, 90, 91, 95, 96, 122, 123, 127–128; and polarities, 2–3, 9, 15, 18–19, 51, 68, 72, 88, 89, 94, 108, 115, 134 n.6, 135 n.9. *See also* Splitting
Ingersoll, Earl, 137 n.1

Introduction to the Work of Melanie Klein (Segal), 135 n.8

Jung, C. G., 15, 75

Kelsey, Nigel, 135 n.1
Kernberg, Otto, 118
Keynes, John Maynard, 134 n.7
Keynes, Milton, 133 n.2
Kinkead-Weekes, Mark, 15, 87, 134 n.7, 138 n.1, 139 n.6, 141 n.9, 142 n.11
Kohut, Heinz, 67, 108, 118, 138 n.4
Klein, Melanie, 16, 17, 62, 123, 134 n.8, 137 n.2

Laing, R. D., 15
Langan, Robert, 82
Langbaum, Robert, 98, 103, 139 n.6, n.8, 141 n.9
Lawrence, Ada, 11
Lawrence, Arthur, 11–13
Lawrence, D. H.: early life, 11–14; Works cited: *Aaron's Rod*, 51; *Apocalypse*, 131; "A Propos of *Lady Chatterley's Lover*," 1; "Art and Morality," 3; "The Blind Man," 38, 61, 64–65, 67, 70, 120, 137 n.4; "The Crown," 138 n.1; *Fantasia of the Unconscious*, 98, 134 n.6; "The Fox," 35, 139 n.7; "Glad Ghosts," 60–61; "The Horse-Dealer's Daughter," 38, 73–77, 113–114, 126; *Kangaroo*, 43, 62–63; *Lady Chatterley's Lover*, 16, 128, 131; ""Love," 125; "The Man Who Loved Islands," 58, 137 n.2; "Morality and the Novel," 1, 17; *Mr. Noon*, 1, 14; "New Eve and Old Adam," 55–57; "Odour of Chrysanthemums," 55, 57; *The Plumed Serpent*, 51, 131, 142 n.2; "The Princess," 38, 61, 65–68, 69, 70, 73, 76, 137 n.5; "The Prussian Officer," 38, 51, 61–63, 68, 70; *Psychoanalysis and the Unconscious*, 134 n.6; *The*

Rainbow, 19, 56, 68, 76, 79–101, 103, 112, 133 n.1, 136 n.8, 138–139; "The Reality of Peace," 124; "The Rocking-Horse Winner," 30–32; "The Shadow in the Rose Garden," 55, 57–59, 60, 70; *Sons and Lovers*, 11, 12, 19, 21–53, 58, 73, 79, 81, 83, 86, 89, 90, 93, 105, 107, 120, 133 n.1, 135–137; "Sun," 55, 59–61, 69, 70, 139 n.7; *Studies in Classic American Literature*, 138 n.1; "Study of Thomas Hardy," 138 n.1, n.5, 142 n.2; "We Need One Another," 1; *The White Peacock*, 51; "The Woman Who Rode Away," 61, 68–73, 110, 116, 137 n.3, n.5, 138 n.7; <u>*Women in Love*</u>, 9, 51, 56, 58, 79, 88, 92, 96, 103–129, 131, <u>139–142</u>

Lawrence, D.H. (Worthen), 11–15, 133 n.3

Lawrence, Frieda Von Richthofen Weekley, 14–15, 87, 101, 103

Lawrence, Lydia, 11–12

Lawrence among the Women (Siegel), 2

Lawrence and the Devouring Mother (Ruderman), 16

Lawrence and the Idea of the Novel (Worthen), 140 n.8

Lawrence and the Trembling Balance (Cowan), 135 n.9

Leavis, F. R., 139 n.8, 140 n.4

Lewiecki-Wilson, Cynthia, 2, 21–22, 135 n.1, 136 n.3

Levy, Eric, 140 n.5

Like Subjects (Benjamin), 109

Literature and the Relational Self (Schapiro), 3, 33, 137 n.4

Lodge, David, 103–104, 131, 133 n.2

Love, Guilt and Reparation (Klein), 134 n.8

Luhan, Mabel, 137 n.5

Maddox, Brenda, 15, 134 n.7

Mahler, Margaret, 6–7, 16

"Marriage of Opposites, The" (Kinkead-Weekes), 87

Martz, Louis, 37

Masochism, 9, 44, 59, 60, 63, 67, 68, 70, 71, 110, 111, 112, 116, 138 n.7, 140 n.7. *See also* Sadomasochism

"Masochism, Submission, Surrender" (Ghent), 59, 109, 116

McDargh, John, 53

Merging fantasies, 15, 16, 27–28, 45, 52, 56, 63, 74, 75, 80, 84, 85, 96–97, 107, 111–112, 114, 115, 117, 118, 119, 120, 121, 126. *See also* Mother, Narcissism

Mermaid and the Minatour (Dinnerstein), 140 n.6

Meyers, Jeffrey, 18, 134 n.7, 140 n.8, 141 n.10

Miko, Stephen, 98

Millett, Kate, 2, 41, 48, 68–69, 70, 133 n.1, 136 n.6

Mitchell, Stephen, 4–5, 7, 32, 36

Morrison, Andrew, 41

Mother: ambivalent feelings toward, 16, 27, 32–36, 43, 53, 60, 81, 85, 86, 91, 119, 124, 134 n.8; and depression, 12, 21–36, 45, 81, 105, 137 n.3; and fragility, 18, 32–36, 41, 45; identification with, 17, 18, 36, 41, 52–53, 79, 83–84, 85; and omnipotence, 10, 16, 17–18, 29, 45, 84, 108, 112, 140 n.6; psychic destruction of, 9, 33–36, 49, 124, 131–132; and shame, 12, 18, 23–31, 41; subjectivity of, 8, 17, 21–36, 60, 64, 82, 84 105, 106, 131–132, 133 n.4, 135 n.1. *See also* Merging fantasies

Moynahan, Julian, 138 n.1, 139 n.6

Murfin, Ross, 37, 137 n.8

Narcissism: and loss, 13, 24, 27, 29, 36, 38–39, 44, 46, 52, 67, 68, 73, 86, 89, 90, 91, 92, 94, 95, 97, 105, 106, 108, 109, 117, 123, 126; and

Narcissism *(continued)*
  omnipotence, 10, 17, 32, 92, 94, 95,
  100, 105, 106, 107, 108, 117, 132;
  and primitive fantasy, 16–17, 19,
  22, 29, 51, 85, 86, 88, 94, 100, 115;
  and rage, 27, 30, 36, 41, 44, 57, 62,
  68, 81, 86, 87, 92, 107, 108, 116,
  126, 127. *See also* Idealization,
  Merging fantasies, Shame
Nin, Anaïs, 1
Nixon, Cornelia, 133 n.1

Oates, Joyce Carol, 105
Object relations, 16, 53, 123
Object use, 8–9, 33–36, 42, 49, 92–93,
  94, 124, 125–126, 131, 133–134 n.5
Oedipus complex, 10, 16, 22, 25, 32,
  49, 112, 136 n.3, 136 n.6
Oedipus in Nottingham (Weiss), 15
Ogden, Thomas, 135 n.8
"Omnipotent Mother, The"
  (Benjamin), 10, 17, 140 n.6
Orality, 27, 28, 52, 62, 63, 137 n.2

Paradox, 3, 8, 19, 51–52, 83, 84, 85,
  103, 104, 111, 116, 128, 131, 135
  n.9
Paranoid-schizoid position, 16, 17,
  43, 123, 134 n.8. *See also* Splitting
Pinkney, Tony, 139 n.1
Playing and Reality (Winnicott), 133
  n.5
Postmodernism, 4, 5
Pritchard, R. E., 137 n.3, 140 n.4,
  n.7, 141 n.9, n.10
Psychoanalytic Explorations
  (Winnicott), 6, 50
Psychotic Core, The (Eigen), 3, 5, 7,
  33, 108, 121, 135 n.8
Pullin, Faith, 133 n.1, 136 n.6

Réage, Pauline, 70
"Recognition and Destruction"
  (Benjamin), 132
Reddick, Bryan, 139–140 n.3
*Relational Concepts in
  Psychoanalysis* (Mitchell), 32

Renewing the Normative (Spilka),
  139 n.2
Ross, Charles, 140 n.8
Rossman, Charles, 136 n.7
Ruderman, Judith, 16, 17, 51, 89,
  119, 137 n.4
Russell, Bertrand, 134 n.7
Ryals, Clyde de L., 75

Sadism, 34–36, 40, 41, 62, 63, 68,
  69, 70, 89, 93–94, 95, 106, 116
Sadomasochism, 9, 18, 59, 68–73,
  88, 89, 103–117, 137 n.1
Sagar, Keith, 98, 139 n.6, n.8
Salgado, Gamini, 104
Sanders, Scott, 133 n.3, 138 n.1, n.2,
  139 n.8, 140 n.8
Savage, Henry, 134 n.7
Schorer, Mark, 21
Schwartz, Murray, 15
Schizoid condition, 3–4, 24–25, 58,
  63, 67, 74, 80, 91, 97, 99, 101,
  133 n.3, 137 n.5
Segal, Hanna, 135 n.8
Sexual Politics (Millett), 2
Sexuality, 18, 32, 36, 37–38, 41–42,
  45–46, 47, 48, 59, 64, 65, 67, 69,
  71, 76, 93, 99, 110, 117, 118
"Shadow of the Other, The"
  (Benjamin), 132
Shame, 12, 13, 14, 18, 27, 27–29, 36,
  37, 38, 40, 41, 44, 46, 47, 57,
  64–68, 70, 73–77, 85, 86, 87, 90,
  91, 96, 97, 99, 106, 109, 110,
  111, 112, 113, 114, 126,
  127–128, 140 n.5, 141 n.10. *See
  also* Narcissism
Siegel, Carol, 2
Simpson, Hilary, 133 n.1
Smalley, Barbara, 137 n.5
Sons and Adversaries (Storch), 16
Spezzano, Charles, 7
Spilka, Mark, 136 n.6, 139 n.6, n.8,
  n.2, 141 n.10
Splitting, 13, 16, 43, 51, 68, 72, 91,
  106, 123, 134 n.8. *See also*
  Paranoid-schizoid position

Sproles, Karyn, 133 n.3
Stern, Daniel, 6, 58
Stewart, Jack, 133 n.2
Stoll, John, 135–136 n.3
Stolorow, Robert, 5–6,
Storch, Margaret, 16, 17, 33, 35, 50, 51, 52, 64, 119, 136 n.3, 136 n.5, 137 n.2
Story of O, The (Réage), 70, 71, 72
Strange Sapience, A (Dervin), 16
Sweetman, Annie, 135 n.8

Through Paediatrics to Psycho-Analysis (Winnicott), 5
Turner, John, 133 n.3

Van Ghent, Dorothy, 135 n.3

Weiss, Daniel, 15, 136 n.6, n.8
Wheeler, Richard, 137 n.4
Widdowson, Peter, 2
Widmer, Kingsley, 138 n.7
Willbern, David, 137 n.2
Williams, Linda, 2, 47, 137 n.1
Winnicott, Donald, 5, 6, 8–9, 15, 16, 33, 34, 35, 36, 50, 59, 83, 93, 101, 111, 121, 125, 128, 133 n.5
Worthen, John, 11–14, 18, 133 n.3
Wurmser, Léon, 41, 67, 74

"The *deficient self*" 37–38
What a term?